First published in Arrow 1987

14 13

© John Dunning 1987

First published 1987

Arrow Books Limited
Random House UK Ltd, 20 Vauxhall Bridge Road, London SW1V 2SA

Random House Australia (Pty) Limited
20 Alfred Street, Milsons Point, Sydney,
New South Wales 2061, Australia

Random House New Zealand Limited
18 Poland Road, Glenfield
Auckland 10, New Zealand

Random House South Africa (Pty) Limited
PO Box 337, Bergvlei, South Africa

Random House UK Limited Reg. No. 954009

A CIP catalogue record for this book
is available from the British Library

Papers used by Random House UK Limited
are natural, recyclable products made from wood grown in
sustainable forests. The manufacturing processes conform to
the environmental regulations of the country of origin

ISBN 0 09 949430 2

Printed and bound in Great Britain by
Cox & Wyman Ltd, Reading, Berkshire

Mindless Murders

John Dunning had a varied and adventurous
career, including service in the US Navy and
the Shanghai Municipal Police. He spent four
years in a Japanese POW camp during the
Second World War and then worked in
American intelligence. He subsequently
became a journalist, travelling to China and
Europe. He was the top selling author of
murder stories for *True Detective* magazines
and wrote over a thousand accounts of true
crime.

He lived in Luxembourg as a full-time
writer, until his death in 1990.

D1514405

Also in Arrow by John Dunning

Carnal Crimes
Deadly Deviates
Madly Murderous
Murderous Women
Strange Deaths
Truly Murderous

MINDLESS
MURDERS

JOHN DUNNING

ARROW

CONTENTS

INTRODUCTION

Be ye not weary of murder?

No indeed. It is one of the most fascinating of subjects. It is the ultimate act of violence. It is final. There is no appeal from this verdict.

And yet, the act of murder itself tends to be repetitive. There are a limited number of ways in which humans can be dispatched into eternity and all have been used countless times.

An isolated description of murder itself lacks meaning. It may be sordid, tragic or even comic, but it is the circumstances leading to the climax of homicide which lend interest to the death of one human being at the hands of another.

The circumstances include the motive, but, sometimes, there is no motive that we can understand. Then, the murder itself is the motive – for there can be no murder when there is no motive. Without motive, the killing is not a deliberate act and, therefore, no murder.

Motives for murder can be reduced to two opposite impulses. The murderer wanted something. The murderer did not want something.

This is so basic that it applies to all human actions and leaves us with no better understanding of the phenomenon of murder than before.

However, murder is not difficult to understand. There are few of us who have not, at one time or another in our lives, wanted to kill someone. Most of us have not done so. Many are incapable of it. Some are, and have killed or will kill.

Are these murderers different from the rest of us?

Some are. There is a deviation of mind or psyche which makes them very different from the average person.

Most are not. They are only men and women who want or do not want something very badly and believe that murder is the only solution to their problem.

Another and larger group consists of persons who have no homicidal intentions at all. They merely hit too hard, squeeze too long, stab too deep or aim too accurately and become killers to their own astonishment and dismay. They are not murderers, but simply clumsy. They can, however, become clumsy again.

There are few humans in which the tendency to violence does not lie close to the surface.

If the cannon is the final argument of kings, the gun, the knife, the cord and the club are the final arguments of his subjects. The difference is in the material employed and not in the act or the intent. The elimination of the opponent is the universal solution of all classes.

Murder is normal human behaviour.

This is not going to be a popular observation in an age where all men are presumed to be of good will and eager to sacrifice their own interests for those of their fellow men, but we are concerned here with murder and not with running for office.

There is little in human history that is not connected with killing other species or our own.

At one time, the killing of animals, birds and fish was a matter of defence or nourishment. Today, apart from the animals and birds which we raise specifically to kill and eat, it is purely recreation.

We kill other living creatures because we enjoy killing them and we call this killing sport.

The relationship between hunter and hunted has been the subject of much mystical rubbish to the effect that animals take as much pleasure in being killed as we do in killing them.

The only relationship between hunter and hunted is that of killer and victim, and anyone who doubts this can easily acquire wisdom by joining one of the groups of several million humans who are, at this moment, being hunted and killed somewhere in the world.

There is no need to hurry. The killing will continue, by organizations and by individuals. Murder competes with sex as one of the best-loved human activities.

Does this seem cynical?

Then why do people go to motor races?

Any psychologist can tell you.

Why are the most popular books, films and television programmes filled with murder and violence?

Why are you reading this?

Regarded dispassionately, murder may be the human's most outstanding characteristic. It is the mastery of murder that has made us the dominant species of the planet. Should we ever reach other worlds, we shall, undoubtedly, dominate them in the same manner.

Unless we encounter a species even more murderous.

Skill in murder is an important survival factor.

However, being expert and enthusiastic killers also presents humans with a problem. Having eliminated competition by other life forms, we are able to breed indiscriminately and this leads to increased density of population.

Dense populations are dangerous. The greater the number of humans in a given space, the higher the incidence of homicide. There are more homicides in New York City than in the state of Ohio, although Ohio has a larger population.

The traditional response to this problem has been society. The individuals within a group strike a sort of truce. Individuals may not kill. Only the representatives of the group as a whole are authorized to execute or neutralize dangerous elements.

Generally, this works about as well as most human institutions. A few individuals are so imprudent or vindictive that they are prepared to risk losing their lives for the satisfaction of depriving others of theirs, but most prefer to suppress their murderous impulses.

As many such unruly offenders are too young to have done much breeding, society is additionally benefited by the elimination of hereditary tendencies to violence.

Unfortunately, social systems appear to bear within themselves the seeds of their own destruction.

As the more violent are eliminated and the proportion of non-violent within a society rises, pressure groups advocating leniency in the treatment of criminals and the abolition of the death penalty come into being.

The ultimate objective of such groups is to relieve the individual of the responsibility for his acts. He or she is regarded not as a danger to society, but as sick, uninformed or a victim of social, racial or economic discrimination.

All that is necessary to eliminate crime is to correct these external circumstances. There is no such thing as a dangerous human.

Unfortunately, there is overwhelming evidence that humans are the most dangerous life form ever to appear on this planet and that the only predator that has ever succeeded in reducing their numbers is the human himself.

Humans who are not sick, uninformed or the subject of discrimination murder with monotonous regularity, and murderers who have been released as cured of their murderous tendencies murder again.

The advocates of criminals' rights either ignore or rationalize such cases. They are ideologues; and the basis of ideology is unwavering faith in the ideal, whether it bears any relation to reality or not.

For those who are not idealists, but merely desirous of a society in which the weaker members, particularly children, can live in relative safety, it is well to remember that such social experiments are being carried out with the lives of others.

It is not enough that nine out of ten rehabilitated murderers fail to murder someone else. If the tenth murders a child, society has failed in its duty.

Why a child precisely?

Because children are weaker than the rest of us and because they have no voice. Adults who vote into office politicians more concerned with ideology than the safety of their constituents are, ultimately, responsible for their own misfortunes.

And yet, in Western Europe today, killing a child, even under the most hideously cruel circumstances, is often regarded as no more than a peccadillo, less severely punished than insurance swindle or tax evasion.

Does this mean that Europeans do not care if their children are murdered?

Indeed they do, but, within large systems, the individual is helpless. Not everyone has time and money to spend in crusades for a more secure society, and for the persons most affected, the relatives of the victims, it is too late.

It is probably too late for the rest of us too. Population density will continue to increase. The proportion of violent elements within society will increase. Official leniency toward murderers will increase.

And so too will the barrage of tearful media accounts of lovable, misunderstood criminals.

Like so many human problems, this one probably has no satisfactory solution. Murder is with us to stay. We shall not lack entertainment.

Nor shall we lack political advocates of criminals' rights and clever lawyers to circumvent the will and intent of the majority of the electorate.

Ours is a government of law and not of men and, if it is possible to manipulate the law to the benefit of the criminal, we must accept it for we have voluntarily chosen law over justice.

As for the countless thousands of children who are

raped, tortured, forced into prostitution and murdered
in every week of the year, they might prefer less law and
more justice.

But, of course, they cannot vote.

You can though, can't you?

John Dunning
Kopstal, 1986

I

AN ACT OF LOVE

On the morning of Monday, 27 February 1984, municipal gardener Karl Mandel found a human foot among the rhododendrons.

The foot was in a plastic container and, although slightly dirty, appeared to be in good condition.

There were many other such containers in the rhododendron bed and Mandel left his tools lying and hurried to the nearest telephone to alert the police.

The police, in the form of a patrol car, arrived swiftly. Moenchengladbach, West Germany, is a town of nearly three hundred thousand inhabitants and, being located just to the west of the teeming Ruhr district, has a relatively high crime rate.

The patrol car officers were, therefore, well versed in dealing with such discoveries and, having determined that what Mandel had found was indeed a human foot, reported to the dispatcher at police headquarters that they were at the scene of a murder.

As a matter of fact, they were not. The homicide squad was immediately able to determine that the murder had not taken place in or near the rhododendron bed in the Bunter Garten, the city's main park.

Bunter Garten means 'colourful garden' and later in the year, the park, stretching northward from the city centre, would be colourful. At the moment, however, it was drab and almost deserted.

Which, suggested Dr Joachim Krause, might explain why it had been chosen for disposal of a heap of human parts.

'They haven't been here long,' said the homicide squad medical expert. 'Six or seven hours at the most.'

'Some time during the night then,' said Inspector Max List. 'How can you tell?'

'They were deep-frozen,' said the doctor. 'The larger pieces still aren't completely thawed out.'

'But will you be able to tell when the person was murdered then?' asked Detective Sergeant Peter Brugge, wrinkling his high forehead in consternation.

'Certainly not with any precision,' replied the doctor. 'We'll have to see what we can do once we have all the parts in the autopsy room. He's been cut up in extremely small pieces.'

'He?' asked the inspector. 'You're certain it's a man?'

The doctor silently held out a plastic container intended for freezing food. It contained a set of male genitals.

'Hmmm, yes,' said the inspector. 'All right. Let's get everything collected up here for transfer to the morgue. Careful about handling the containers. There may be prints.'

The order was directed at the detachment of technicians and specialists from the police laboratory and other departments who were standing by waiting for the doctor to finish his preliminary inspection of the corpse as found.

The doctor, a brisk, broad-shouldered little man with a great deal of black hair on head, face and hands, went off to the morgue to prepare for the autopsy. The inspector and sergeant withdrew a short distance so as not to interfere with the operations.

It was a mild day for late February and a weak sun was peeping cautiously through the typical central German haze. The temperature stood at five degrees above freezing and a light south-east wind was moving the branches of the still leafless trees. A few optimistic sparrows were looking for crumbs along the gravel paths.

The inspector, a quiet, slightly stoop-shouldered man, clean-shaven and neat, with the appearance and manner of a civil servant, brought out a short, stubby pipe and began thumbing tobacco into the bowl.

'It will be mainly a question of identification,' he remarked. 'Once we know who he is, the identity of the murderer should be obvious.'

The sergeant, tall, hawk-faced, painfully thin, nodded in silent agreement. If the murderer had gone to such pains to cut up the victim and conceal the parts in a public park, it could only be because there was a connection which could be traced.

'We have the fingers,' said the white-smocked technician in charge of the detail, coming over to where the inspector and the sergeant were standing. 'If the prints are on record, we'll have identification within an hour.'

'Good,' said the inspector. 'I'm going back to the office. Let me know the results as soon as possible.'

He went to his car and was driven off in the direction of police headquarters.

The sergeant remained behind in case anything of significance should turn up, but nothing did and, the operations at the scene being completed, he too returned to the office which he and the inspector shared in the department of criminal investigations.

'They think they have all the parts,' he remarked, hanging his anorak on the back of the door. 'The head has been skinned and, they think, cooked.'

'Unusual,' said the inspector. 'Could be a ritual murder or, maybe, another cannibal case.'

There had been a number of cannibal cases in recent years in West Germany, although, generally, the victims were females, adult or children.

The cannibalism theory received some support when the preliminary autopsy report was sent over late that afternoon.

According to Dr Krause, the head and hands had been grilled or roasted and some other fleshy parts of the body had been boiled. Pieces of the arms, thighs and buttocks were missing altogether.

'All prime meat cuts,' observed the inspector sagely.

In all, the technicians had recovered forty-four parts of the body. They had been reassembled on the autopsy slab like a gruesome jigsaw puzzle and represented the corpse of a rather slight man under the age of forty who had stood approximately five feet five inches tall and had weighed roughly one hundred and forty pounds.

There were no particular identifying marks on the body, and the face, having been grilled and skinned, was not recognizable. However, the tips of the fingers were intact, and satisfactory fingerprints had been obtained and sent to the records section.

The records section had been able to identify the victim immediately as he had a police record in connection with a minor financial swindle.

His name was Hans Josef Wirtz. He was thirty-three years old and a professional hairdresser. His last known address was a block of flats near the main railway station.

Although it was, by now, early evening, Sergeant Brugge immediately went with a team of detectives to the address given, where he found that the flat was occupied by a Mrs Martina Zimmermann, aged twenty-eight, and her sons, eleven-year-old Brian and nine-year-old Joe. Mrs Zimmermann stated that she was separated from her husband, Wilhelm Zimmermann.

She had known Hans Josef Wirtz, she said, but not very well. He had rented a room from her at one time, but he had moved out and she had not seen him for over a year.

'And the residents' registry office?' asked the inspector when he had heard the sergeant's report on the interview. 'Did he unregister?'

Registration of residence is compulsory in West Germany. A person changing address must unregister at the old address and reregister at the new.

'There's nobody there at this hour,' said the sergeant. 'I'll check it out in the morning.'

Mrs Zimmermann, a handsome, striking and charming woman, had made a good impression on the sergeant and he was surprised and dismayed to learn that, according to the records of the residents' registry office, Hans Josef Wirtz was still living in her flat.

'Either she's lying or Wirtz moved without registering,' said the sergeant, 'but that would mean he was up to something crooked.'

'We'll check on that first and give Mrs Zimmermann the benefit of the doubt,' said the inspector. 'From what you tell me, she doesn't seem like a woman who would be dining off her lodgers and Wirtz did have a record even if it was for a petty offence.'

'I'll take a look at the hairdressing places,' said the sergeant. 'If he was working anywhere in Moenchengladbach, it would have been in one of them. He's trained for nothing else.'

Hans Josef Wirtz had been working in Moenchengladbach and the sergeant soon found out where. Ominously, however, he had not been seen at his place of work after the evening of 29 April the preceding year. The day had been a Friday and he should have reported for work on Saturday morning, a busy time for hairdressers. He had not and a telephone call to the flat where he rented a room had produced only the reply that Mr Wirtz did not live there any more. He had never come back to work and had had nearly a full month's salary on the books at the time of his disappearance.

'Which, of course, is why the owner didn't report him missing,' said the sergeant. 'A little saved here, a little saved there . . .'

'Was it Mrs Zimmermann who answered the telephone when the boss called?' said the inspector.

'It wasn't the boss,' said the sergeant. 'They don't remember who called or who answered. After all, this was close to a year ago.'

'Yes, I suppose so,' said the inspector. 'Well, all right. It's Mrs Zimmermann then. Bring her in for questioning. No charge yet, of course. And pick up a warrant to search the flat. Maybe we'll find something interesting.'

The inspector had just uttered one of the greatest

understatements of his career. The search of Martina Zimmermann's flat would produce something a great deal more than merely interesting.

'No wonder she stood out in the hall and talked to us,' said the sergeant. 'The place is a combination of a menagerie and a house of horrors at an amusement park.'

He had just returned from the flat, which was still being searched by a team from the police laboratory. They were not yet finished, by any means, but what they had already found was enough to convert Martina Zimmermann from a respectable landlady into a murder suspect.

The sergeant's account was sufficiently startling that the inspector hurried personally to the scene, where his first act was to order the removal of the Zimmermann children to the juvenile shelter of the social welfare department.

'Not that it makes a lot of difference,' he remarked. 'After all, they've apparently grown up in this. But I can't justify leaving minors in such an environment.'

The environment within the Zimmermann flat was, indeed, scarcely suitable to minors and not even to most adults. Martina Zimmermann had been attached to animals, but not the conventional ones. Her pets were snakes, rats and giant tropical spiders. The only innocent creatures were a few hamsters, but, as it later turned out, they were intended as food for the snakes and spiders and not as pets.

The pets had, however, not had it much better than the hamsters. A freezer in the kitchen contained partially eaten remains of raw snakes, spiders, rats and hamsters and a few pieces of boiled human flesh.

'Those are human tooth marks,' said the technician in charge of the search party, gagging slightly. 'I have seen some things in this business, but . . .'

'Remarkable,' observed the inspector. 'I've never heard of anyone eating tropical spiders before either. The things are rather expensive, I think. Anything else?'

'A complete library on witchcraft and black magic,'

said the technician. 'And one of the biggest collections of horror and sex video films I've ever seen. We haven't had time to view any of this stuff yet, but there are things there that I've only heard of. I wouldn't have believed they were available in Germany.'

Curiously, despite the collection of occult books, horror films and strange pets, the flat was not dirty or untidy. The boys had their own room and it was in perfect order, as was the clothing hanging in their wardrobe. Both were attending school and, as would later be determined, doing well. Whatever Martina Zimmermann's other interests, she was apparently a good housewife and mother.

She was also a good murderess, as she now admitted, although she denied that it had been murder. Hans Josef Wirtz had merely been helped into another plane of existence, she explained. He had been her lover, but they could not live together because it would not have been respectable for her sons. Unable to accept separation, Wirtz had asked her to kill him and she had merely complied with his wishes. Anyway, as far as she was concerned, he was not dead, but simply elsewhere. She had promised to join him, once the boys were old enough to look after themselves, and she intended to keep her promise.

As she was not, however, going to keep it immediately, the police were interested in determining the true circumstances of the murder. Mrs Zimmermann was an attractive woman, but they doubted that Hans Josef would have preferred death to separation from her.

They were hoping to extract this information from Mrs Zimmermann herself as they did not suspect that anyone else would know the details of the crime.

In this, they were mistaken. Wilhelm Zimmermann was still on excellent terms with his wife and he had not only known of the murder, but had supplied the electric saw with which she cut up the more resistant parts of the body.

He had not taken part in the actual cutting up as

Martina preferred to do this personally, but he had helped transport parts of the corpse to the park – in suitcases mounted on the luggage racks of their bicycles – and conceal them in the rhododendrons.

He was indicted on a charge of acting as an accessory after the fact to homicide and released pending trial. Eventually tried and convicted, he was given a suspended sentence as compensation for his cooperation with the investigation.

As a matter of fact, his exhaustive statement concerning what he knew of the murder, together with details of his wife's interests, activities and background, was not needed for Martina proved remarkably loquacious once she had confessed to helping her lover into a better world.

The murder, she stated, had been carried out formally and with dignity. Hans Josef had had certain sexual problems in that he could achieve orgasm only if he was naked in the bathtub while she, naked under an open dressing gown, held his head under water and simultaneously handed him an apple. As this represented a pleasant experience for him, he had decided to die in the same manner.

On the evening of Friday, 29 April 1983, he had taken five strong sleeping tablets and, as he became drowsy, undressed and got into the bathtub. Martina had stripped, perfumed herself, put on her jewelry and donned the open dressing gown.

She had entered the bathroom carrying the obligatory apple and a length of plastic cord tied into a slipnoose, which she put around Hans Josef's neck.

After having pushed his head under the water, she had given him his apple and pulled the noose tight.

Hans Josef had achieved orgasm and oblivion more or less simultaneously.

Leaving the corpse in the bathtub, she had gone about her housework and, when her husband, who was apparently living, at least part of the time, in the flat, arrived home, she asked him if he could find something to help her cut up Hans Josef, who was lying in the bathtub and who would have to be refrigerated if he was not to go bad.

Wilhelm had provided her with an electric circular saw and an electric carving knife. With these and the butcher's knives and meat saw from the kitchen, she had succeeded in cutting Hans Josef up into satisfactorily small pieces.

This had taken some time and Hans Josef was, indeed, a little bad by the time that all of him was in either the refrigerator or the freezer.

Such parts as she had eaten, she had boiled, but the head and hands she had baked in the oven in the belief that the heat would shrink them like the South American shrunken heads of which she had seen pictures.

Had this worked out well, she would have kept Hans Josef's head as a permanent souvenir of their relationship, but, instead of shrinking, the flesh had become soft and drooped so badly that he had looked more like a basset hound than a human being.

'I was no longer able to recognize him,' said Martina sadly.

She had, therefore, skinned the head and kept it in a small freezer, which she bought especially for the purpose and she set up next to her bed.

'Often,' she told the stupefied investigations officers, 'I would take him into my bed, play with him, kiss him and talk to him. Merely because he was on another plane was no reason for our sexual relations to cease.'

The investigators did not press her as to the precise form these sexual relations had taken. The details which they already had were quite revolting enough.

For Martina Zimmermann was apparently a person with even more unusual tastes in sex than her late lover. She had sometimes obtained sexual relief by watching one of her snakes or spiders devour a hamster or rat. At other times, she herself had torn the heart out of a living hamster or rat and eaten it with the same result. A regular purchaser of ox blood from the butcher, she had masturbated while bathing and washing her hair in it and she had once beaten a masochistic pharmacist nearly to unconsciousness, a process which she enjoyed as much as he.

All of these activities, including the sex games with her lover's skinned and cooked head, were, she maintained, exciting but normal and she had never felt nauseated by them in any way.

What did nauseate her was her own body, which displayed a tendency to become over plump. According to her doctor, she suffered from the compulsory eating disorder known as anorexia nervosa and her weight vacillated between a hundred and nearly two hundred pounds as she ate ravenously or dieted savagely.

Unable to cope with this problem, she had become a heavy user of Vallium, captogan and other stimulant, depressant or hallucinogenic drugs.

As is customary today, Martina Zimmermann blamed her troubles on an unhappy childhood, but, for once, the claim appeared to be justified.

Born into an unconventional family, she had been taught masturbation at the age of five by her grandfather and required by her stepfather to perform stripteases at the age of eleven.

This precocious sexual activity having come to the notice of the authorities, Martina was placed in a home for unwanted children, not an entirely apt designation in her case.

She was returned to her family at the age of fourteen, promptly raped by a second stepfather and sent back to the home, where she remained for a little more than a year before final release. By the age of sixteen, she was already pregnant with Brian.

A woman of many and varied interests, in addition to the largely sedentary pets, horror films and black magic, she went in for the more strenuous pursuits of fencing, yoga and tennis. Despite this balance between intellectual and physical activities, she had not been satisfied with her life, and her medical history included four known suicide attempts. Although she insisted that she did not regret the passing of Hans Josef, in the week following the murder she had stabbed herself in the chest and arms so seriously as to require medical treatment.

For the police, the most important question concerning this family history was whether it was true. Evidence of such a background would certainly have an influence on the decision concerning Martina Zimmermann's competence to stand trial.

It seemed that it was true. Much of what Martina said could be verified from the records of the juvenile section of the social welfare department, and witnesses' statements, including that of her thirty-five-year-old husband, tended to indicate that she was simply telling the literal truth. There was no need to embroider her life story. It was already more weird than any product of the imagination.

None the less, Martina Zimmermann was found competent to stand trial. Maintained under psychiatric observation for nearly two years, she was described by the doctors as being of higher than average intelligence and capable of understanding the illegality and consequences of her act.

She was brought to trial for murder on 9 December 1985 and for nine days a crowded courtroom listened to her description of what was undoubtedly, even for West Germany, an unusual life.

Having made a complete and, to a degree, verifiable confession, she did not deny the murder, but threw herself on the mercy of the court, pleading extenuating circumstances.

Hans Josef, she repeated, had wanted to die. He could not live without her and she could not live with him because of the bad example this would make for her children. She had, therefore, helped him to another plane of existence in the joyous manner which he had chosen for his departure. She did not regret her act because it was what he himself had wanted and it was her intention to join him as soon as her responsibilities toward her sons were ended. Killing Hans Josef had not been murder. It had been an act of love.

This was not an original defence, but the court was apparently impressed by Martina's sincerity and, although it was never possible to confirm her claim that Hans Josef had been murdered at his own request and that she had merely complied with his wishes, the charge against her was reduced from murder to manslaughter.

On Wednesday, 18 December 1985, she was found guilty on this charge and sentenced to eight years' imprisonment.

Neither verdict nor sentence were appealed and for good reason. As the counsel for the defence pointed out, she had already served two years in pre-trial detention, which reduced the sentence to six. Then, no one was expected to serve more than two-thirds of their sentence, assuming good behaviour, which accounted for another three years. This left three years to serve, but, after one year of the psychiatric treatment ordered by the court, Martina would be eligible for release on probation. It is, therefore, probable that she will be able to return to society, a changed and better person, any minute now.

2

BROKEN ENGAGEMENT

At ten-thirty in the evening of Saturday, 19 March 1983, a young woman occupying a flat on the first floor of the brick building at 162 Kuikenstraat in Drogenbos, a suburb of the city of Brussels, remembered that she had not put her car into the garage.

She descended and did so, encountering no one.

The front entrance door, normally locked after ten in the evening, was still open and, before going upstairs, she locked it.

She had barely regained her flat when there came the sound of four explosions, three very close followed a moment later by a fourth which seemed to come from the hall.

Frightened and uncertain as to the nature and origin of the reports, she double-locked her door, but did not call the police. The time was precisely ten-forty-five.

At ten-fifty, Jean-Claude and Simone Aerts, a young couple living in a flat on the ground floor, drove up to the front of the building.

They found the glass pane of the entrance door lying in shards and assumed that there had been a visit by vandals. Brussels is a city of over a million inhabitants. Vandalism is not unknown.

Aerts did not realize the significance of the fact that the broken pieces of glass were lying outside the door, indicating that someone had broken out rather than in. Fearing that the vandal might still be in the building, he left his wife outside and entered alone.

The entrance hall was empty, but there were faint

noises coming from the first-floor landing, and, ascending cautiously, he saw thirty-seven-year-old Cecile Josse-Vandenbosh, the tenant of a first-floor flat, lying on the tile floor in a pool of blood.

She was moaning softly and her breath had fogged over the cold surface of the tiles.

Unable to speak, or even, perhaps, to see, she was aware of Aerts' presence and, drawing on some last reserve of strength, moved a trembling hand to trace, slowly and painfully, the letters 'A.G.' with her index finger on the misted tiles.

As the horrified Aerts bent forward to read what she had written, the hand fell limp and motionless to the floor. The moaning stopped.

In that instant, from the open door of the flat arose a high-pitched, keening wail.

Nerves taut with shock, Aerts raised his head and saw on the floor of the entrance hall, huddled against the motionless body of a man, a tiny Yorkshire terrier crying out his sorrow with all his heart. Brutus had just lost his two best friends.

'Don't come in here, Simone!' shouted Aerts, who thought he heard his wife entering the building. 'Go back to the car!'

He ran down the stairs, fumbled the key into the lock of his own flat, snatched up the telephone and dialled 900, the emergency number of the Brussels police. Having made his report to the police, Aerts returned to the car, where his wife was anxiously waiting. Without going into detail, he informed her that their neighbours on the first floor, Yvon Josse-Vandenbosh and his wife, were dead, murdered, and that it would be best to remain in the car until the police arrived. He did not know whether the murderer was still in the building or not.

It was a short wait and, under other circumstances, would have been agreeable. Although only the middle of March, the weather was mild and Drogenbos, nestled between the Charleroi Canal and the Senne river to the south-west of the city, was fragrant with the coming spring.

A pleasant, upper-middle-class, residential suburb, Drogenbos had never seemed sinister to them, but it did now.

They were much relieved when the first patrol car arrived, followed shortly by the ambulance and then by a great many cars and vans. The duty homicide squad was moving in on the case.

Unaware of the activity in the Kuikenstraat, a baker who had just got up to go to work was drinking coffee and gazing idly at the intersection outside his window. Traffic was still brisk and he saw that there was even a hitchhiker, a rather haggard-looking young man.

Presently, a car stopped, the young man got in and the vehicle disappeared into the stream of cars. The baker noted neither the make, the colour nor the number of occupants.

In the building in Kuikenstraat, a police photographer was hurriedly snapping shots of the letters 'A.G.' traced in the moisture from the dying woman's breath. They were fading rapidly, but he was able to obtain a legible record of them.

'The initials of the murderer, beyond a doubt,' said Inspector Gerard Trautmann, bending his tall, angular body over the inscription. 'She sensed that she didn't have time to write out the name in full.'

Detective Sergeant Jacques Haan came out of the flat, holding the little Yorkshire terrier in his arms. The dog was whimpering and frightened, but it had stopped howling.

'What should I do with him?' he asked.

'See if somebody else in the building will look after him until we've notified the next of kin,' said the inspector, stretching out a long, bony hand to stroke the hairy, unhappy head. 'Pity he can't talk. He must have been a witness.'

'If he could, he'd be dead too,' said the sergeant, heading down the stairs.

He was a sober, round-faced, young man with the ends of a square, black moustache hooked down around the corners of his mouth so that he looked deceptively fierce.

A steady stream of technicians from the police laboratory was passing into the flat and the inspector stood aside to let them pass. Too thin, too sallow, too mournful of expression, he looked more like an undertaker waiting to remove the corpses than an inspector of police responsible for determining what had produced the corpses in the first place.

'Single heavy-calibre bullet through the throat at close range,' called Dr Emiles Martens, the squad's stocky, elderly, grey-haired medical officer. 'Same weapon as the woman, I expect.'

He had already concluded his examination of the corpse of Cecile Josse-Vandenbosh and was now occupied with that of her thirty-six-year-old husband. Mrs Josse-Vanderbosh, he reported, had been shot twice in the upper chest. It was a miracle that she had lived long enough to trace the initials of her murderer on the tiles.

'Time would be around ten-forty-five,' he added. 'No indication of any struggle. The woman wasn't molested sexually.'

'Exactly ten-forty-five,' said a detective who had been taking a statement from the woman in the other flat on the first floor. 'The neighbour heard the shots.'

The inspector nodded and went on into the flat. Technicians and detectives were going through the drawers and cupboards, looking for the names and addresses of the next of kin and for any potential clues to the identity of the murderer.

'Apparently someone known to them,' said the technician in charge, coming up to the inspector to report. 'There are two dirty glasses and a dirty cup on the coffee table in the living room. They had a drink together before the shooting. Robbery was not the motive. There's money and valuables to some considerable amount here and nothing's been touched.'

The inspector nodded again. 'Probably the woman,' he said. 'She was young and pretty. Triangle, I expect.'

He began to walk through the large, tastefully furnished flat, fixing the scene of the crime under investigation in his mind.

After a time, he was joined by the sergeant.

'People downstairs took the dog,' he said. 'Any developments?'

'The technicians think it was a love triangle,' said the inspector. 'I imagine about all we have to do is determine who among Mrs Josse-Vandenbosh's friends has the initials A.G.'

He knew the names of the victims. They had been identified by Jean-Claude Aerts in his initial call to the police.

'Must have been a gun collector,' remarked the sergeant, pointing with his chin at the rifles and pistols mounted on the walls of the living room and in racks.

Their survey of the scene completed, the officers left the flat. Dr Martens was already gone, on his way to the police morgue to make preparations for the autopsies. Four technicians in smocks were loading the corpses into the metal coffins used by the police for transporting bodies.

'His visitors didn't believe in signs,' said the sergeant, pointing to a small plaque on the wall beside the door to the flat. It read, 'Check your guns here'.

'It was meant as a joke,' said the inspector soberly.

Eleven miles to the north-east, too far for the inspector and the sergeant to hear, the sirens of the fire engines were howling as they raced through the streets of the suburb of Etterbeek in response to an alarm.

The fire was in a studio on the third floor of a building at 78 rue de Tervaete. It was soon put out and there was no damage to the vast collection of firearms which covered the walls.

'Either there's a permit I never heard of or he's illegal,' said one of the firemen. 'Those are hand grenades there.'

There was no one in the studio, but the firemen had not had to break in. The door was unlocked.

It did not occur to them that leaving open the door to a room containing such an expensive weapons collection was a remarkably careless act. Their job was to put out fires. They put out this one and left.

The following day, Dr Martens turned in the autopsy reports, and the documents section reported on the investigation into the background of the victims.

The autopsy reports contained nothing of value. Yvon Josse-Vandenbosh had been shot through the throat. His wife had been shot through the chest. He had died within a minute, the main arteries to the brain having been severed. She had lived a few moments longer before succumbing to loss of blood from the perforated blood vessels around the heart. Both had apparently been trying to leave the flat and there were blood stains on the telephone, indicating that one or the other had tried to call for help.

All three bullets had been recovered and sent to the ballistics experts, who reported that they were nine-milli-metre slugs fired from a pistol of which the police had no record.

The background reports on the victims were longer, but equally valueless.

The only son of an upper-middle-class family, Yvon Josse-Vandenbosh took a degree in industrial design and then found a position with the postal checking depart-ment of the Brussels post office. He had been there for the past twelve years and his career was the normal, uneventful one of an upper-level civil servant.

Privately, he was a passionate collector of firearms and a ham radio fan with contacts all over the world.

On 13 July 1968, he married Cecile Laurent and, by all accounts, the marriage was an ideally happy one.

Yvon and Cecile shared a love of nature and of animals and the investigators found, in addition to Brutus, the Yorkshire terrier, squirrels, birds and other pets in the flat.

They were fond of long walks in the countryside, sometimes alone, but often with one of the many walking clubs found everywhere in Europe.

They had many friends and no one could believe that either Yvon or Cecile was romantically involved with another person.

There were no financial problems. Yvon's job was well-paid and Cecile worked full-time as head of the accounting department of a firm called Mach III in downtown Brussels.

'Then why were they killed?' said the inspector in some irritation. 'No lovers. No mistresses. No debts. Lots of friends. No trouble with anybody. Where's the motive?'

'We don't know,' said the technician who had handed in the report and was waiting for the inspector's reaction. 'Obviously, someone had strong feelings about them, but we haven't been able to identify the person or to determine the reason for the strong feelings.'

'And that's all you have to report?' said the inspector. 'Who's A.G.?'

'No one mentioned in any of their personal papers,' said the technician. 'The document people have gone through everything. There's not an A.G. among them.'

'Prints?' asked the sergeant hopefully.

'Theirs on the glasses, an index and thumb on the handle of the coffee cup,' said the technician. 'Records reports no record.'

'The neighbour said she heard four shots,' said the inspector.

'The entrance door was locked and he shot out the glass,' said the technician. 'We weren't able to recover the bullet.'

There were no further questions and the technician left.

'We have to identify A.G.,' said the inspector glumly.

'But the lab people couldn't,' said the sergeant. 'How could he be so close to them, if nobody they knew had those initials?'

'And, if he wasn't so close to them, why did he kill them?' added the inspector. 'The case doesn't make sense.'

There was a long, thoughful silence in the office.

'Maybe A.G. isn't a person,' said the inspector finally. 'Maybe it refers to something else.'

'That must be it,' said the sergeant. 'If the lab is certain that she didn't know anybody with those initials . . .'

'The lab is not always right,' said the inspector. 'I think we'll begin by taking a look at her connections ourselves.'

A rather thorough look was taken, mostly by the sergeant. It produced only what the technician had said. Cecile Josse-Vandenbosh had known no one with the initials A.G. and neither had her husband, with one exception, a ham radio fan in Australia.

'It's ridiculous,' said the inspector, 'But ask the Australian embassy. We can't leave the question unanswered.'

It did not remain unanswered long. The embassy was able to report within twenty-four hours that the Australian A.G. was in Australia and had not left the country.

'We could put it down to the act of a total lunatic,' said the sergeant, 'if it wasn't that they obviously knew him well enough to invite him for a cup of coffee.'

'And to ask him in at close to eleven o'clock at night,' said the inspector. 'We must be overlooking some person one of them knew.'

'Maybe Josse-Vandenbosh had trouble with somebody at the post office,' suggested the sergeant.

'I doubt it,' said the inspector. 'He wasn't dealing with the public in his job. Anyway, the lab will have checked that.'

'I'll ask them,' said the sergeant.

To the inspector's indignation, it turned out that the lab had not contacted any of Josse-Vandenboshes' professional contacts.

'That's your job,' they told the sergeant. 'We handle documents and material evidence. The leg work is up to you.'

'That solves our mystery then,' said the sergeant. 'It'll be somebody he worked with.'

'I don't think so,' said the inspector. 'She was the one who wrote the initials. It was somebody she knew. Start with her office.'

The sergeant drove over to the offices of Mach III and returned within a half-hour with a suspect.

'Six assistant accountants in the office,' he said, 'One of them is named Alain Goens. Twenty-three years old. Single. Quiet. Nice guy. Very highly regarded in his job.'

'And Cecile Josse-Vandenbosch was his boss,' said the inspector. 'What happened? Did she tell him off for something?'

'Not at all,' said the sergeant. 'They got on well. He'd even been to her house. Not to see her, but her husband. He was a gun collector too.'

'Still no motive,' said the inspector. 'Well, why didn't you bring him in?'

'He wasn't there,' said the sergeant. 'Not been back to work since the night of the murder.'

The sergeant had obtained Goens' private address from the company and he now proceeded to 78 rue de Tervaete in Etterbeek with a team of detectives.

He did not expect to find Goens there and he did not. The building superintendent did not know where he was and was of the opinion that he had not been home since the night of the nineteenth.

'His studio caught fire that night,' he said. 'No serious damage, but, if he'd been back since, he'd have come to ask me about it. The firemen wet things down a little.'

The sergeant went up to look at the studio. Considering the circumstances, it seemed probable that Goens had set the fire himself.

There was no evidence of this, but he was impressed by Goens' weapon collection, which was bigger and better than Josse-Vandenbosh's. Like the fireman, he immediately noticed the hand grenades, but he knew there was no special permit. They were illegal.

Rummaging about in Goens' personal effects in search of recent photographs of the young man, he was astonished to discover many pictures of Cecile Josse-Vandenbosh.

More astonishing yet, some of them showed Goens and Cecile together in the room he was in and in more informal poses than would normally be expected of an assistant accountant and his boss. Neither was undressed nor was there anything which could be described as improper, but the attitudes were far from professional and there were many of the photographs.

There was no indication where Goens might have gone, and the sergeant returned to headquarters with the photographs. He found the inspector conducting a canvas of the Drogenbos area with patrol cars bearing loud speakers on their roofs. They were requesting information from anyone who might have seen a man answering to Goens' description between the hours of ten and eleven on the night of March the nineteenth.

The sergeant reported what he had found in Etterbeek and showed the inspector the photographs.

The inspector responded by losing his temper and went storming down the hall to the laboratory. He shoved the photographs under the nose of the chief technician and demanded to know why he had been assured that Mrs Josse-Vandenbosh had had no extra-marital contacts, when she had been spending her afternoons in the studio of one of her assistant accountants.

The chief technician was unable to answer, but said, very stiffly, that he would check his men's findings and forward a written report.

The inspector returned growling to his office, where a telephone call had just been received from the baker who had seen a young man hitchhiking in the neighbourhood shortly after the time of the crime.

The report was useful for it placed Goens, or at least

someone who looked like him, in the area at the time in question.

The fact that he had been hitchhiking was, however, strange. As an assistant accountant, he made quite enough money to own a car.

It was the sergeant, acting on a hunch, who cleared up this mystery by calling the traffic department.

Goens had owned a car up until March the twentieth of the preceding year. On that date, he had driven it into a stone wall in an apparent suicide attempt which had failed, but which had resulted in severe injuries to a pedestrian nearby. Goens' driving licence had been withdrawn and he had been fined.

'March the twentieth last year, he tried to commit suicide and March the nineteenth this year, he murders his boss,' said the inspector. 'There's a connection there of some kind.'

'Maybe they were having an affair and she tried to break it off last year,' said the sergeant. 'His suicide attempt made her change her mind, but this year she decided to break off after all so he killed her.'

'Something like that,' said the inspector. 'Although the specific date seems suspicious. It must be some kind of an anniversary.'

If it was, it was no anniversary shared by Alain Goens and Cecile Josse-Vandenbosh. She had been on a two-week holiday in the Canary Islands during the last half of March 1982.

'Well, hell . . . !' said the inspector, shocking the sergeant with the first profane expression he had ever heard from his chief's mouth.

There was worse to come. The laboratory had made a study of the pictures taken from Goens' studio and they now reported that an analysis of the degree of aging showed that two of them had been taken at a time when Cecile Josse-Vandenbosh was in the hospital following a minor operation.

'We have no explanation for it either,' said the chief

technician. 'The woman couldn't be in two places at once.'

'Unless she was twins?' said the sergeant, grasping at straws.

'She was an only child,' said the inspector. 'You talked to the family yourself.'

At four o'clock the following morning, the inspector was roused from a sound sleep by the ringing of the telephone beside his bed.

On the other end of the line was the sergeant in a state of great excitement.

'They don't have to be twins to look alike!' he yelled into his startled chief's ear. 'He just had a girl friend who looked like Mrs Josse-Vandenbosh.'

The inspector thought it over.

'Well, perhaps,' he said finally. 'But I don't see it helps our case.'

And hung up.

'What would help the case was the apprehension of Alain Goens, who was now being sought all over Belgium and in the neighbouring countries of Germany, France, Holland and Luxemburg.

As it turned out, Goens was in none of those places, but in the flat of a friend named François Jaumotte, who lived at 57 rue de Tervaete, less than a block away from Goens' studio.

This having been determined, the sergeant led a squad of heavily armed detectives on a raid of the flat, brushing the startled Jaumotte, who had opened the door, out of the way.

In the living room, Goens saw the police burst through the door, instantly drew a heavy .357 magnum pistol from his waist band and opened fire.

One slug hit the sergeant square in the middle of the chest and would have ended his career had he not been wearing a bullet-proof vest.

The sergeant promptly returned the fire, striking Goens to the right and four inches above the navel with a single round from his 7.65-mm service pistol.

Gravely wounded, Goens fell to the floor, but remained conscious. With an enormous effort, he raised his gun, tucked the muzzle under his chin and pulled the trigger.

The result was devastating. Goens' jaw was smashed, his tongue was torn away and a part of his brain was reduced to jelly.

Incredibly, he was still alive and, the ambulance having been standing by during the raid, he arrived very quickly at the hospital where, all predictions to the contrary, he survived.

But not in any condition to be of use to either the police or himself. In addition to the shredded tongue, which rendered him permanently mute, the brain damage was so severe that Goens was reduced to the state of a vegetable. Speechless, mindless, unaware of the world around him, he lies motionless day after day waiting for the death which may be many years yet in coming.

The case was solved and it was not solved. Without question Alain Goens had murdered Yvon and Cecile Josse-Vandenbosh, but there was no answer to why.

Cecile resembled strongly a girl named Martine with whom Goens had associated for roughly a year. They had shared the studio flat and Goens had expected them to marry.

On 19 March 1982, a year to the day before the murders, Martine had left Goens and broken off their engagement.

His suicide attempt, which had ended in the loss of his driver's licence, followed.

What took place in the Josse-Vandenbosh flat will never be known. Goens knew Yvon as they often exchanged information on guns and weapon collecting, but they were not friends. The difference in ages and backgrounds was too great.

On that night, he had gone there armed with the 9-mm revolver later found in Jaumotte's flat and had been invited in and offered a cup of coffee.

He had finished the coffee and then murdered his hosts.

Two theories concerning his motives were developed.

According to the first, the loss of Martine had so preyed on Goens' mind that he had lost touch with reality and sincerely believed that the woman he killed was the faithless Martine.

According to the second, he had planned to kill Martine and told the Josse-Vandenboshes of his intentions. Horrified, they had tried to disarm him and had been killed in the attempt.

In either case, the murders had taken place on the anniversary of Martine's departure and were, undoubtedly, the result of it.

Said Martine's father,' He seemed like such a nice boy. He was one of the very few that I would allow her to live with.'

3

MAKE WAY FOR YOUTH

It was a moving funeral and hugely attended. Mourners had come from Chassenneuil-sur-Bonnieure, La Roche-foucauld, St Claud, even as far away as Confolens. As for Cellefrouin, the entire population was, of course, present.

René Cailler had been well-known, modestly famous even, in the Charente, the sparsely populated, flat country between Limoges and Angoulême some eighty miles inland from the French Atlantic coast.

Immediately following the coffin came the family, fifty-three-year-old Sylvie Cailler, René's wife of thirty years, supported on the arm of her younger son, twenty-year-old Christian. Behind them walked her two other children, Solange, who was twenty-five and married, and Jean-Paul, twenty-three, who was not married but no longer living at home.

'A pity that they could not be buried together,' whispered a woman at the back of the crowd.

'But no! What a humiliation for the family,' replied her companion. 'The priest would not permit it.'

René Cailler was laid to rest in glorious early autumn sunshine on 3 October 1983. He was fifty-seven years old at the time of his death and in excellent health. He had, undoubtedly, expected to live longer.

On the day following, Jeanne Metayer was buried only a few graves away in the same cemetery of Cellefrouin, the tiny village where both she and René were born and where Jeanne had lived all her life. She too had been in radiant health and was barely fifty years old.

René had lived only the beginning and the end of his life in Cellefrouin. As a young man, he went out to Gabon, one of France's African colonies where he served as an officer in the gendarmerie. All the children were born in the town of Mayumba and it was only in 1965 that he retired from the gendarmerie and returned to Cellefrouin to go into the insurance business.

Being clever, industrious and having a pleasing personality, he was an immediate success and, being public spirited, he combined his professional career with an active role in local politics. Needless to say, he was conservative.

In 1968, he sold Jeanne Metayer an insurance policy, and one of those inexplicable sparks of emotional empathy flashed between them so that they immediately became and remained lovers.

She was married to a man named Bernard Metayer who worked in a factory in La Rochefoucauld and, although there were no children, the marriage was a happy one. There was never any suggestion of divorce.

Nor was there in the case of René Cailler.

But René loved Jeanne and Jeanne loved René and there was no concealing the fact. Even after fifteen years, they were like two love-sick adolescents. They could scarcely bear to be separated.

The affair had, of course, instantly become known to everyone in the Charente, including Bernard and Sylvie. They had been, understandably, lacking in enthusiasm, but with typical French tolerance they succeeded in accepting the relationship.

Bernard worked shifts at the factory and, three times a week, René spent a night or a day with Jeanne, depending upon the shift that Bernard was working.

The arrangement did nothing to affect René's reputation nor that of Jeanne. Indeed, she was regarded as something of a minor saint because of her phenomenal kindness and local charity work. At the time of her death she was housing an old woman in her spare bedroom simply because she was too poor to pay rent elsewhere.

René and Jeanne were, therefore, a respectable and respected couple, even if they did happen to be married to other people, and it would never have occurred to anyone that they would become the first persons ever to be murdered in Cellefrouin.

Murder certainly did not cross the mind of Bernard Metayer when he arrived home at five-thirty on the morning of September the twenty-eighth and found the metallic grey Peugeot 505 belonging to René Cailler parked in front of the house.

He was, however, astonished. The lovers had always been discreetly considerate of his feelings. René had never before been there when he arrived home.

His astonishment was quickly replaced by alarm when he arrived at the front door and saw that the glass panes were smashed and the door was standing half-open.

Calling out his wife's name, he charged into the house and came to an abrupt halt outside the kitchen door.

René and Jeanne were lying on the floor near the table. They were both fully dressed and they were both dead.

There was no doubt about that. Their throats had been cut literally from ear to ear, the wounds below the chins gaping like huge grinning red mouths.

To the stunned Metayer it seemed impossible that so much blood could have come from only two human bodies. The entire kitchen was coated with it. Walls, floor, furniture, everything was smeared with the bright red glistening substance. Even the ceiling was splashed by the jets from the severed arteries.

Gasping as if he had been struck a violent blow in the pit of the stomach, Metayer backed away from the kitchen door, ran out of the house, climbed into his car and raced away in the direction of Confolens, nearly twenty miles to the north-east. His house was on the edge of Cellefrouin and there were other communities nearby, but, in his state of profound shock, all he could think of was the gendarmerie post at Confolens.

He did not, however, get there. The familiar demands of driving exercised a calming effect and, regaining some control of his emotions, he stopped at the nearest house to telephone the gendarmerie.

The gendarmes did not believe him. Metayer's description of the bodies was far too graphic and they knew Cellefrouin perfectly well. It was not the sort of place in which people's throats were savagely cut.

The general conclusion was that Metayer was drunk, a theory supported by the fact that he was almost unintelligible with excitement and sorrow.

Bernard had loved his wife and he had been fond of René. After fifteen years as Jeanne's lover, René was practically a member of the family.

The sergeant on the duty desk, therefore, urged Metayer to remain where he was and sent a car to investigate. He did not believe that anyone had been murdered, but the report was official and had to be followed up.

To the consternation of the two gendarmes in the car, Metayer was obviously not drunk at all and, when he led them back to his house, they were able to confirm his statement in all respects. It was a murder, a double murder, a horrible one.

The duty sergeant's response to this report was to send in half a dozen more cars and notify the criminal investigations department of the Angoulême police.

Angoulême, a city of some fifty thousand, is nearly as far to the south-west of Cellefrouin as Confolens is to the north-east, but its criminal investigations department has responsibility for the area.

Which, generally, does not amount to a great deal of work for the homicide squad. The district is rural and peaceful, and the relatively small number of inhabitants are more concerned with making a living than with murdering each other.

As a result, on night duty at the criminal investigations department was a single extremely junior detective and, from nine in the evening until eight-thirty in the morning, there was no homicide squad at all.

It was now, however, barely seven and the homicide squad was, if out of bed at all, having breakfast and morosely scanning the customary horrors of the morning papers.

The junior detective on duty did not know what to do. He could scarcely initiate an investigation of what appeared to be one of the most important cases with which the department had ever been presented; nor could he stall until the homicide squad came on duty in another hour and a half.

The logical and, indeed, prescribed response was to call out the members of the homicide squad. They were, after all, on permanent stand-by.

But the detective was afraid to do this because he did not know which of the two permanent officers of the squad to call out first.

Inspector Louis Bouton was the senior officer-in-charge and the detective was not afraid of him at all. A mild-mannered, elderly man with sweeping white moustaches and a fine head of snow-white hair, he was one of the most popular officers in the force and particularly so with the younger detectives, in whom he took a fatherly sort of interest. There was nothing to be feared from Inspector Bouton.

Not so his assistant and second-in-command, Sergeant Paul Mougenou. A short, remarkably handsome man, invariably well-groomed and nattily dressed, he was the youngest officer ever to have achieved the rank of sergeant of detectives in the history of the Angoulême police.

He had not achieved it as a result of a gentle nature. Brilliant, aggressive and ambitious, he was a dangerous man to cross and his immediate goal was the command of the homicide squad.

This was, however, only possible if Inspector Bouton retired and Inspector Bouton, although already at an age when he could gracefully do so, showed no inclination to retire.

Sergeant Mougenou was left chafing helplessly at the bit and, if there was anything that the sergeant did not like it was the sensation of being helpless.

The situation did not improve his temper and he was treated very gingerly by the junior members of the department.

The duty detective's problem was that, if he were not given the opportunity to decide whether his superior be called out or left to come in at eight-thirty, Sergeant Mougenou would be unhappy. Knowing the sergeant, he had no doubt what the decision would be.

However, the inspector, who was quite aware of his assistant's ambitions to replace him, if necessary, even before he retired, had issued orders that no action affecting his section was to be taken without his knowledge, and to disobey would be unthinkable as well as harmful to his career.

Confronted with this insoluble problem, the detective did what all good civil servants do. He passed the buck to his immediate superior, the on-call inspector for the night shift.

Inspector Bouton was, therefore, informed at a little after seven-thirty, just as he was finishing his breakfast, that a double murder had taken place in the village of Cellefrouin.

He issued instructions that his assistant and the appropriate technical sections be alerted, and departed immediately for the scene.

As none of the technical personnel was yet on duty, he found no one present other than Bernard Metayer, fourteen gendarmes from the Confolens post and Sergeant Mougenou, who had been notified only a few moments after his chief, but who had dressed and driven a good deal faster.

The gendarmes had set up a cordon around the house and Metayer was sitting in his car crying.

The inspector came over, put a comforting hand on his shoulder and asked if he was prepared to make a statement. The circumstances being unknown, it was possible that Metayer was the murderer.

Metayer said he had no statement to make. He had

come home from working the night shift and found his wife and her lover murdered.

The two officers exchanged glances. Gallic tolerance aside, a great many wives and their lovers are murdered by outraged husbands in France.

Metayer did not appear prepared to confess, however, and the investigators entered the house – cautiously, as they did not want to risk destroying any potential clues.

They did not enter the kitchen at all, the view from the door being sufficient to confirm the reports of a double murder.

Inspector Bouton then went back outside to talk with Metayer. He had seen that the blood was dried in places, indicating that the murders had taken place some considerable time earlier, so that, if Metayer's claim of working the night shift was true, he could be eliminated as a suspect.

Sergeant Mougenou remained in the house, going through the downstairs rooms and then ascending to the first floor. Presently, he came out again with a somewhat puzzled expression and joined the inspector and Metayer.

Who, he wanted to know, was the old woman sleeping in the front bedroom upstairs?

Metayer said that it was Mrs Paulette Vault, a poor woman with no place to go. She had been living in their spare bedroom.

'But she must have been in the house when the murders took place,' said the inspector.

Metayer said he supposed so. Mrs Vault went out very little and certainly not at night. She was eighty-one years old.

'She has good nerves for her age,' said the sergeant. 'She's sound asleep up there.'

'She may not even know about the murders,' said the inspector. 'Wake her up gently and ask her if she noticed anything. Don't tell her that anyone was killed.'

The inspector was right. Mrs Paulette Vault had slept straight through two bloody murders committed ten feet below her bed. If she had heard nothing, it was hardly strange. The old woman was almost completely deaf.

'Lucky for her,' remarked the sergeant. 'He'd have killed her too, if she'd been a witness. If you want to go back to the office, I can handle things here. It'll take them hours to go over the house and Descroix isn't even here yet.'

Descroix was the department's medical expert who would have to examine the bodies before they could be moved. A solid, square-built man with a clean-shaven, emotionless face, he was not actually attached to the police, but worked on the basis of a contract with the city. He had, so far, not responded to the alert.

Those going over the house were, of course, the technicians from the police laboratory, the fingerprint experts and the photographer.

The inspector gave the sergeant a thoughtful glance and went silently to his car. It was true that there was nothing to be done other than stand around and wait for the reports of the specialists, but he doubted that the sergeant's sole motive was his chief's comfort.

This was, undoubtedly, the biggest case that either he or the sergeant would ever face and there would be much credit due to whoever was most active in solving it.

In short, he might yet retire as chief inspector, or he might retire sooner than he wanted while the sergeant became Inspector Mougenou, officer-in-charge of the homicide squad.

There was also a third possibility. The case might not be solved and there would be no credit at all.

On the basis of the reports when he finally received them at the office, the third possibility seemed the most likely.

Dr Descroix had found nothing of significance on the bodies, either at the scene or during the course of the autopsies, other than proof of the innocence of Bernard Metayer. The murders had taken place at approximately eleven-thirty on the preceding night, when he had been at work in La Rochefoucauld.

It was not possible to say which of the two victims had been killed first. Both had cuts on arms and hands where they had attempted to ward off what the doctor said was an extremely sharp, double-edged, rigid blade at least ten inches long.

In addition to their cut throats, René had been stabbed thirty-seven times, mostly in the chest and upper abdomen, and Jeanne had been stabbed thirty-three times in the belly and stomach.

A great many of the stab wounds would have been fatal eventually, but the actual cause of death in both cases was massive blood loss.

The technicians reported that there were signs of a desperate struggle in the kitchen, but no indications that the murderer had been anywhere in the house other than the entrance hall and the kitchen.

Robbery was not a motive, for money and valuables had been left untouched.

The glass panes of the front door had been broken with a stone left lying on the steps and the murderer had then reached through to open the locked door from the inside. The handle of the door had been wiped, presumably when he was leaving.

They had found one clue. The murderer's footprints in blood. He had been wearing tennis shoes.

'Size ten,' said the sergeant. 'He must be a big rascal. Should help in eliminating potentials.'

'Well, he was wearing big shoes,' said the inspector mildly. 'What size the feet in them were . . .'

The sergeant looked annoyed. It was the sort of observation a young, dynamic investigator should have made.

'But, I dare say, that occurred to you too,' said the inspector. 'How are things going with the interrogations?'

The entire population of Cellefrouin was being interrogated, as would be the bulk of the population of the other communities nearby. The murderer was believed to be, with almost total certainty, a local man.

'Or woman,' said the inspector.

'With size ten shoes?' said the sergeant.

'Shoes, not necessarily feet,' said the inspector, causing the sergeant to wince slightly.

'We've turned up no potential suspects at all,' he said. 'As far as we've been able to determine, Cailler didn't have an enemy in the Charente. As for the woman, everybody loved her.'

'Some more than others,' observed the inspector. 'Mr Cailler, for example. Where was Mrs Cailler that evening?'

'At home and not alone,' said the sergeant. 'The youngest son is the only one living at home and he'd gone out on a date, but the neighbours had come over and they were playing cards until after midnight.'

'That disposes of the two obvious suspects,' said the inspector pensively. 'The husband at work. The wife at home. Who else?'

'Nobody,' said the sergeant. 'That is, no suspects.'

'And no motive,' said the inspector. 'And yet, they were murdered.'

'There has to be a motive and there have to be suspects,' said the sergeant. 'We just haven't found them out yet.'

'Do you think we will?' said the inspector.

The sergeant looked unhappy and remained silent.

In fact, he was not as unhappy as he looked. Although he had not seen fit to mention it to the inspector, the laboratory report also stated that the tennis shoes worn by the murderer were not new and that, if they could be located, they could be identified. One of his teams of detectives was now making up a list of names of men in Cellefrouin and other villages who wore size ten tennis shoes. Practically speaking, this meant large, young men. The sergeant did not agree that the feet of the murderer might not match the shoes. That would indicate a degree of sophistication which he thought unlikely in the district.

On the other hand, the murders appeared to be deliberate. The murderer had come armed. He had broken into the house. He had stolen nothing. Moreover, the number of stab wounds, far greater than needed simply to kill, indicated an overwhelming hatred of the victims. The motive was clearly emotional.

Unfortunately, no one in the entire area was known to have hated either René Cailler or Jeanne Metayer. The only two persons who might have hated them, Bernard Metayer and Sylvie Cailler, were unquestionably innocent.

But could one of them have hired a killer?

The sergeant did not think so. In the first place, the affair had already been going on for fifteen years and had been long since accepted by everyone concerned. If Metayer or Mrs Cailler had been going to hire a killer, it would seem that they would have done it a good deal earlier.

Secondly, a hired killer would have had no reason to hate the victims. He would, presumably, not even have known them. He would have stabbed them once or twice, cut their throats and left, probably taking with him everything of value in the house.

No, it was someone from the immediate circle of the victims' contacts, someone who had hated them, and it was merely a matter of identifying him.

The sergeant was confident and optimistic. There were not that many young men who wore size ten tennis shoes in such a sparsely populated area.

It was, however, important to locate the suspect quickly. The same line of thought could well occur to the inspector.

As a matter of fact, it had not or, rather, the inspector had been too preoccupied with his own theory to give much attention to anything else.

His theory rested upon the somewhat unusual background of René Cailler.

The man had been a gendarme in Africa for many years. Gendarmes and police officers often made enemies in the course of carrying out their duties, as the inspector had good reason to know. René Cailler had very probably had enemies in Gabon.

France was now full of Africans. The arrival of the socialists to power had resulted in such lax policies on immigration that Africans were pouring into France in a flood to avail themselves of the generous welfare benefits financed by French taxpayers. Among them were certainly some from Gabon.

And among those immigrants from Gabon might well be one of René Cailler's old enemies – or, perhaps, the son of one of his enemies – who had learned where Cailler was and had come to settle the score. Jeanne Metayer had, of course, been killed simply to eliminate a witness.

If this theory was correct, then there would have been a black man in the area around Cellefrouin on September the twenty-seventh and he would surely have been noticed. In a big city, such as Marseille, blacks were more common than whites, but a black in the little villages of the Charente was a rarity.

The inspector sent out a team of his own to search for witnesses who had seen a black man wearing tennis shoes. He did not specify a large man as he did not know how African shoe sizes ran. However, he was under the impression that they were rather larger than in France.

The inspector and the sergeant were, therefore, carrying out quiet, separate investigations and this could not, of course, last. The Angoulême police department of criminal investigations was not large enough for secrets. In the end, the inspector called in the sergeant and asked him if he had found any tennis shoes matching the pattern of the prints in blood and the sergeant replied that he had not, but that he had reports of the sighting of a black man in the area on September the twenty-sixth.

This was bad news for it meant that the case would probably not be solved. Many of the Africans in France were there illegally and it would be impossible to trace the man, even if he had remained in the country, which was not likely.

As the only description of him was that he was black and rather small, not much could be done in that direction. The investigators, now reunited in misfortune, turned to the tennis shoe lead, not because they thought it would result in anything but in order to show for the record that they had left no stone unturned.

The sergeant obtained fairly complete lists of all the size ten tennis shoe wearers in the district and it turned out that not all of them were big men. Even Christian Cailler, who was rather puny, wore size ten tennis shoes.

'And of the same sole pattern as the ones at the scene,' remarked the sergeant, 'but, of course, not the same ones. The shoe style is common around here. About eighty per cent of the tennis shoes are from the same manufacturer.'

'But you checked his shoes anyway?' said the inspector.

'Didn't have to,' said the sergeant. 'He has an alibi for the time of the murders. He was with his date. She's a seventeen-year-old girl named Estelle Petit.'

'You have a statement from her?' persisted the inspector.

'No,' said the sergeant in some irritation. 'We didn't consider the boy a valid suspect. Why would he murder his father and his father's mistress?'

'I don't know,' said the inspector. 'Let's ask him.'

They did not ask him immediately, but, after Estelle denied that she had laid eyes on Christian on the evening of September the twenty-seventh, and after it was learned that Christian was a passionate collector of knives and daggers, and after it was determined that one of his daggers, a double-edged weapon with a rigid ten-inch blade, and a pair of his tennis shoes were missing, they did.

Christian whined, protested his innocence and then broke down and confessed. He had been tired, he said, of his father pushing him around. He had not had very good marks at school and his father had been too critical.

The investigators found this a feeble motive and continued the interrogation.

Christian said that the true motive was that he could no longer stand to see his mother humiliated by his father's affair with another woman. He had murdered to revenge his mother.

The investigators were still not satisfied, but they were unable to obtain any further admissions.

Christian was placed under psychiatric observation to see if he was competent to stand trial, and the real motive of the murders was gradually extracted from him by the psychologists.

It had been jealousy pure and simple.

René Cailler had been a forceful, able leader of men, widely admired and respected, successful in business and popular with women.

Christian had been a physical weakling, mediocre at school, a mama's boy and frustratingly unsuccessful with women.

He had simply not been able to bear the comparison between himself and his father.

Following the crime, he had thrown his blood-stained tennis shoes and the dagger into a nearby pond, from which they were eventually recovered by the police.

The court recognized that he had been under considerable emotional stress, but, as he had been found competent to stand trial and the crimes had been deliberate and premeditated, there was little choice but to sentence him to life imprisonment and this was done on 2 November 1984.

As for Inspector Bouton, he retired with the rank of chief inspector, a week after the trial ended. Inspector Paul Mougenou is now chief of the Angoulême homicide squad.

4

A HAIR IN THE HAND

On the evening of Monday, 22 March 1982, a plump but not unattractive woman of thirty-eight was climbing the stairs of the Résidence Ile de France, located at 35 rue Guy de Maupassant in the French city of Rouen.

Mrs Thérèse Rangée had finished work at the insurance company, done her shopping and was now going to prepare dinner for herself and her thirteen-year-old daughter, Roselyne. The time was a quarter to eight.

Roselyne did not answer the doorbell and Mrs Rangée put down her bag of groceries and opened the door with her key. She was not too surprised that Roselyne was not at home. She was not a girl to sit around in the flat alone, and her father had left following the divorce two years earlier.

Dropping off the groceries in the kitchen, Mrs Rangée continued down the hall to Roselyne's room. Being an experienced mother of a teenage daughter, she suspected that the room would be a shambles and, if so, she intended to have a word with Roselyne about it when she turned up.

Shuddering slightly at the horrors she expected to encounter inside, Mrs Rangée opened the door and found herself confronted with a horror beyond anything that she could have imagined.

The room was a shambles and, in the middle of it, on the floor next to her bed, lay Roselyne. Her knitted blouse was open to the waist, exposing her adolescent breasts, as yet not subjected to the restraint of a brassière. Her short skirt was pushed up around her waist, leaving her naked from the navel down, and a pair of white nylon panties lay on the floor beside her.

Breasts and belly were stained with dark-brown dried blood.

Thérèse Rangée staggered back as if she had been struck, clutched her temples and, throwing back her head in a primeval gesture of unendurable sorrow, gave vent to a long, wailing cry almost like that of a howling she-wolf.

In the flat next door, Mrs Paulette Garaud, just beginning her evening meal, froze with the fork halfway to her mouth. The cry was not loud, but it was very penetrating and, like many modern buildings, this one was not acoustically insulated.

Mrs Garaud did not recognize the sound as human. Rather, she thought that someone had abandoned a dog in the corridors and, being fond of animals, she put down her fork and went to investigate.

As she emerged from her flat, the adjoining door was flung violently open and Mrs Rangée stumbled out, gasping, weeping and crying out 'Roselyne's dead! Roselyne's dead!'

Although Mrs Garaud did not know the Rangées well, she knew that Roselyne was Mrs Rangee's daughter and, as the hysterical woman collapsed against the wall of the corridor, she rushed past her into the flat, where, after looking through two wrong doors, she located Roselyne's room.

The sight of the girl's body was nearly as much of a shock to her as it had been to Mrs Rangée. She had been expecting some kind of an accident, but this was clearly rape and murder.

Running back to her own flat, she hurriedly dialled the combined emergency number of the ambulance, police and fire department.

Distances in Rouen, an ancient city famed for its cathedral, are short and the response to Mrs Garaud's call was swift. Although its population is under a hundred and twenty thousand, the community, ninety miles to the north-west of Paris, is prosperous and the public services are generally excellent.

She had barely had time to hang up the telephone and go to see what she could do for Mrs Rangée when a patrol car arrived in front of the building.

As she had given the flat number in her report, the policemen came straight up, entered the flat and immediately came out again to confirm the murder report over Mrs Garaud's telephone.

By this time, the ambulance too had arrived and a paramedic came running up the stairs, followed by two stretcher-bearers.

While the stretcher-bearers waited in the hall, the paramedic went in to the body together with one of the police officers, but came out again after only a few minutes. The girl, he said, was not only dead; she had been dead for some time.

As there was nothing for the ambulance crew to do, they returned to their base.

In the meantime, at police headquarters the report had been forwarded to the department of criminal investigations and the evening duty homicide squad was preparing to leave for the scene of the crime.

It consisted of Inspector of Detectives René Savarois, a relatively slight man with reddish-blond hair and brilliant blue eyes who looked younger than he was, and Medical Officer Maurice Depetry who was short, stocky, black-haired, black-moustached and black-browed so that he looked like the villain in a second-rate melodrama. A third member of the basic squad, Detective Sergeant Julien Barente, had not been in the office when the report was received and would follow as soon as he could be located.

Also alerted, but not yet called away until the circumstances of the case had been determined, were a detachment from the police laboratory, a fingerprint expert, the police photographer and a weapons specialist.

At the block of flats, the homicide squad found no one present other than the two uniformed officers from the patrol car. Mrs Garaud had taken Mrs Rangée into her flat, where she was plying her with neat brandy by the water glass. This had already produced a calming or, perhaps, numbing effect.

While the doctor began his inspection of the corpse, the inspector wandered slowly through the flat, looking at everything but touching nothing. He was not searching for anything in particular, but experience had shown that a survey of the scene sometimes produced unexpected benefits later.

He finished shortly as the flat was not large, and went to stand silently watching the doctor, who had completed his determination of the cause of death and turned his attention to the sexual aspects of the case.

'She doesn't appear to have been raped,' he commented. 'Her hymen has been ruptured, but not recently and I see no signs of penetration or any traces of semen, either in the sex organs or on the body.'

'Impotent or frightened off,' said the inspector.

'Perhaps neither,' said the doctor. 'The thing looks staged to me. We may have an attempted cover-up for another motive here.'

'Time and cause?' said the inspector.

'Not less than eight hours,' said the doctor. 'Possibly more. Immediate cause was probably internal bleeding, although some of the vital organs may have been damaged as well. I don't see anything that would be of much use to you.'

'No, I suppose not,' said the inspector. 'Do you think the knife there on the floor was the murder weapon?'

'Very probably,' said the doctor. 'Ho! What's this?'

The girl's long black hair had been lying down over her face, and the doctor had lifted it and turned it back. Against the white skin of the forehead, red scratches stood out clearly in a crooked row of strange signs like some sort of exotic script.

'Is that writing?' said the inspector, bending down to look. 'What do you make of it?'

'No form of writing familiar to me,' said the doctor. 'It's possible that this is a ritual murder of some kind.'

The sergeant stuck his long, thin face in through the door. 'Got here as quick as I could,' he said, his metal-rimmed glasses glinting. 'Did you say ritual murder?'

'Could be,' said the inspector. 'Call headquarters and tell them we'll need the full squad. This is not something we're going to solve by looking at it.'

By the following day, he was beginning to wonder if they were going to solve it at all.

The specialists and technicians had poured into the flat, and what they found left them nearly as confused as their report would leave the inspector. The indications were, to say the least, contradictory.

To begin with, the sexual aspects of the crime were definitely faked. The blood on the breasts and pubic area had been deliberately smeared there – possibly, suggested the laboratory, by someone who believed the girl to be a virgin and thought that blood on the genitals would constitute proof of rape.

Secondly, the girl's blouse had not been torn open, but unbuttoned after she had been stabbed. There was a slit in it where the knife had gone through under the left breast.

Even the nylon panties lying beside the body had not been removed by the murderer, but had apparently been taken out of the chest of drawers. The lab tests showed that they had not been worn since laundering.

Partially covered by the corpse was a large coloured poster of the popular, but aging, French rock singer Johnny Hallyday. It had been torn from the wall, where there were other posters of rock singers and musicians.

A record player, a collection of stuffed animals, a tennis racket, books, magazines and scattered articles of clothing completed the typical décor of an adolescent girl's room.

Lying on the Johnny Hallyday poster was a large, single-edged kitchen knife, which tests showed had been the murder weapon. There was a small amount of blood on the blade. Mrs Rangée subsequently identified the knife as having come from her own kitchen.

The strange marks on the girl's forehead had been photographed and the pictures submitted to language experts at the University of the Sorbonne in Paris. They had been unable to identify them, but several had remarked that they bore a resemblance to the occult signs used by practitioners of black magic.

The signs had been made with an ice pick from the kitchen, which had been returned to the drawer where it was usually kept. Although the handle, as in the case of the knife, had been wiped clean of fingerprints, there were visible traces of blood on the point.

The specialists were at a loss as to how to interpret these findings.

The murderer had obviously gone to very considerable lengths to confuse the circumstances of the crime, but his motives for so doing were unclear.

He had staged a sex crime, but had apparently not been sexually interested in the victim at all. There was no indication that he had touched the body any more than absolutely necessary.

Nothing had been stolen from the flat and there were no indications of a forcible entry. The murder had not been committed by a surprised burglar.

Strangest of all, however, was the matter of the knife and the ice pick. The knife had been used for the murder, the ice pick to scratch the unidentified marks on the victim's forehead. The handles of both had been wiped, obviously to eliminate fingerprints, but why had the blades then been left conspicuously bloody? And why had the ice pick been put carefully back in the drawer in the kitchen while the knife was left beside the body?

Because of these inconsistencies, the laboratory was inclined to the theory of a mentally deranged killer, but even this, they admitted, did not fit fully the circumstances of the case.

For example, the murder appeared to be deliberate

and not the uncontrolled act of a psychopath, for the single knife-wound was to the hilt and in a fatal area.

The only conclusion that they were able to draw was that Roselyne had been murdered by someone who knew the flat well enough to know where the knives were kept, but this was not certain either. Even a total stranger would have expected the knives to be in the drawers of the kitchen counter.

Neither sex nor money had been a motive and they could suggest no other. It seemed unlikely that a thirteen-year-old girl would have an enemy who hated her enough to kill her.

The autopsy report was scarcely more helpful. It confirmed that Roselyne had not been sexually molested in any way and that the cause of death had been massive internal bleeding as a result of the severing of major blood vessels near the heart. The heart itself had not been touched.

Roselyne, said Dr Depetry, had fought for her life. Two of the fingernails on her right hand and one on her left were broken and her hands and forearms were bruised.

She had been found with her right hand clenched in a fist and, when the doctor opened it at the morgue, he found it to contain a single long black hair, which he, at first, thought to be one of Roselyne's own.

A microscopic examination of the hair revealed, however, that it was, although very similar to Roselyne's, from an older person.

The murder appeared to have taken place shortly after Mrs Rangée left the flat to go to work at a quarter past eight in the morning.

Under normal circumstances, Roselyne would have left half an hour later. She was a pupil at the Pasteur Technical School in Petit Couronne, the suburb to the south-west of the city where the Résidence Ile de France was located, and her first class would have been at nine-thirty.

She had not attended it, and this fixed, with some

precision, the time of death at between eight-fifteen and eight-forty-five of that Monday.

It was the only thing that could be fixed with precision.

Questioning of Mrs Rangée had produced a statement to the effect that she herself had had no intimate male contacts since her divorce and that her daughter had been too young for any.

This was undoubtedly true, but the autopsy showed that Roselyne had had at least one intimate contact, for she had not been a virgin for some time.

Roselyne, said her mother, was a rather shy, timid girl and she was quite certain that she would never have let a stranger into the flat, particularly when she was alone there.

Her schoolmates, however, told the police that she was anything but shy and timid, particularly where men were concerned. Some thought that she would have let any male into the flat in her mother's absence, if he were reasonably attractive physically.

'But at eight-thirty of a Monday morning?' said the sergeant. 'The girl wasn't a nymphomaniac and she would have been getting ready to go to school. Whatever she let him in for, it wasn't sex.'

'You've checked the utility people and the postman?' said the inspector. 'Nearly anyone will let in somebody who says they're from the electricity company, even if they don't have any identification at all.'

'We checked the real utility men and the postman,' said the sergeant. 'They're all clear. There's no way of checking if one turned up who wasn't authentic.'

'Well, maybe there is,' said the inspector. 'As we don't know the motive, we don't know whether he was a stranger or not, but, assuming that he was, he couldn't know who was in that third floor flat. He'd have had to try doors at random to find one where there was a female alone. It's a common pattern in that type of crime. All right. He starts at the top of the house and works down or he starts at the bottom and works up. For psychological reasons, it's usually from the top floor down. In any case, unless we have absolutely rotten luck, he rang some other door bells in that building between eight and eight-forty-five. If we interrogate all the occupants, we may turn up a witness.'

He had, it seemed, worked from the top down. The sergeant also began at the top, and by the time he reached the third floor had already collected three witnesses.

Two of these were a husband and wife living on the fifth floor. A husky young man with a black beard had rung their doorbell at approximately eight-fifteen and asked if Mr Courtoux was there.

The wife, who had answered the doorbell, said that she did not know any Mr Courtoux and called her husband to ask if he knew any person by that name living in the building.

He did not either, and the young man had thanked them politely and gone off down the stairs.

On the floor below, he had rung the doorbell of a Mrs Annie Trebuchon, a widow in her late sixties living alone.

Mrs Trebuchon, keenly conscious of the number of elderly persons killed for their savings each week in France, had a very sophisticated system of locks on her door, but opened it on the chain to see who was calling.

The young man asked the same question and Mrs Trebuchon said that Mr Courtoux lived on the ground floor. She admitted to the police that she had never before heard the name, but she was unable to explain why she had given the young man false information. Her description of him was the same as that furnished by the couple on the floor above, with the added detail that he was wearing a very loud checked shirt.

'Well, that's our man,' said the inspector, 'but what is he?'

'Has to be a psychopath of some kind,' said the sergeant. 'Otherwise, why is he going through blocks of flats at random, looking for somebody to kill?'

'For no reason at all? Just for the pure joy of killing?' said the inspector. 'Ask records to run a search on the *modus operandi*, but I can't recall ever having heard of a case like that. Generally, it's sex, weird sex maybe, but identifiable sex. Depetry was sure that sex wasn't a motive in this case.'

The records section proved to be unable to produce any similar case and, when the inspector questioned Dr Depetry on the matter, he hedged slightly on his previous statements.

'It's hard to say what form deviant sex might take,' he said. 'I don't know of any other such case, but it's possible that the killing itself provided the sexual relief. Or it may be the struggle with the girl. The murder may even have been unintentional or for the purpose of eliminating the witness.'

'But, if the motive was deviant sex, then he'd have done it before or, if this was the first time, he'd do it again, wouldn't he?' said the inspector.

'Yes,' said the doctor slowly. 'If it was compulsive, he'd have done it before or he'd do it again.'

This assessment of the possible motive lent the case a certain urgency, for it could be established with considerable certainty that no similar murder had taken place anywhere in the north of France during the past ten years.

'All that we can hope for is that it wasn't compulsive and that Depetry is right about it being an accident or to get rid of the witness,' said the inspector. 'No report of the young man with the black whiskers, I suppose?'

As a matter of fact, there was not only one report but several. The hippy look having gone largely out of style, beards were not all that common, and it had been possible for the sergeant's detectives to obtain witness sightings of the potential suspect from the street and from a tavern two turnings away from the Résidence Ile de France.

'Cool character,' observed the sergeant. 'He's murdered a young girl less than an hour earlier and he spends the next two hours in a tavern two turnings away, drinking coffee, eating croissants and reading the papers.'

'From what time to what time?' said the inspector.

'Roughly nine-thirty to eleven-thirty,' said the sergeant. 'Nobody knew the exact time.'

'I don't like it,' said the inspector. 'It's not a pattern of behaviour that I can imagine. Anything more on Mrs Rangée's boy friends?'

Thérèse Rangée, it developed, had not been entirely truthful in her statements concerning male friends. In fact, she had had several, all from the company where she worked as a switchboard operator. Some of her colleagues had described them as 'overnight friends'.

The inspector had.not been too troubled by this lack of candour. Many divorced mothers of teenage girls were inclined to pretend to be morally conservative, presumably as an example.

What did concern him was the possibility that Roselyne had known one of her mother's 'friends', whether she knew how close a friend he was or not, and had let him into the flat.

Were this the case, the man might have made sexual overtures to the girl, been repulsed, attempted the use of force and ended by murdering her. Then, after faking the motive for the crime and eliminating any traces of his presence, he had fled.

It was obvious that Mrs Rangée did not suspect any of her friends, but the inspector had more reason. His investigations showed that one man, at least, should have been at work that morning and was not. It was, however, a Monday, a day on which absenteeism was, in any case, high.

The sergeant was concentrating on the young man with the beard – who, he pointed out, was reported to have relatively long black hair such as the single hair found in the dead girl's hand – and was making some progress.

It was now known that the young man's first name

was Robert and that he lived somewhere in the northern part of the city.

With this much information, it was eventually possible to locate and identify him. He was a student at the Centre Universitaire and his name was Robert Courtoux.

'The name he was asking for in the Résidence Ile de France,' said the sergeant with satisfaction. 'I think we've got him. We have the three witnesses from the building. If they pick him out of a line-up . . .'

'Well, we'll have to try it,' said the inspector. 'I agree, he sounds good, but, somehow or other, I still don't like it.'

He was going to like it less following the arrest of Robert Courtoux, although the young man unhesitatingly admitted that he had been in the Résidence Ile de France on the morning of the murder.

'I was looking for my uncle,' he said. 'I knew he lived in the building, but I didn't know what floor. I thought it was the fifth, but the people up there didn't know him. A lady on the fourth told me he lived on the ground floor.'

And to the sergeant's consternation, he did. Robert Courtoux, after whom the suspect was called, had received his nephew that Monday morning at a little before half-past eight and sat chatting with him until nine o'clock, when he went off to work. As his uncle had offered him no more than a cup of coffee, Courtoux went to the nearest café for a leisurely breakfast.

'But the old lady on the fourth floor said she'd never heard the name of Courtoux!' said the sergeant. 'How could there be such a coincidence?'

'It wasn't a coincidence,' said the inspector. 'She had heard the name, but she just didn't remember it. Happens to all of us. As for you, you started at the top of the house and stopped when you got to the third floor. If you'd started at the bottom, you'd have already encountered the name.'

The investigation was left with no suspects other than Pierre-Louis Massegrain, Thérèse Rangée's friend who had not been to work that Monday, but he was not considered to be very promising. The inspector, therefore, fell back upon a stratagem which he had tried before, sometimes with success, sometimes not.

Everything known in the case was, of course, already committed to paper, and the inspector and the sergeant sat down in the office and read the whole file off alternately, section by section, with the one not reading trying to pick holes in what was being read.

This produced, as usual, a great many inconsistencies and, also as usual, most of them were of no value to the investigation. One, however, was.

It concerned Roselyne Rangée's personal hygiene.

Roselyne, according to her mother, was in the habit of taking a shower in the morning before going to school.

The autopsy report, however, had stated that there were traces of dirt and a minor scratch on her left knee as if she had fallen down somewhere outside.

As she had not been out of the flat that morning, the dirt was from the day before – meaning she had not taken a shower, although she was already dressed.

Why? asked the inspector.

Thérèse Rangée was questioned. She said that Roselyne had taken her shower that morning as usual.

'Then, she went out after her mother left and came back,' said the inspector. 'Tell Depetry we need a more exact time of death.'

The doctor said that he could only provide an exact time of death by running an analysis of the internal organs, but, as they had been preserved separately, he would try. He had not troubled before as the time was known from other sources.

Or was believed to be known. The following day, an apologetic doctor called the inspector to inform him that Roselyne Rangée had not been murdered on Monday morning, but on Sunday evening between the hours of ten and eleven o'clock.

There was only one possible conclusion to be drawn

from this and Thérèse Rangée was taken into custody and formally charged with the murder of her daughter.

She denied it, admitted to it and then denied it again.

'I couldn't have killed Roselyne,' she wept. 'She was my own daughter!'

She had though, and, although she insisted that she did not know why or even if she really had committed the crime, the psychiatrists were able to reconstruct, to some extent, the course of events on the evening of the murder.

Both Mrs Rangée and her daughter, it seemed, had been rather active in their intimate relations with the opposite sex and both found this reprehensible in the other, Roselyne because she thought her mother too old for such activities and Thérèse because she thought her daughter too young.

There had been frequent quarrels, and on that evening they degenerated into physical combat. Mother and daughter fought it out like bar room brawlers and the adult woman was more than a match for the thirteen-year-old, who seized the knife to defend herself.

Thérèse got it away from her and, accidentally or otherwise, stabbed her to death with it. The black hair in Roselyne's hand was her mother's.

The court was inclined to accept Thérèse's word that she had not intended to kill her daughter, but her attempt to mislead the investigation and the fact that she had spent the night following the murder in the flat with the corpse weighed heavily. On 4 May 1984, she was sentenced to twenty years' imprisonment.

5

OUR FLESH AND BLOOD

A hard-bitten lot, the farmers of Lower Austria, reflected the duty sergeant of the missing persons section. Their only son and they were reporting him missing with all the visible emotion of reporting a strayed pig.

Of course, the emotion was there. A farmer with one son would be as devoted to the boy as to the Virgin Mary, and that was saying a lot in a place as catholic as St Poelten. After all, the town had been founded around an abbey.

They stood awkwardly in front of the desk, refusing to sit down in the presence of what they obviously regarded as an important official. Sixty-four-year-old Franz Reich, grey-haired, stoop-shouldered, but still with peasant strength in his rawhide body and work-gnarled hands, and his wife of forty years, Christine, seven years younger but looking older with her heavy, shapeless body, plump, sagging cheeks and double chins. Typical small farmers of the fertile plains stretching from St Poelten to the Danube river, twenty miles to the north. They were, of course, dressed in their Sunday best clothes.

'Rudolf Reich,' read the sergeant, going over the entries he had made on the standard missing person form. 'Born 7 February 1963, last seen at Reich farm on Herzogenburg Road outside St Poelten on 19 May 1983. Five feet eleven inches tall. Weight one hundred and eighty-five pounds. Hair colour, brown. Eyes, brown. Particular distinguishing characteristics, none.'

'He's very strong,' said Christine.

Her husband turned to look silently at her for a brief moment.

It seemed to the sergeant that she reddened, but she had a normally high complexion and it was hard to say.

They're more worried about this than they let on, he thought, as the Reichs marched stiffly out of the office. There's something else bothering them.

He picked up the photograph they had brought with them, attached it to the form and dropped both into the cases-to-be-investigated basket. There would probably not be a great deal done with it until Monday. It was a Friday, 20 May 1983, and there would only be a skeleton staff over the weekend. St Poelten is a town of under fifty thousand population and the police force is not large.

One of the detectives picked up the report on Monday morning, spent the best part of the week investigating it and, on the following Friday, turned it in with the notation that no trace of the missing man had been found.

This was hardly good enough and, when the report landed on the desk of Inspector Anton Grybek on Monday morning, he called in the detective and asked for a detailed account of the investigation.

As the detective had been expecting this, it was already typed out and he handed it over.

He had been thorough. He had questioned the Reichs, their hired man, fifty-one-year-old Alfred Koenig, all the neighbours within a mile of the farm and the young people of Rudolf's age with whom he associated and with whom he had gone to school.

He had not found out where Rudolf was or why he might have suddenly disappeared, but he had found out a good deal about Rudolf.

The young man was very attached to cars and had totally wrecked no less than five of them. All of the accidents had been caused by excessive speed, had involved no other vehicles and the insurance company had refused payment. At the time of his disappearance,

56

Rudolf had no car because his driving licence had been revoked following the last accident. The traffic department regarded him as a menace to the public.

Cars were practically the only thing to which Rudolf was attached. He was not known to have ever had a date with a girl, and some of his former schoolmates insisted that he had never spoken to one. No one believed, however, that he was homosexual.

He was quarrelsome and bad-tempered, particularly when he had been drinking, which was often, but he was no bar fighter unless his opponent was a great deal smaller and weaker than himself.

'I wonder why they bother looking for him,' said the inspector. He was a large, overweight man with a round, red face and a not entirely serious manner. 'Or do they need his help on the farm?'

'They don't even need the hired man,' said the detective. 'It's a very small farm, about a quarter of an acre.'

'That's barely enough for a garden,' said the inspector. 'How do they live?'

'Poorly,' said the detective. 'Poorly.'

'Well, I suppose that's not our problem,' said the inspector. 'Do you have any ideas personally about what might have happened to the boy?'

The detective hesitated.

'Could be the business with the cars,' he said. 'He'd lost his licence here, so maybe he thought that if he went over to Vienna, he could work an angle and get one. Big city and all that. Or . . .'

'Or?' prompted the inspector.

'I got the impression there was something wrong with him,' said the detective. 'Pervert of some kind, maybe. The business about not liking girls . . . If he was abnormal, there's not much outlet for that sort of thing here, whereas in Vienna . . .'

'In short, you think he went to Vienna,' said the inspector. 'All right. I'll get in touch with them and see if they can locate him. Hang on to the file. You're not off the case yet.'

The detective took the file and left the office. He was not entirely displeased at being kept on the case. In the first place, working directly with the inspector was not going to harm his prospects for promotion to sergeant and, secondly, he was more than a little intrigued by the strange character and mysterious disappearance of Rudolf Reich.

Four days later, he was once again summoned to the inspector's office. The Vienna police had reported no trace of Rudolf Reich in the cäpital, and the inspector wanted him to check on the various means of public transport to see if anyone had noticed Reich when he was leaving town.

The detective did not think that this would be an easy task. St Poelten was small, but it was not small enough that the booking clerks at the railway station and bus depot would remember a young man as inconspicuous as Rudolf Reich.

He was not, however, taking into consideration the element of chance and, to his astonishment, the booking clerk at the railway station knew Reich well, having been at school with him. The booking clerk at the bus depot did not, but it turned out that, as the result of a bus drivers' strike, there had been no bus service out of St Poelten between May the fifteenth and twenty-fifth.

'He would hardly have set off for Vienna on a bicycle,' said the inspector, upon learning this. 'So, he's still here.'

'He could have hitch-hiked,' said the detective. He was a rather handsome man, short-haired, neatly dressed, in his middle thirties and the happily married father of two little girls. His name was Peter Mueller and he was a career police officer.

'Very good,' said the inspector approvingly. 'See if you can find any evidence of that.'

Mueller left the office a little less cheerfully. The assignments were getting more difficult all the time. How was he supposed to find out if one of the fifty thousand inhabitants of St Poelten had been hitch-hiking on a given day or days?

Having thought the matter over, however, he came to the conclusion that it was not quite as hopeless as it looked at first glance. He did know with some certainty the day on which Reich had disappeared and he could assume that he was heading in the direction of Vienna. That meant National Route E5, the great motorway leading from Vienna in the east to the German border in the west. From St Poelten into Vienna, there was an older secondary road which ran parallel to the highway, but Reich would presumably have chosen the more heavily trafficked motorway.

The detective drove out to the edge of the city, to the approach to the motorway. Reich would have been walking or he would have taken the city bus to the last stop. It was only the inter-city buses that had been affected by the strike.

There was a filling station at the entry and a hitch-hiker standing beside the road, thirty yards away. He was bearded, remarkably dressed and carried a guitar slung over his back. He did not seem to be having much luck with lifts.

'Been there for an hour and a half,' said the filling station attendant, pointing with his chin. 'He'll never get a lift in that get-up. People think he's on drugs.'

A Mercedes slowed and pulled in to a stop beyond the hitch-hiker, who ran forward, spoke briefly to the driver through the open window and then climbed in. The Mercedes slid back out into the traffic and disappeared down the motorway, gathering speed.

'Damn fool!' said the filling station attendant in disgust.

'One born every minute,' said Mueller tactfully. 'Do most of them wait out there?'

'All of them,' said the attendant. 'They've worn a bare spot in the grass. It's about the only point where they can hope to get a lift. Traffic's moving too fast further on.'

'But I suppose you get a good look at them before they do get a lift?' said the detective.

'Pretty good,' said the attendant. 'To tell the truth, there's not a lot else to do here. What do you want him for? He rob somebody or something?'

'I don't want him,' said Mueller. 'His parents do. They don't know where he's got to.'

'You have a picture?' said the attendant. 'I never forget a face. When would it have been?'

'About two weeks ago, Thursday or Friday,' said the detective, handing him the photograph of Rudolf Reich.

'Why, hell! That's Rudolf Reich, isn't it?' said the attendant. 'I was at school with him. Nasty piece of work. Why do his parents want him back?'

'They love him,' said the detective. 'Has he been out here hitch-hiking?'

'Not unless it was in the middle of the night,' said the attendant. 'I haven't laid eyes on him.'

Mueller returned to headquarters, pondering the possibilities of coincidence in a small community. Granted, there was only one high school so everybody who went to high school at all had been at school with everybody else, but even so . . .

Inspector Grybek did not apparently find the coincidence as unusual as Mueller did.

'Well, that about wraps it up then,' he said. 'There's good reason to believe that Rudolf Reich has not left St Poelten at all.'

'We drop the case then?' said Mueller, disappointed.

It seemed a sorry sort of trailing off of the investigation, although he knew that many investigations did trail off in just that manner.

'Not at all,' said the inspector briskly. 'If he's still in St Poelten, but he's disappeared, it's not unlikely that he'd been murdered. That or some kind of a freak accident. I want you to investigate. Use whatever men and facilities you need, but keep in mind that we don't have an inexhaustible budget.'

Mueller left the office in a state of exhilaration.

Advancement was slow in a force the size of St Poelten's and the cases to be investigated were usually piffling – assault, robbery, burglary, occasionally rape or attempted rape. Now, all of a sudden, he found himself investigating a potential homicide. Even if it turned out that it wasn't homicide after all, it could hardly do him any harm and it was certainly going to make the job more interesting for a time at least.

However, after having had a cup of coffee and an apple tart in the police canteen while thinking the matter over, he realized that he had no idea where he should begin. Everything that could have been done in a homicide investigation had already been done in the missing-person case.

Start all over again? Question everybody a second time? For what? None of the persons he had questioned could be remotely suspected of murdering Rudolf Reich.

Perhaps he should look for a motive? That was something that had not yet been done because it had been assumed that Reich was still alive, but now that it was assumed that he was not . . .

It was all assumption. There was not a solid fact in the case other than the bare circumstance that Reich was missing. He could be dead. He could be somewhere else in Austria. He could be anywhere in the world. There was no evidence, no indication even, of anything.

There was, moreover, another point. The Reichs were as poor as church mice. A quarter of an acre of land was not even enough to feed three of them, let alone the hired man. Rudolf had never held a job. How could he afford to travel anywhere? He would have had no money at all.

Unless, of course, he had stolen it.

Mueller went to the records section and asked for a computer printout on unsolved robberies and burglaries from the middle of May to the present.

There was none. St Poelten does not have a high crime rate.

The only remaining possibility was that a theft had

taken place, but it had not been reported, perhaps because the injured party was not yet aware of it.

It was possible but, all in all, the theory of an accident or homicide seemed more likely.

Very well, assuming that it was an accident. Where and how could it have taken place? It would be necessary to know more about Rudolf Reich's activities and movements to answer that question.

Mueller set about trying to trace them and found that he had an easy task. Rudolf engaged in hardly any activities and he had moved about very little since losing his driving licence. Mostly, he hung around second-hand car garages or the show windows of the motor dealers. When he had any money, which was surprisingly often, he went to one of the two taverns that he frequented and drank it up. He did not stand other people drinks.

All of this was exactly what the detective would have expected to learn concerning a twenty-year-old who was crazy about cars, held no job and had no driving licence. The only thing remarkable was the money. Where did Rudolf get it?

And, for that matter, where had he got the money to buy the cars? It was true that they had all been very much second-hand, but they had cost something and, if he had no income at all . . . ?

For the first time, Detective First Class Peter Mueller began to have the feeling that he was on to something.

Rudolf had some source of money and it was neither his parents nor a job. In St Poelten, almost anything else would have to be illegal, and it was because he was mixed up in something illegal that he had been murdered or, at least, was missing.

So what would it have been?

Mueller could think of only one thing. Drugs. What else was there, legal or illegal, that would bring in money without working?

On the other hand, St Poelten did not have much of a drug problem, in so far as he knew, and where would the boy be getting it? Big-time gangsters operating out of Vienna? The Mafia?

The whole thing began to strike Mueller as slightly ridiculous. What big-time gangster would be interested in St Poelten? There was hardly enough money in town to support a cinema, let alone a profitable drug operation.

Still, it was all that he could think of and he took his suspicions to Inspector Grybek, who considered the matter and decided it was at least possible. He sent the detective over to talk to the section that dealt with narcotics.

To his surprise, he learned that there was more of a narcotics problem in St Poelten than he would have thought. The modern world-wide network of instant communications had enabled young people to follow the trend even in relatively out-of-the-way places.

The numbers, however, remained modest. Many of the young residents of St Poelten were of hard-headed peasant stock and their inclinations ran more to improving their lot in this world than to escaping from it.

'Who are you looking for?' asked the sergeant in charge of the section. 'If he's in the trade, we know it.'

'Rudolf Reich,' said Mueller. 'Age twenty. Last address, the Reich farm to the north of the city. He's been missing since May the nineteenth.'

The sergeant punched keys on his computer terminal.

'No record,' he said. 'And that means he's never pushed so much as a gram in St Poelten. What makes you think he did?'

'Oh, just a hunch,' said Mueller disconsolately. 'Thanks a lot.'

He left the office, but paused for a moment in the doorway.

'Is there much money in the narcotics business here?' he asked.

'Very little,' said the sergeant dryly. 'The pushers are their own best customers and they shoot up the profits. You'd do better in some other line.'

'I wasn't thinking of myself,' said the detective and closed the door. He was in no mood to respond to humour. The case seemed now more mysterious than ever.

'I don't feel I'm making any progress,' he told the inspector. 'All that's happening is that I'm getting more and more confused. I haven't the foggiest notion as to what happened to Rudolf Reich or if anything happened to him at all.'

'You're no worse off than I am,' said the inspector, 'but don't let it worry you. I didn't expect you to solve it in an afternoon.'

'I'll never solve it,' said Mueller miserably.

'Never is a long time,' said the inspector. 'Even for a civil servant. We'll try another line now. There's reason enough to believe that something fatal may have happened to Reich. We'll begin a search for his body.'

'Where?' said the detective in astonishment.

'Why, the last place he was seen,' said the inspector. 'His father's farm.'

It was already the first week of June when the search parties began to fan out from around the Reich farm. They did not move very fast and there were not very many of them. As the inspector had said, the police budget was not inexhaustible.

The search parties moved slowly because there were a great many clumps of bushes, small groves, ravines, ponds, old wells and other places where a body could be hidden, and all had to be examined carefully.

Normally, the search parties would have been larger as there would have been volunteers from among the missing man's friends and neighbours. Few, however, appeared to be interested in finding Rudolf Reich and the search was carried out mainly by off-duty firemen and police.

Detective First Class Peter Mueller did not take part in the search. Encouraged by the inspector's irrepressible optimism, he resumed investigation of the lead which he had dropped when the narcotics section assured him that

Rudolf Reich was not engaged in the drug trade – the question of where Rudolf had got the money to buy cars.

And, much to his own surprise, he was successful.

'There's no doubt about it,' he told the inspector. 'The Reichs were selling off their land to pay for their son's cars. They originally had twelve acres and every time that Rudolf bought a new car, the farm shrank. The dates of the bills of sale on the fields correspond precisely with the dates of the car purchases.'

'I can't believe it,' said the inspector. 'An Austrian farmer will sell anything in the world, but not his land. You can torture them to death and they won't part with a square centimetre.'

'The Reichs did,' said Mueller, 'and I think this had something to do with the boy's disappearance. The trouble is, I don't know what.'

'Nor I,' said the inspector, 'but maybe we'll have an indication when we find his body.'

The inspector had become convinced that Reich had been murdered and, with his customary optimism, was quite certain that the body would be found.

The sergeant was less so, but he was wrong. While he was still pondering what overwhelming force could have brought the Reichs to sell their very livelihood from under them, one of the search parties came upon a suspicious oblong of freshly turned earth in the extreme back corner of what had once been the Reichs' farm.

Digging down, they struck first a crucifix and, a little further, in a rough wooden coffin, the remains of Rudolf Reich.

As he had now been dead for nearly three weeks, he was in poor condition, but still recognizable. His parents were, however, spared the painful duty of identifying his corpse officially as they immediately confirmed that it was they who had buried him there.

The treatment to render him suitable for burial had, however, been carried out by the hired man, Alfred Koenig.

Taken into custody and questioned separately, the

Reichs and Alfred Koenig told identical stories, which were believed by the police simply because they were too strange to have been invented by unsophisticated farmers.

Detective Mueller's impression was correct. There had been something very wrong with Rudolf Reich. Although the son of quiet, gentle parents, through some quirk of the genes, he had been born a raging sadist whose greatest joy in life was the suffering of others.

However, the suffering of others can seldom be enjoyed without a degree of personal risk and Rudolf was a coward. Longing to hurt but fearing to be hurt, he had been an intensely frustrated youth.

Until he realized that there was at least one person in the world whom he could hurt without fear of retaliation.

His mother.

The discovery had been a revelation and a release to Rudolf. Particularly when he found out that his father either would not or could not stop him.

From that point on, Christine Reich had been subjected to the most humiliating tortures. Beaten with a cattle whip, kicked, punched, forced to crawl about the floor on all fours and, possibly, worse as there were things that neither of the Reichs were willing to discuss, she had believed her son to be totally mad.

So too had his father, and he had sold field after field of the farm in an attempt to placate him. It had, of course, merely led to more exorbitant demands and greater violence.

Finally, on May the nineteenth, after undergoing terrible torments at her son's hands, Christine could stand no more.

Creeping to the barn with her clothing half torn off her body, she had climbed a ladder to the hay mows, fastened a rope around her neck and was about to hang herself when Alfred Koenig intervened. He had often been a witness to the tortures and beatings and, suspecting her intentions, had followed her to the barn.

Christine was saved from suicide, but, at a family

council with Franz and Alfred, it was agreed that the situation could not continue any longer.

Typically, it did not occur to any of them to seek the help of a doctor or to go to the authorities. Rudolf had become an unacceptable menace. He had to be removed.

Alfred Koenig was chosen to do the job. In the first place, he was the youngest and strongest. In the second place, he was not related to Rudolf. And, finally, he had had experience in such matters as it was he who always butchered the pigs.

Koenig raised no objections. Humbly conscious of his position as family retainer, he accepted the decisions of his employers without question.

He therefore went to prepare the necessary utensils, sharpening the axe on the grindstone and putting a fine edge to the long, thin blade of the butchering knife.

The butcher's tools were prepared in the kitchen practically in the presence of the victim who, exhausted by his efforts with his mother, had lain down to take a nap on the bench there.

When the preparations, including the oilcloth to prevent staining the floor and the tub to catch the blood, were completed, Koenig simply raised the axe and split the sleeping man's head with a single, practised blow.

This, of course, killed him instantly, but the hired man knew only one way of butchering and he continued by cutting Rudolf's throat so that the blood could drain out of his body into the tub.

In the case of a pig, the blood would have been used for making blood sausage, but, in the case of Rudolf, it was thrown away.

The boy's parents were not present during the slaughtering, but came in afterwards to wash the body and place it in the rough wooden coffin which Franz and Alfred knocked together. It was then carried out to the fields and buried with the crucifix on top as a substitute for a proper Christian burial.

All three of the accused admitted that they had known that what they were doing was murder and illegal and that they had tried to conceal the crime. They had had no choice, however, they said. Rudolf was killing them.

The court did not go so far as to accept that they had acted in legitimate self-defence, but it did find that there were very substantial extenuating circumstances.

On 2 March 1984, Franz and Christine Reich were each sentenced to two years' imprisonment for ordering the murder of their son. Alfred Koenig, who had killed because his employers asked him to kill, was sentenced to five years.

6

SPIDER!

It was a splendid wedding that took place on that Sunday of 16 February 1975. The Fichardts were rich, great land-holders in the fertile plains to the south-west of the Cape, and they were marrying off two daughters in a double ceremony.

As South Africa lies in the southern hemisphere, February is, of course, high summer. The weather was hot, a trifle muggy with a threat of thunderheads gathering on the horizon in late afternoon.

The threat failed to develop, however, and Georgina Fichardt, twenty-two years old and darkly beautiful, was married to twenty-seven-year-old Adrian Dreyer in glorious summer sunshine while her sister, Carolyn, two years younger, equally dark and lovely, became the wife of twenty-six-year-old Daniel Laurens.

Two highly suitable marriages, as all of the hundreds of guests would agree. Adrian and Daniel were wealthy in their own right and both had graduated only recently from the agricultural engineering school in Cape Town. Like the Fichardts, their land holdings lay near the little town of Worcester.

All of which made them logical and desirable husbands for the Fichardt girls. In the tightly knit society of the great landowning families, such marriages were little short of affairs of state, to be arranged well in advance. Georgina and Adrian had been destined for each other by their families and by themselves since they were in primary school.

Exceptionally, that had not been the case with Carolyn

and Daniel. Their marriage was a surprise, something regarded with scant approval by some. Surprises were not altogether respectable.

They had, of course, known each other all their lives, but there had never been any suggestion of a romance until Georgina's and Adrian's formal engagement party on the twelfth of June the preceeding year.

Daniel, Adrian's classmate in the agricultural college, had asked Carolyn to dance. They had danced. They had danced again. Then they had danced only with each other for the rest of the evening. Something unexpected had taken place.

By the time that the preparations for Georgina's and Adrian's wedding began, it was time to prepare for Carolyn and Daniel as well.

In any case, everything worked out to a satisfactory conclusion, everyone was happy and the celebrations lasted until dawn, by which time there were few sober enough to remember who was getting married.

There was no reason to suspect then that within a scant seven years both of these happy, suitable marriages would end in death or that the youngest couple would be the first to be separated.

On 28 January 1980, Daniel and Carolyn went to have dinner at a restaurant in Wellington on the other side of the nearby mountain range.

Daniel had rather too much to drink at dinner and, as the couple set out for home, the friends who had been dining with them entreated him to let Carolyn take the wheel. The road over the high mountain pass was dangerous.

Daniel would not hear of it. He had not had too much to drink. He was in perfect command of himself. He knew what he was doing.

They set off shortly before midnight with Daniel at the wheel of the Toyota. At shortly after three in the morning, Carolyn came limping in to Wellington, cut, bruised, hysterical, her clothing torn and her shoes missing.

Daniel had lost control of the car and it had gone over the edge of a three hundred foot cliff. Carolyn had barely had time to jump as the car tottered on the edge. She had fallen on to a ledge and managed to crawl back to the road. As there was no traffic at that time of night, she had been forced to walk all the way in to Wellington, a distance of over five miles, in her stocking feet.

A banal traffic accident, brought on by Daniel's refusal to recognize that he had had too much to drink to be driving. At least there had been no children.

Two years later, tragedy struck again, this time due not to carelessness on the part of anyone, but to a bizarre accident.

On the evening of 19 February 1982, three days after her seventh wedding anniversary, Georgina Dreyer had gone to bed with her three-year-old daughter, Deborah, in a crib beside her.

Hidden in the bed clothes was a button spider, the dreaded *Lostrodectus indistinctus*, no larger than a pea, but deadly.

Although Georgina had taken a strong sleeping potion before going to bed, the agony of the spider's venom resulted in such frightful moans that Adrian rushed in to see what was wrong, discovered the spider and killed it.

It was, however, too late for Georgina and she died even before the arrival of the ambulance.

There was no question as to the cause of death, for the spider was not so badly crushed that it could not be identified by Dr Morris Vander Houten, the Worcester coroner.

However, although the doctor, a plump man with a high complexion and very fair, thinning hair, entered 'spider bite' as the cause of death on the death certificate, he was not entirely satisfied with the circumstances and sent a report, together with the dead spider, to the offices of the criminal police in Cape Town.

The button spider, he wrote, was an uncommon species and, to the best of his knowledge, found only in the area around the town of Malmesbury, fifty miles to the north of Cape Town and roughly the same distance from Worcester. He had been unable to find any previous reports of button spiders in Worcester.

The criminal police did not know exactly what to make of this.

'Is he saying that he considers the death suspicious or is he warning us that there are button spiders where there were no button spiders before?' said Inspector Johann Groote, the investigations officer who had been handed the report and spider.

His assistant, to whom the question had been directed, looked thoughtful but made no reply. A large young man with regular features and long sideburns, he was aware that the question was rhetorical. The inspector was merely thinking out loud.

'A small creature like that, it could have been carried over to Worcester by almost anything,' continued the inspector. 'Someone moving house. A shipment of agricultural produce. On a vehicle. Where do the things live anyway? In holes in the ground?'

This was a question meant to be answered.

'I don't know,' said Sergeant Harry Kleaver. 'I could go over to the university and find out.'

'Do,' said the inspector. 'We have to file some kind of action on this.'

The sergeant was gone for some time and the inspector, who had other matters to occupy his attention, had forgotten about the button spider by the time he returned.

'Almost never seen outside the area,' said the sergeant without preamble. 'Shy beasts. They say it's a chance in a million for one to turn up in somebody's bed in Worcester.'

The inspector looked at him silently for a moment. He was a very large man, heavy but not fat, and his hands were the size of small frying pans.

'Ah!' he said finally. 'The button spider. Right. They think it's impossible then.'

'Not impossible. Unlikely,' said the sergeant. 'I suppose you want me to take a run over to Worcester and take a look?'

'Yes, do that, Harry,' said the inspector. 'I can't get away right now. Who's the expert on these animals?'

'Nobody here,' said the sergeant. 'They say that there's a centre up at Malmesbury where they study them. Maybe I should go there first.'

The inspector thought this was a good idea and the sergeant left. It would be another two days before he returned.

This time, the inspector had not forgotten.

'You should be an expert on button spiders by now,' he observed. 'What did you find out?'

'Something very strange,' said the sergeant. 'Either there was a remarkable coincidence, an improbable accident or Mrs Dreyer was murdered by a Dr Helena Dippenser of the University of Witwatersrand.'

The inspector sat digesting this silently for some minutes, his large, round face completely expressionless.

'I'm very busy now,' he said, fixing his eyes thoughtfully and a little reproachfully on his assistant. 'Perhaps you'd best make me a written report on the results of your investigations.'

The sergeant hastened to comply and, by that afternoon, was able to present his chief with a typed report running to some three pages.

He had gone first to the agricultural college at Malmesbury, where he found a small team of entomologists engaged in a study of the button spider. It was not, it seemed, a very widely dispersed spider, but it was a very poisonous one and the scientists were plotting means to bring about its extinction.

So far, they had had little success and had, indeed, increased the button spider population slightly by breeding them in the laboratory for their research purposes.

They were, however, not the only scientists interested in the button spider for, some two weeks earlier, on

February the fifth, a Dr Helena Dippenser from the University of Witwatersrand had called and asked for one or two specimens for a research project.

She had been given two female and one male so that she could begin breeding her own collection.

They described Dr Dippenser as a tall, statuesque woman with blonde hair drawn tightly back under a hat, her eyes concealed by dark sun-glasses. She had been wearing an extremely severe tweed suit and sensible shoes with low heels.

The sergeant asked what the chances were of a button spider turning up in Worcester and the entomologists replied roughly zero.

The sergeant had then gone to the University of Witwatersrand, where he was informed that there was no Dr Helena Dippenser on the staff nor was there any person resembling the woman who had been given the spiders in Malmesbury.

From the university he had gone to Worcester and spoken to most of the surviving family members, including the husband.

None of the women was blonde and, although Dreyer was, he was not tall or statuesque. The sergeant thought his horror and grief over the manner of his wife's death sincere.

'Did you ask if anyone in the family had ever heard the name Dr Helena Dippenser?' said the inspector.

The sergeant nodded. 'Negative in all cases.'

'But you believe that she may be responsible for Mrs Dreyer's death,' said the inspector. 'Why and how?'

'I have not the faintest idea,' said the sergeant. 'Dreyer and other members of the family were in the house at the time of Mrs Dreyer's death. They saw no blonde woman and it is almost impossible for anyone to have entered without being seen. They all insist that Mrs Dreyer had not had an enemy in the world.'

'In short, no motive for a murder,' said the inspector. 'Do you think it was that?'

'I don't know,' said the sergeant slowly. 'It can hardly

be a coincidence that a woman giving a false identity obtains three comparatively rare spiders on February the fifth and that another woman is killed by just such a spider on February the nineteenth. I think it certain that it was one of the Malmesbury spiders in Worcester, but how it got there is another question. It could have been an accident.'

'I doubt it,' said the inspector. 'If this Helena Dippenser obtained the spiders under false pretences, it was because she had illegal intentions for them. It's not the sort of thing that anybody would do to amuse themselves.'

'But why would she have wanted to murder Mrs Dreyer when all her relatives say that she knew no one by that name?' said the sergeant. 'And how could she have got the spider into her bed?'

'The answer to the first question is that her name is obviously not Dr Helena Dippenser,' said the inspector. 'That was as false as the rest of her story. As for the second question, there is only one thing to do in such cases.'

'And that is?' prompted the sergeant when the inspector showed no inclination to continue.

'Why, question the servants, of course,' said the inspector. 'They always know everything.'

The sergeant understood very well what the inspector meant by this and he knew how to go about it. It was, therefore, not very long before he was able to make a pronouncement.

'Mr Dreyer is having an affair with his sister-in-law,' he said. 'The servants have observed them actually engaged in intercourse.'

'Well, I suppose there's no real reason why they shouldn't,' said the inspector. 'They're both unattached now.'

'They may have unattached themselves,' said the sergeant.

The inspector laid down his pencil and leaned back in his chair, causing it to creak alarmingly.

'You think or you have reason to think?' he inquired.

'The affair seems to have been going on since they were married,' said the sergeant.

'Since which one was married?' said the inspector.

'Both,' said the sergeant. 'It was a double ceremony. Either the affair started shortly after the weddings or it was already going on before.'

'But then, why didn't Dreyer marry the sister he was having the affair with?' said the inspector. 'The thing doesn't make sense.'

The sergeant shrugged. 'Big land owning families,' he said. 'The marriages were probably arranged by the parents. The girls may not have had a lot of choice in the matter.'

The inspector thought it over.

'It looks like you have the basis for a homicide investigation,' he said. 'Possible motive. Peculiar circumstances in connection with the death. Can you handle it by yourself? I can't give it a lot of time and it's going to be one of those things that take a lot of rooting around and leg work.'

'I can handle it,' said the sergeant. 'I'll start with Mrs Dreyer's brother-in-law.'

'You think he may be involved?' said the inspector.

'No,' said the sergeant. 'I think he may have been murdered.'

He was going to find support for his suspicions, but no evidence. Daniel Laurens had definitely died as the result of his car going off the cliff and the autopsy had shown a high level of alcohol in his blood. He should not have been driving.

The sergeant was able to locate the friends who had been at the dinner in Wellington and they confirmed that he had been drunk. They had pleaded with him to let Carolyn drive, but he had been adamant.

There was only one remark of possible significance.

'It was almost as if he didn't want to live,' said the man. 'He never drank anything to speak of until about a year before.'

The sergeant checked on this statement and found it was true. Approximately eleven months before his death, Daniel Laurens had suddenly begun drinking heavily, a departure from his normal pattern of behaviour so abrupt that it was noticed by many.

He had not been a happy drinker and seemed morose and depressed, but there appeared to be no reason why.

Unless, of course, he had learned of his wife's infidelity. It was possible that Daniel had committed suicide and sought to take his faithless wife with him, but there was no proof of it.

In the end, the sergeant was forced to give up on Daniel Laurens. He still thought the circumstances of his death suspicious, particularly in view of later developments, but there was only one person in the world who knew what had actually taken place that night when Daniel's Toyota went over the edge of the cliff and he was not going to ask her.

It was important Carolyn did not learn that there was an investigation. If Georgina had been murdered, she had probably been involved in it even if she could not be the mysterious Dr Helena Dippenser, who was blonde and drove a Ford while Carolyn was brunette and drove a Buick.

The person the sergeant suspected of murdering Georgina was her husband, Adrian Dreyer. Whether the death of Daniel had been an accident or not, the deaths of both Daniel and Georgina were too convenient for the lovers to be simply chance.

The sergeant, therefore, set about searching for a tall, blonde woman who could have obtained the spiders for Dreyer.

And found no one. Dreyer was a serious farmer who spent nearly all of his time at the farm and there was no tall, blonde woman within his circle of friends, relatives and acquaintances.

Frustrated and forced to admit that he could not, after all, handle the case alone, the sergeant returned to the inspector for suggestions and advice.

'The longer I work on this, the more I'm convinced that Mrs Dreyer and, probably, Daniel Laurens were murdered,' he said, 'but there's no evidence of it. All I know with certainty is that Dreyer and Mrs Laurens have been having an affair for six or seven years.'

'You also know that someone tricked the people in Malmesbury into giving her spiders of the kind that killed Mrs Dreyer,' said the inspector. 'Is there nothing more you can do with that?'

'I don't know what,' said the sergeant. 'I've gone through every person with whom either Mrs Laurens or Mr Dreyer had any contact and there's not a tall blonde among them.'

'So perhaps it wasn't a blonde,' said the inspector. 'The woman was also wearing sun-glasses, wasn't she? What about Mrs Laurens? Is she tall and statuesque?'

'Yes,' said the sergeant. 'You mean a disguise, a blonde wig?'

'It's only logical,' said the inspector. 'The woman used a false name and title. She'd have wanted to conceal her appearance as well. Check the car rental agencies in Malmesbury. You may find a rental to a Mrs Carolyn Laurens for the afternoon of February the fifth.'

The sergeant found no record of a Ford rented to a Mrs Laurens on February the fifth, but he did find one rented to Dr Helena Dippenser, and the employee who had rented it remembered the customer well.

'I thought she was crazy,' he said. 'Tall, blonde woman with sun-glasses. She drove up in a Buick. Parked it. Rented the Ford and drove away. I reckoned she must have a date with a married man or else she was married herself, but she didn't look the type.'

'Did you see her driving licence or any of her papers?' asked the sergeant, his heart in his mouth. Carolyn Laurens drove a Buick.

'Didn't need to,' said the car rental employee. 'The Buick was guarantee enough for me. I didn't think she was about to swap it for a Ford.'

'If he'd just noted the licence number on the Buick!'

lamented the sergeant. 'Damn sloppy business practices . . .'

The inspector looked grave.

'She covered very thoroughly,' he muttered. 'Didn't leave a trace. I suppose we'll have to chance it.'

'Chance what?' said the sergeant. 'I don't see anything to chance.'

'Chance carrying out a search of her house,' said the inspector. 'It's the only hope of finding anything incriminating. If we fail, it's the end of the case.'

The sergeant thought that it was already the end of the case. He could not see anything incriminating being found in Carolyn Laurens' house or anywhere else. If the button spider had been a murder weapon, it was already in police hands.

'No,' said the inspector. 'There are several things. A blonde wig. A tweed suit. And don't forget, she was given three spiders. She may have kept the other two.'

The sergeant remained doubtful. If Carolyn Laurens was a murderess, she was a cool and clever one. She had left no traces so far and he did not think that she would have been so foolish as to keep the incriminating spiders or the wig.

And, even if she had, would that be enough to bring a charge of homicide? One *Lostrodectus indistinctus* looked much like another. How to prove that any specific one was from the Malmesbury laboratory?

It was not, however, his decision. If the inspector said, 'Search', he searched, and he proceeded with a detachment of specialists from the police technical section to the Laurens' farm, where they carried out an extremely thorough search of the house and outbuildings.

They did not find any blonde wig, and any spiders encountered were local and not *Lostrodectus indistinctus*.

The species were easily determined as Carolyn Laurens had a remarkably complete set of reference works on spiders, snakes and other poisonous creatures. All were new, but all had obviously been well read.

The rest of her library was devoted to great crime cases, both fictional and real. These too were new and well read.

Carolyn Laurens had not been at home when the search-party descended upon her house, and her servants said that she was at Mr Dreyer's farm. She had, they added, lived there nearly all the time since Mr Laurens' death.

Although the search operation was not yet completed, the sergeant left the Laurens' farm and drove to Adrian Dreyer's farm, some four miles distant.

It was late afternoon and he found Carolyn Laurens and Adrian Dreyer having tea on the veranda of the house.

The sergeant introduced himself, said that he was investigating the circumstances of the death of Georgina Dreyer and informed Mrs Laurens that his men were now engaged in searching her house. They were equipped, of course, with a search warrant.

Adrian Dreyer looked extremely startled and said that his wife had died from the bite of a poisonous spider. The coroner had issued a death certificate to that effect.

Carolyn Laurens said nothing and did not change expression at all. After a time, she excused herself and went into the house and upstairs.

The sergeant was left in an awkward situation. He was not in a position to arrest Carolyn Laurens. Her choice of reading material might be ominous under the circumstances, but it was no proof of murder and the reference works on spiders could even have been bought after Georgina's death.

Nor could he follow her into the house. She might be simply going to the toilet.

Dreyer did not appear to be inclined to conversation and the sergeant sat fidgeting uncomfortably on the edge of his chair, sipping tea and trying to think of something to say. He had hoped and expected the announcement that he was investigating Georgina's death and the knowledge that her house was being searched would produce some kind of a reaction from Carolyn, but it had not.

Or had she gone down the back stairs and out of the back door, and was now fleeing in her Buick?

It seemed unlikely, although it would, of course, be the best thing that could happen. She could not escape and it would be a clear admission of guilt.

Nearly half an hour had passed when there came from the upper storey of the house the heavy boom of a twelve-gauge shotgun going off.

Dreyer and the sergeant leaped to their feet, exchanged appalled glances and ran into the house.

Carolyn was lying on the floor of Adrian's bedroom, the best part of her head blown away by the shotgun charge. On the table near the window lay a block of notepaper, two pages of which were covered with her clear, firm handwriting.

Carolyn Laurens had fled, but to a place where the law could not follow and, before leaving, she had written out the history of her star-crossed love and the confession to her murders.

For Daniel Laurens had indeed been murdered. On that night, Carolyn had grasped her opportunity and deliberately goaded Daniel into drinking and driving while drunk. As they reached the dangerous stretch along the edge of the cliff, she had suddenly twisted the wheel with all her strength and jumped. Taken by surprise, Daniel had not been able to stop the car from going over the cliff.

Perhaps he had not tried very hard. He had learned the circumstances of his marriage only a year before and drinking was his response to it.

Carolyn had never wanted to marry him. She had been in love with Adrian Dreyer since she was a little girl, but Adrian was destined for Georgina.

Filled with bitterness on the night of the engagement, she had surrendered her virginity to Daniel in her own bedroom.

Daniel had taken this for love, but it had really been a sort of revenge.

The day following the double wedding Carolyn had finally achieved her heart's desire by seducing Adrian and they had remained lovers ever since.

He had, however, known nothing of her murderous plans to free both of them for marriage to each other. The crimes had been carried out by her alone and with no one else's knowledge.

'And,' said the inspector, 'if she hadn't lost her nerve at the very end, she'd have got away with it.'

7

WELL DONE WIFE!

Far, far to the north, where the chill waters of the Skagerrak mingle with the equally chill waters of the Kattegat, lies Gothenburg, with a population of close to half a million, the second largest city in Sweden.

There are, of course, communities even further north, but Gothenburg is quite north enough for the climate to have a profound effect on the emotions of its inhabitants.

In winter, the sun scarcely rises. In July, it scarcely sets. People remain up all night. There are revels and celebrations. The summer is relished to the full. There will be little enough of it.

It was, consequently, three o'clock in the morning but not yet dark when seventeen-year-old Eric Larson returned home to his parents' house in the little town of Overlida, some thirty miles to the east of Gothenburg.

Eric had been taking part in the customary summer festivities with a group of friends of his own age and was now preparing to get some sleep.

To his surprise, he found his father sprawled over the kitchen table of the big, single-storey, eight-room house, drunk and nearly unconscious.

The situation was the more amazing in that his father, unlike many Swedes, was not a heavy drinker and would normally have been either working or sleeping.

'Where's Ma?' demanded Eric, largely because he did not know what else to say.

He assumed that she would be awake. She generally tried to keep the same somewhat erratic hours as her independent taxi-driver husband.

'Quarrel,' babbled his father. 'Gone to sit in the sauna.'

That explained everything. Eric knew that his parents sometimes quarrelled, just as did all married couples, and he knew that the quarrels upset them both. They had had a row. His father had got drunk and his mother had gone off to sulk in the sauna in the basement.

His father put his head back down on the table and appeared to pass out.

Eric left the kitchen and headed for the basement to see what his mother had to say to this. As he started down the basement stairs, he noticed a strange odour as of burned wood mingled with something else which he could not identify, but which made the short hairs at the nape of his neck stand up.

The door to the sauna, a massive ten-foot cube of wood which his father had assembled from a kit, was closed and, as he opened it, he noted mechanically that the temperature was set for the normal temperature for use, but the heating unit was turned off and the thermometer was at room temperature.

The thought flashed across his mind that, if the sauna was not hot, what was causing the smell of burning wood mingled with something else that made his stomach churn?

Then he forgot the question for the door was open and he was gazing into the brightly lit little room.

His mother was lying on the floor in front of the door. She was, of course, naked.

The sight did not shock him. He was accustomed to seeing his parents naked, but her appearance did.

Karine Larson was fifty-two years old, but she still had the slender, beautifully formed body of a dancer. She wore her blonde, curly hair short and, in summer, she was invariably tanned over her entire body.

But not like this. The skin was nearly the colour of mahogany.

Something had happened! The wooden bench had been knocked over and lay upside down and broken on the floor. The thick blocks of lava had been pulled off the oil-fired heating element and lay scattered about the floor.

With horror, Eric saw that his mother's hands were blackened and crusted with dried blood. There was more of it on her shoulders and her face was distorted in a hideous grimace.

Frightened, uncomprehending, he bent over, caught her by the arms and tried to lift her to her feet.

The arms came away in his hands.

'Cooked,' said Dr Leif Halverstrom unbelievingly. 'She's cooked completely through. Even the internal organs.'

The stocky, greying medical examiner from the town of Boras, fifteen miles to the east of Overlida, had just completed an examination of the corpse of Karine Larson and was finding it difficult to retain his professional calm.

'That poor kid!' muttered Inspector Bjorn Svensson, chief of the Boras police homicide squad. 'What a shock! It'll be a wonder if he ever recovers from this completely.'

Eric Larson had been found raving outside the house by neighbours, who summoned the emergency ambulance, his condition obviously requiring hospitalization.

They had ended in nearly as bad shape themselves. Entering the Larsons' home, they had found fifty-four-year-old Anders Larson unconscious in the kitchen, thought that he had suffered a heart attack and assumed that this was the cause of Eric's distress.

Upon examination, however, it turned out that Larson was merely drunk, which was certainly no reason for his son to become hysterical.

Suspecting, therefore, that the boy's mother had suffered some sort of accident, they searched the house and found her in the sauna, her arms largely separated from her body.

Too horrified to even describe what they had seen, they sent the ambulance crew to the basement, and it was the paramedic from the ambulance who had called the police.

The response had been somewhat delayed. It was early in the morning of a Saturday and it was summer. Boras has a population of under seventy-five thousand and the crime rate is not high. The members of the homicide squad all had to be summoned from their homes.

There was, in any case, no great urgency. At the moment, no one knew what had brought about Karine Larson's death, only that it had not been natural. It could have been accident, suicide or murder.

The homicide squad found no one at the scene who could inform them. Eric was gone, taken to the hospital under sedation. It would be a long time before psychiatric therapy could even partially overcome the emotional shock resulting from his mother's terrible death.

Anders Larson was lying unconscious across the kitchen table; and the neighbours had returned to their own house, where they were drinking neat brandy by the water glass and trying to forget what they had seen.

Scarcely able to believe the report by the paramedic, the doctor and Inspector Svensson, a huge, slow-moving, blond man with very clear wide-set blue eyes, had hurried directly to the basement while Detective Sergeant Nils Sorenson, tall, raw-boned and hawk-faced, remained in the kitchen with Larson.

By the time they came back up, the sergeant had succeeded in reviving Larson by holding his head under the tap, rendering him conscious but indignant.

'Who are you? What do you want?' he demanded, his voice still slurred from the effects of alcohol.

'Inspector Svensson, Boras criminal police,' said the inspector, holding out his official identification. 'What is your name? Are you the owner of this house?'

Larson stated his name and said that he was the owner.

'What do you want with me?' he said. 'It's not against the law to take a drink in your own home, is it? Or did Karine call you? Just because of a quarrel?'

'You quarrelled with your wife, Mr Larson?' said the inspector. 'Where is she?'

'In the sauna,' said Larson. 'Anyway, that's where she was going. Why?'

'You are under arrest on suspicion of murder,' said the inspector formally. 'You are warned that anything you say will be taken down in writing and may be used against you. You are not required to make any statements and you are entitled to legal counsel if you wish. I call upon you to accompany me peaceably.'

Larson stared at him with bulging eyes. He too was a big man, thick set, big-bellied, bald.

In an instant he turned cold sober and great beads of sweat popped out across his lined forehead.

'Karine!' he exclaimed hoarsely. 'What's happened to Karine?'

The inspector did not tell him. Either he knew and there was no need or he did not and the truth was more than a man should be asked to bear.

Larson was taken to police headquarters in Boras and subjected to interrogation. He was not, however, immediately charged. No one knew whether Karine Larson had died from suicide following a quarrel with her husband.

In the meantime, the entire technical staff of the criminal police descended upon the house in Overlida in an attempt to determine what could have taken place.

The corpse was still lying in the sauna as it could not be removed until the investigations had been completed.

Dr Halverstrom had scarcely touched it. His primary task was to determine whether the woman was dead and, if so, under what circumstances, but she had been so obviously dead and the circumstances so bizarre that he postponed any further examination until the autopsy.

Eric had, however, partly lifted his mother before the softened flesh of the arms gave way, so the body no longer lay exactly over the brown silhouette formed by the liquids that had cooked out of it on to the floor, and this puzzled the investigators as they could not imagine who would have moved the corpse.

The neighbours, who had, by now, made statements, knew nothing of the circumstances of the discovery of the body and Eric could not be questioned.

The technical report was, therefore, somewhat distorted by this lack of information.

Karine Larson, they said, had not committed suicide, but had fought for her life like a tigress.

A strong, athletic woman, she had used the bench as a battering ram, smashing it against the door with such force that splinters from it were embedded in the planks.

Either before or after, she had charged the door wildly with her bare shoulders, splitting open the flesh and leaving traces of blood on the wood.

Finally, in an act of near insane desperation, she had torn the burning-hot blocks of lava from the heating unit and, the seared flesh peeling from her fingers, hammered on the door with them.

Nothing had worked. The door had remained closed and Karine had slowly cooked to death.

The laboratory was conducting tests to see how long and at what temperature she would have had to be in the sauna to arrive at the state in which she was found.

The report stated that both sauna and body had been at room temperature when found. The sauna temperature control was set at one hundred and seventy-five degrees Fahrenheit, the usual temperature when in use. There was, however, extensive charring of the inside walls, particularly near the heating unit. This would indicate that the temperature had been over two hundred degrees for a considerable length of time. Tests were being carried out to permit an estimate of what temperature and for how long.

Finally, there was no indication of what had prevented Karine from leaving the sauna. The door opened outwards and, as was legally required in Sweden, there was no means of fastening the door from the outside. She had failed to smash her way out because the door, like the walls, was made of two layers of inch-and-a-half-thick planking laid diagonally to each other and secured with screws.

'Doesn't make sense,' grunted the inspector. 'The woman was fighting like a trapped animal in there and they say there's no indication of why she couldn't get out. What does Halverstrom say?'

The sergeant had been going through the autopsy report while the inspector read the findings from the laboratory.

'Nothing,' he said. 'She was cooked to death, but there's practically no precedent for it in forensic medicine and he doesn't know the time of death or even how long it took her to die. Somebody pulled her arms off after she was dead. Their fingers sank right into the flesh of her forearms. He suggests that it may have been her son. He probably found her, but he's still in the psychiatric ward at the hospital and can't be questioned.'

'It was finding her that put him there,' said the inspector. 'I doubt that there would be any point in questioning him, even if the doctors would let us. He obviously doesn't know anything about it.'

'And Larson?' said the sergeant.

'The first suspect in a homicide is always the spouse,' said the inspector, shrugging. 'But was this homicide?'

'You mean it could have been an accident,' said the sergeant. 'The door got jammed in some way.'

The inspector remained silent for a few moments, lost in thought.

'No,' he said finally. 'I suppose I don't. Mrs Larson didn't turn the temperature control up above two hundred and she certainly didn't turn it back down again. It couldn't have been an accident. It couldn't have been suicide. It was murder.'

'Are you going to charge Larson?' asked the sergeant.

'Not yet,' said the inspector. 'We don't have a motive and we don't know how the door was blocked. It's possible that somebody else had a reason to kill her. The place was wide open. Anybody could have walked in and they wouldn't even have had to go through the house. There's an outside entrance to the basement.'

'It would have had to be a pretty good reason,' said the sergeant, shaking his head.

He did not think that anyone other than Anders Larson would have had such a good reason. How could a fifty-two-year-old mother and housewife make an enemy so ruthless that he would cook her alive?

The sergeant was, understandably, thinking in terms of he and not she, although it should have occurred to him that a woman could have blocked the door of the sauna and turned up the temperature controls as well as a man.

'Deadlier than the male, as they say,' said the inspector. 'He may not look like Romeo to us, but she apparently found him irresistible.'

'She' was forty-one-year-old Gerda Andreson, whose name had joined the suspect list the moment the sergeant's men began asking questions in Overlida.

Everyone in the village had known about Gerda Andreson and Anders Larson and they had all found the matter uproariously funny, It had been a standard joke for years.

It had been no joke for Gerda or for Anders either. In just such a mad summer month of July in 1976, Gerda had been a fare in Anders' cab. Both had been younger at the time and, carried away by glandular impulse, they left the cab at the edge of a green meadow and spent the afternoon in sex frolics.

Anders apparently regretted this immediately and bitterly. He had met Karine in much the same manner ten years earlier, but that turned out to be true love. Both had married young. Both had had disappointments with their partners. Both were divorced. With Eric six months on the way, they married and lived happily ever after.

Or, at least, up to the incident with Gerda. She. it seemed, had been so impressed with her afternoon of love that she could neither forget it nor let him either.

She wanted Anders to divorce Karine and marry her and, as she was not a woman to hide her feelings, there was no one in Overlida who did not know it.

This frankness was not, however, the innocent plaint of unrequited love, but a deliberate and obvious attempt to foment trouble between Anders and his wife.

It had not succeeded. Anders had been embarrassed and apologetic, but Karine had simply ignored the whole thing.

'She must have been frustrated to the point of madness,' said the inspector. 'She'd made a laughing-stock of herself in the village and the Larsons simply ignored her. See if you can find anybody who saw her near the Larsons' house on Saturday and I'll work on Halverstrom for a more precise time of death. We've got the motive. Now we have to show opportunity.'

This turned out to be rather more difficult, although Gerda Andreson had, indeed, been seen within a few hundred yards of the Larsons' home on that Saturday. Unfortunately, the time had been approximately midnight.

'Too late,' said the inspector. 'Halverstrom and the lab people have been running tests and they have come to the conclusion that Mrs Larson was shut into the sauna at around seven o'clock in the evening. By midnight, she was already unconscious and nearly dead.'

'How did they arrive at that conclusion?' said the sergeant in some astonishment.

The inspector silently held out the typewritten report of the results of the tests made on the carcass of a calf with approximately the same weight as Karine Larson.

The tests had been made in the sauna where Karine had died and they indicated that the start of her torment had been not later than seven in the evening, when she began her frantic struggle to escape from the death-trap.

This struggle had lasted for three hours before she finally and mercifully lost consciousness. The time would then have been ten o'clock.

Following loss of consciousness, it had taken another

three hours before death took place, bringing the time up to one in the morning.

Finally, it required a minimum of two hours for the sauna and the body to return to room temperature, which was what it had been at the time of the arrival of the police and, presumably, when it had been discovered by Eric Larson.

'In short, it could have been before seven in the evening that this started, but not later,' said the sergeant, handing back the sheet. 'And that checks with Larson's statement. He said that she went off to the sauna at seven o'clock. However, the only sighting we have for Gerda Andreson is at around midnight.'

The inspector consulted the time schedule on the sheet.

'If it had been a little later, she could have been turning the thermostat back down and removing whatever was blocking the door,' he said, 'but, at midnight, Mrs Larson wouldn't have been dead yet.'

'Andreson wouldn't know that,' said the sergeant. 'And, after five hours in that inferno, Mrs Larson couldn't have survived. She may have died after the temperature was turned back down.'

'That sounds logical,' said the inspector. 'I'll see what Halverstrom and the technicians have to say.'

The doctor and the laboratory specialists agreed that the sergeant's theory was possible and the inspector ordered Gerda Andreson to be taken into custody.

Held at first without charge, she was cautioned on her rights and asked if she was prepared to make a statement.

Miss Andreson said that she was. If she was suspected of involvement in the death of Karine Larson, she wanted to state that she was innocent of any wrongdoing and that she had had no reason to wish Karine dead.

The inspector suggested that Anders Larson might be a reason.

'No,' said Miss Andreson. 'I am no longer interested in Anders. Eight years is a long time and he is not the same any more. Even if she was divorcing him, I . . .'

'She was divorcing him?' interrupted the inspector in utter astonishment. 'Why? Because of you?'

Gerda Andreson laughed, but without humour.

'Because of her own lover,' she said. 'She wasn't quite so faithful to Anders as he was to her.'

'Did he know that she had a lover?' said the inspector.

'Of course,' said Gerda. 'I told him. I said, "If you want to spend an interesting afternoon, come home without Karine knowing it and follow her. Maybe you can get your head examined for free." '

'Head examined?' said the inspector.

'Karine's boy friend is a doctor,' said Gerda. 'Dr Arnold Joestrom. He has his practice just outside Boras here, on the road to Overlida.'

'Well, what now?' said the sergeant.

He had just returned from conducting Gerda Andreson to the detention cells. Although the inspector no longer considered her a suspect, he did not want to release her immediately for fear that she might talk about what she had told the police.

'We have to check her statements,' said the inspector. 'If what she says is true, Larson is the murderer. It's still hard for me to believe that he could have sat there in the kitchen, drinking himself unconscious, with the knowledge that his wife was slowly cooking to death ten feet under him, but he admits himself that he was there at seven o'clock and, if anybody knows how to block the sauna door, he does.'

'It's never been shown that it can be blocked,' said the sergeant. 'Wouldn't we need that for an indictment?'

'Probably,' said the inspector. 'But we know that it *was* blocked so you go out there and find out how. I'm going to call on Dr Joestrom.'

As a matter of fact, the inspector did not call on Dr Joestrom – who, it turned out, was not qualified to examine Anders Larson's head, as Gerda Andreson had suggested, because he was a gynaecologist – but obtained all the information he needed from the doctor's secretary.

The secretary, who appeared to be remarkably well

informed about her employer's private life, said that she had seen Anders Larson's picture in the newspaper and had recognized him as the man who had come to the office on January the twenty-fifth of that year.

There had been a scene of sorts. The doctor was entertaining his fiancée in the examination room and Larson burst in despite the efforts of the secretary to stop him. Mrs Larson was on the examination table and the doctor was partially undressed.

Mrs Larson, said the secretary, had taken the matter calmly and told Larson that it was just as well that he knew as she was planning to divorce him.

She and the doctor then continued the activities which had been interrupted by Larson's appearance.

'Continued?' said the inspector. 'What did Larson do?'

'He left,' said the secretary. 'What else could he do?'

The inspector was afraid that he knew very well what Larson could do, but he was far from certain that he could prove it to the satisfaction of a jury.

Granted he now had a valid motive for the murder, but the manner in which it had been carried out was so barbarous that, unless Larson confessed, it might be hard to convince the court that this overweight, balding taxi driver who had never been charged with even so much as a traffic offence in his life was capable of it.

And the inspector did not think that Larson was going to confess. He had not done so up to now and his story was so simple that it was difficult to disprove. He and Karine had had a quarrel. He had gone to the kitchen to get drunk. She had gone to the sauna to sulk. That was all he knew.

Arriving back in his office, the inspector was informed that the sergeant had gone to the Larsons' house with a team of laboratory technicians and that they would be trying various possible ways of blocking the sauna door.

The inspector began on some of his other paperwork, but was unable to concentrate and finally set off for Overlida himself.

There, he found the sergeant and the technicians

experimenting with a number of heavy planks which they had found piled at the other end of the basement. They were trying to see if they could be arranged in such a manner as to block the door of the sauna by wedging them against the opposite wall.

This proved to be impossible as the distance was too great. The planks would have had to be fastened together and there were no nail or screw holes in them.

It was actually the inspector who noticed that the ends of two of the planks had been cut at an angle while all the others were cut square across.

The significance of this was not immediately clear, but, by a process of trial and error, it was eventually possible to determine that the planks, if placed in an X over the sauna door, could be wedged into the frame in such a manner that the door could not be opened. The mystery of the blocked door had been solved.

And so too, after another two hours of interrogation, had the case.

Confronted with the statements of Dr Joestrom's secretary and Gerda Andreson, and told of the discovery of the manner in which the door had been blocked, Larson broke down and confessed to the murder. He had not, he said, been able to accept the idea of a divorce.

On 10 May 1985, a jury found that the cruelty of his reaction had been out of all proportion to the provocation and, although they acknowledged that there had been extenuating circumstances, sentenced him to life imprisonment.

8

DOING THE MAMBA

On the morning of Tuesday, 13 November 1984, Christine Albert rose at her usual hour of six-thirty, washed, dressed and prepared to set off to mass. A practising Catholic, the seventy-eight-year-old widow rarely missed services at the Damm church.

Damm is an old, residential suburb on the northern edge of Aschaffenburg, West Germany, a community of some sixty thousand inhabitants located on the Main river to the east of Frankfurt.

It was precisely seven-fifteen when Mrs Albert emerged from her house at 9 Haselmuehl Way into the clammy mists of the early winter day. Central Germany does not have the most delightful climate in the world and the humid cold cut to the bone.

Despite her faith in a righteous God, Mrs Albert felt somewhat nervous. The extensive garden surrounding the old villa was a pool of darkness in which trees and shrubs took on eerie, indistinct, unnatural shapes.

Treading quickly along the white gravel path, which was barely visible in the darkness, she felt her flesh turn cold and her heartbeat speed up dangerously as a faint sound of crackling dead leaves came to her ears.

Something was moving in the garden!

A cat? A stray dog?

Or one of the thousands of young drug addicts who killed and tortured old people for their few miserable savings.

Mrs Albert clutched her purse. She did not, of course, have her savings on her, only a modest sum for the collection plate, but so much the worse. The young killers were at their most violent when they failed to get as much as they had hoped.

What could an old woman do? She could scarcely walk, let alone run, and as for fighting, her only weapon was her purse.

Screaming would not help. The house stood a good five hundred yards from the nearest neighbours. Even if they heard her, she could be murdered a dozen times over before they got there.

Assuming that they came at all. In the jungle of modern society, nobody wanted to get involved. People were murdered, women were raped practically in the middle of a ring of onlookers and no one did anything.

Behind her, something hard and heavy crunched on the gravel.

That was no cat or dog! It was something – somebody – wearing shoes or boots, someone heavy, strong, ruthless.

The confused thoughts of terror were tumbling through her mind. Why had she let Helga go off to spend the night with her girl friend? She had felt confident yesterday evening in the house, but she had forgotten that she would have to come out the next morning to go to church alone.

It was Helga's fault! She should have been more considerate of her old mother. She should not have let her make such a fatal mistake. She should . . .

The footsteps on the gravel were close behind. Christine Albert gave an involuntary screech and tottered forward in a pathetic attempt at flight.

Out of the corner of her eye, she saw the black shadow, darker against the darkness, loom up behind her and she squealed like a rabbit in the jaws of the ferret as she felt herself seized by the shoulders.

'It's all your fault!' bawled a familiar voice, shaking with fury. 'You're the one who destroyed my marriage!'

His grasp on her shoulders tightened and he shook her violently.

'Let me alone! Get off my property!' shrieked Mrs Albert. 'I'll report you to the police, Heinrich Birzer!'

Her fear replaced by rage, she began to struggle, striking out with hooked fingers and kicking at the man's shins.

Suddenly, there was a sharp, pricking sensation in her right shoulder and then her assailant was gone, melting into the darkness of the garden that he knew so well.

Shaken and gasping for breath, Mrs Albert returned to the house and examined her shoulder in the bathroom. In the mirror she could see a very small wound like a prick from a large pin. Only a few drops of blood had escaped.

Touching it with disinfectant, she stuck a plaster over it and went off to church.

'Heinrich attacked me in the garden this morning,' she told her daughter as they entered the church together. 'He acted as if he was insane.'

'If he does it again, we'll go to the police,' said Helga Birzer, who had been born Helga Albert. 'He didn't hurt you, did he?'

Mrs Albert said that her former son-in-law had not hurt her, but, by the time that mass was over, she was beginning to feel decidedly queer.

'I think maybe I should see the doctor,' she told Helga.

The doctor listened to Mrs Albert's account of the attack, examined her shoulder and recommended rest and a cup of camomile tea. The wound, he said, was not serious.

Mrs Albert had her cup of camomile tea and lay resting on the sofa until five o'clock, when she found that she could not keep her eyes open. Her eyelids had become paralyzed.

Helga, who came in response to her call, was alarmed and summoned the emergency ambulance.

Christine Albert was taken to the hospital where, despite the efforts of the doctors, her condition worsened rapidly.

At a little before midnight, she died.

Although she had been under observation for close to seven hours, the doctors were unable to diagnose an exact cause of death. The death certificate was, therefore, not issued and permission for burial was refused.

As a result, the death was classed as not natural, which required that it be reported to the Aschaffenburg police department of criminal investigations, where an autopsy was ordered.

Mrs Albert's body was removed to the police morgue and the autopsy was subsequently performed by Dr Milton Berger, a pudgy, snub-nosed police medical expert who had graduated only recently from medical school and still wore his medium-brown hair down to his collar.

Dr Berger's conclusions were startling. Mrs Albert, he said in his report, had died from the effects of the venom of a black mamba. The venom had, presumably, entered her bloodstream through the puncture wound in her right shoulder as he had been unable to find any other wounds on the body.

'A black mamba?' said Inspector Georg Hermann, chief of the Aschaffenburg homicide squad. 'But that's an African snake. Had she been on vacation in Africa or what?'

'I don't know,' said his assistant, Sergeant of Detectives Franz Tauber. 'Do you want me to find out?'

'By all means,' said the inspector. 'This is the weirdest report that has ever landed on my desk.'

Which was saying a great deal. Aschaffenburg is not a large community, but it is in the heavily populated area where the rivers Rhine and Main meet and the crime rate is high.

Inspector Hermann had been coping with this crime rate for many years. A stocky, broad-chested man with a high, deeply-lined forehead and patches of grey at the temples, he had thought that there was no form of murder he had not encountered, but African serpents *were* something new.

Particularly in connection with persons who had never been in Africa in their lives.

'Her daughter says that she never even went for a holiday there,' said the sergeant when he returned from his initial investigation into the case. 'She thinks her ex-husband killed her.'

'Whose ex-husband?' said the inspector.

'The daughter's,' said the sergeant.

'Any suggestion how he got the snake to bite her?' said the inspector. 'Or where he got it in the first place? What is he? A scientist? A zoo keeper?'

'A bus driver,' said the sergeant. 'Should I bring him in?'

'Do,' said the inspector.

Fifty-five-year-old Heinrich Birzer was arrested at the home of Mathilde and Karl Milis, from whom he rented a room, in the village of Sulzbach, twelve miles up the Main river from Aschaffenburg. He admitted that he was delighted at his former mother-in-law's death and said that he hoped it had been painful. He admitted having scuffled with her in the garden on the morning of the day she died. He denied that he had killed her.

'How?' he said.

'With the venom of a black mamba,' said the inspector, hoping to startle Birzer with the exposure of his *modus operandi*.

'What's a black mamba?' said Heinrich Birzer.

He was sent to the detention cells and, a search warrant having been obtained, his room at the Milises' house was searched.

A small bottle, believed to be of North African origin, and a hypodermic syringe were found.

'Where did you get the bottle?' asked the inspector.

'In Tunisia,' said Birzer. 'I was there with the Milises on holiday last year.'

'And the syringe?' said the inspector.

'Found it under a seat,' said Birzer. 'I get a lot of high school kids in the bus. They're all shooting heroin or something and they leave their things lying around.'

The statement was inaccurate. Not all of the high school pupils were drug addicts.

The hypodermic and the bottle were sent to the police laboratory, which reported that there were no traces of anything in either of them. If there ever had been, they had been very thoroughly washed since.

'Go down to Sulzbach and get statements from the Milises,' said the inspector. 'Ask them if Birzer really did go to Tunisia with them last year and see if they can recall seeing the bottle.'

The Milises could. They confirmed that Birzer had not only gone with them to Tunisia, but also to the Costa Brava and to Lake Chiemsee in southern Germany. They had been with him when he bought the bottle at a souvenir stand in Tunisia. There had been nothing in it.

'They must be remarkably good friends if they take him along on all their holidays,' said the inspector. 'You better get me an in-depth background on all these people. I don't understand the relationships.'

The sergeant, a lean, quietly laconic man with regular features but a slightly sorrowful expression, set out immediately to do as he was told, but the process lasted for some time as the situation was complex.

Heinrich and Helga Birzer, it seemed, had been married for over thirty years and were the parents of three grown children. Rainer, thirty-two, was a computer programmer. Reinhilde, the daughter, was twenty-seven and a medical assistant. And Edgar, twenty-five, was a car mechanic.

All had already left home by the time that Helga and Heinrich obtained their final divorce decree on 12 May 1982.

The divorce action had been initiated by Helga and contested by Heinrich. Although she had offered no concrete grounds for wanting a divorce, it had been granted anyway.

Heinrich was obviously not lucky in legal matters and he was going to be less so.

Following the divorce, he had brought civil suit for

the recovery of time and money spent on the villa at 9 Haselmuehl Way.

According to the complaint, at the time of his marriage, Christine Albert had verbally promised to will the house to him and Helga if he would repair and modernize it.

The villa had been little more than a ruin and Birzer spent every free moment of his time over the next thirty years as well as twenty thousand pounds of his own money putting it into perfect shape.

No sooner had Helga filed for divorce, however, than Mrs Albert made the villa over in her name and served Birzer with an eviction notice.

Birzer moved to Sulzbach and filed his claim, offering in support of it the receipts for the construction materials he had purchased.

Mrs Albert did not contest Heinrich's claim, but brought a counter suit for twenty thousand pounds rent, covering the period of thirty years that Birzer and his family had lived in the house.

As both claims were recognized by the court, Birzer received nothing and had to pay his own court costs.

He was very bitter about this and told the Milises that he had wasted his life repairing Mrs Albert's villa for nothing. He still loved his wife, however, and regretted the divorce.

Despite the fact that he had contested the divorce and declared himself ready to resume the marriage at any time, his children appeared to hold him responsible.

Divorced by his wife, rejected by his children, kicked out of the house he had occupied for thirty years, Birzer was left without family or friends, other than the Milises, as he had always been too busy working on the house to make any.

'The friendship with the Milises is a pretty unusual relationship too,' said the sergeant. 'I've prepared a separate report on it.'

Heinrich Birzer, it seemed, had known Mathilde Milis longer than he had known his wife. They had met thirty-three years earlier at a dance in a tavern called At the Sign of the Angel in Sulzbach and, so they said, fallen instantly in love.

They did not, however, marry – at least not each other. Heinrich went off to marry Helga Albert and Mathilde remained single until 1956, when her mother, for whom she had been caring, died of cancer of the gall bladder.

She then married crane operator Karl Milis and they produced four children.

The marriage was reportedly happy, but Mathilde and Heinrich remained in love, it seemed, although on a purely platonic basis. There was never any suggestion of a physical relationship between them and none was cited in the divorce case.

Karl Milis had known about the tender feelings between Heinrich Birzer and Mathilde even before his marriage to her. It appeared not to have troubled him and he and Birzer were close friends.

It was, therefore, to the Milises that Heinrich Birzer retreated following his eviction from the house which he had spent so many years renovating.

The Milises promptly took him in, comforted him and carted him off with them on their holidays.

'This is a very confusing case,' said the inspector when he had finished reading the reports. 'God knows, Birzer appears to have had more than an adequate motive, but where could he get black mamba venom? I doubt that it's something you can buy on the open market.'

'I'll see,' said the sergeant.

This time, he took even longer than before and the inspector, becoming impatient, called him in and demanded to know what was being done about the black mamba poison business.

The sergeant replied that nothing was being done about it because there was no uncontrolled source of black mamba poison in Germany and probably not in all Europe. There was one snake farm near Munich where black mamba venom was produced for scientific and medical purposes. It was produced in very small amounts and every drop was registered and accounted for. An ordinary doctor could not obtain a sample of it.

'Black market?' inquired the inspector thoughtlessly.

The sergeant gazed at him without speaking.

'No, I suppose not,' said the inspector. 'Wouldn't be much demand, would there?'

'None,' said the sergeant.

'Then what are you doing?' said the inspector.

'I'm trying to find out if there would be any source of the venom in Tunisia,' said the sergeant. 'It's the only place in Africa that he ever visited. I've checked that very thoroughly.'

'Where did they go for the holiday in Tunisia?' asked the inspector.

'Gabes,' said the sergeant. 'A package tour.'

'I've been there,' said the inspector. 'It's nothing but a tourist resort. Or, at least, the parts I saw. The only Tunisians he'd have met would be waiters. I think you're wasting your time.'

The sergeant raised his eyebrows inquiringly.

'Think about it,' said the inspector. 'Can you imagine a waiter at a resort hotel sidling up to a tourist and whispering, "You want some black mamba venom cheap?" Snake venom isn't an unlikely black market item just in Germany. There'll be damn few peddling it in Africa either.'

'True,' said the sergeant. 'And, anyway, according to the experts, there isn't a black mamba north of the Sahara, unless it's in a zoo. Should I give up?'

'Never,' said the inspector firmly. 'Even if it wasn't our job, I'd want to get to the bottom of this out of sheer curiosity.'

'Then what shall I do?' said the sergeant. 'All I was still working on was the Tunisian angle.'

'Let's start from the beginning and go over the whole case,' said the inspector. 'First. Mrs Albert is dead. Berger says she died from black mamba venom entering her bloodstream and that she had only one small wound on her right shoulder. Second. Mrs Albert before she died said that her ex-son-in-law, Heinrich Birzer, caused the small wound on her right shoulder that same morning. Third. Birzer had a potent reason for wanting to kill Mrs Albert. How much of that can we confirm independently?'

'All of it,' said the sergeant. 'Berger is our own medical expert. He must know what he's talking about. Nobody witnessed the attack on Mrs Albert, but Birzer admitted it himself.'

'He didn't admit wounding her or injecting her with black mamba poison,' said the inspector.

The sergeant, not having been asked a question, made no reply.

'Well?' said the inspector. 'What do you think?'

'I think he may or may not be guilty, but if we can't show where he got the poison, he'll either not come to trial or be acquitted,' said the sergeant stolidly.

'That's about it,' said the inspector. 'So start by having another expert or, better, two experts check Berger's findings, He's a good man, but he hasn't had much experience.'

'I doubt anybody has with black mamba venom,' said the sergeant.

'Then,' said the inspector, 'you might check the garden there in Damm. See what other possibilities there are for Mrs Albert to have received a puncture wound on the shoulder. Thorn trees or bushes or, maybe, a fence. Mrs Albert may have been mistaken or she may have been deliberately trying to get Birzer into trouble. She didn't like him any better than he did her.'

'She didn't know she was going to die when she told her daughter and the doctor about the attack,' said the sergeant.

'She could have got him into trouble without dying,' said the inspector.

She had certainly got him into trouble with dying. Although there was still no proof that Heinrich Birzer had injected his former mother-in-law with anything, the examining magistrate found adequate grounds formally to indict him for murder and order him held for trial.

The inspector was dubious. He did not like acquittals as they indicated insufficient preparation by the police, and he did not believe that Birzer could be convicted unless the mystery of the source of the black mamba venom was solved.

The sergeant was, therefore, assigned more men and urged to greater efforts.

The findings of Dr Berger were checked, with the usual inconclusive results. Some of the experts supported his view that the lethal agent had been black mamba venom. Others disagreed. Several pointed out that Mrs Albert had not been a young woman and that she had had an exciting morning.

The records of the one snake farm producing black mamba venom were reexamined and every shipment within the past three years traced to its ultimate destination.

There was not a molecule of the venom which could not be accounted for and there was no point in going back further than three years as Birzer had had no inkling before then that he was to lose his wife, his family, his thirty years' work and his money.

Even the Tunisian angle was checked with the cooperation of the Tunisian police. They were unable to find any evidence of black mamba venom ever having been in the country, let along sold on the black market.

The garden of the villa at 9 Haselmuehl Way was gone over by the square centimetre. No thorn trees or bushes were found and the only fence was of wood and some distance from the path. One tree along the path had a splintered twig with a sharp point.

It was cut off and taken to the police laboratory as it was thought that if it had in some manner penetrated Mrs Albert's shoulder, it would show microscopic traces of blood or skin.

It showed neither.

Birzer was grilled as intensively as the law allowed and

continued to protest his innocence. He admitted that he had often thought of murdering Mrs Albert, but said it had been no more than a pleasant day-dream. In any case, if he had been going to murder her, he would not have done it in the comparatively painless manner in which he understood it had been done.

He had, he admitted, waited in the garden for Mrs Albert to come out to go to mass. He had known that Helga was spending the night with a friend and he knew that Mrs Albert would go to mass if she had to crawl.

He had not intended to harm her physically or even to show himself. The idea was simply to scare her by making her think someone was following her. He had, however, become so enraged at the sight of the person he considered to be at the root of all his troubles that he had seized and shaken her, but not roughly. It was, he added, not the first time he had waylaid his ex-mother-in-law in the garden.

Helga confirmed this statement. Birzer, she said, had been sneaking around the garden at night ever since the divorce. She had wanted to go to the police, but her mother had opposed it.

The investigations continued for over a year and, at the end of that time, were at precisely the point where they had begun. A majority of the medical experts said that Mrs Albert had died as the result of black mamba venom entering her bloodstream. The only wound ever found on Mrs Albert's body was the one on her right shoulder which she said had been made by Heinrich Birzer. Birzer denied that he had wounded her and said that he did not even know what a black mamba was. He had had no possible means of obtaining black mamba venom.

For all that the investigators could determine, he was right. There were perhaps half a dozen people in West Germany who had access to the venom and he was not one of them.

Several reenactments of the incident in the garden

were performed using a smallish policewoman as a substitute for the victim.

As reenactments, they were successful. Birzer seized the policewoman by the shoulders, shook her violently and bawled, 'It's all your fault! You have destroyed my marriage!'

As proof of anything, they were useless. Asked what he had had in his hand at the time, Birzer replied, 'What I have now' and held up his empty palm.

'They'll have to go to trial without proof of possession of the poison,' said the sergeant. 'What do you think will happen?'

'He'll be acquitted,' said the inspector.

And he was.

9

TO DIE IN VENICE

Drawn by the invisible power of the moon, the waters of the Adriatic Sea swelled and rose between the rocky coasts of Yugoslavia and the flat sandy beaches of Italy to pour through the narrow entrances of the Venetian lagoon.

It was the afternoon of 2 December 1982 and the tides were not high. Sweeping around the long barrier of the Lido, they barely rocked the Sant' Elena pontoon, where shoppers and office workers were waiting for the vaporetto to take them home.

The incoming tide had brought with it the usual plastic trash and, less usual, a large wooden trunk, obviously heavy as it floated just at the surface of the water.

The trunk was bumping along the concrete edge of the quay and some of the male passengers left the landing platform and urged it along with kicks and pushes to where a flight of steps led down into the water.

There, it was lifted with considerable difficulty on to the quay, the cords binding it removed and the lid lifted.

Within was something bulky wrapped in blue plastic, and two large dolls.

One of the men produced a pocket knife and made a long slit in the plastic.

The face of a woman with regular, attractive features and wavy dark-brown hair appeared. Her eyes were open and staring at her rescuers, but she saw them not for the trunk was full of water and the woman was obviously dead.

'Something over twenty-four hours,' said the forensic

medicine specialist Dr Giuseppe Rosso, Medical Adviser to the Venice police department of criminal investigations. 'Strangulation, I would say.'

The body of the dead woman had been lifted out of the trunk and now lay on a plastic sheet on the quay. It was nude except for a very short baby-doll nightdress.

Canvas screens had been set up around the area to conceal the operations from the gaze of the idly curious, and technicians from the police laboratory were carefully removing the remaining objects from the trunk. The police launch which had brought them and the homicide squad to the scene was tied up at the quay nearby.

'Any reason why it can't be sent to the morgue now?' asked Inspector Dario Geraldi.

The doctor shook his head. 'I know of none,' he said. 'The laboratory people perhaps . . . ?'

The technicians had no objections and the body was wrapped in the plastic sheet and taken away to the morgue in the police launch, the doctor going with it to begin the autopsy.

The inspector came over to join his assistant, who was watching the technicians at work on the trunk.

'What's in the packages?' he asked.

There were half a dozen brown paper packages lying on the plastic sheet which the technicians had spread out on the quay. They were bound with plastic tape and had proved very resistant to immersion in the water.

'Nails,' said Sergeant of Detectives Marco Cristetto. 'Six one-kilo packages of nails. Intended as weights, no doubt.'

'Hard thing to trace,' observed the inspector.

He was a lean man, a little above average height, long-faced and sallow-skinned with a prominent nose. Although he headed the only murder unit in a city of three hundred and fifty thousand residents and close to a million visitors a year, he was not particularly hard pressed. Venice does not have a high murder rate.

There were various theories to explain this. Some said that it was because the Venetians were too sophisticated to become homicidally upset over the infidelities of their wives, a common motive for murder elsewhere.

Others maintained that it was due to the climate, the joy of living in one of the most delightful cities in the world, the absence of cars or the religious piety, to which the many churches bore witness.

The inspector thought that it was a simple matter of transport.

Or, rather, lack of it. In a city where there were no streets capable of wheeled traffic, the sole means of transporting a corpse was by water – in a gondola, launch or one of the bus-like vaporettos, all conspicuously open to witnesses. As a consequence, anyone wanting to murder someone took them elsewhere to do it.

The statistics bore him out. Such murders as took place in Venice were mainly those committed on impulse and with no thought given to disposal of the body.

This was, therefore, a highly exceptional case. The body had been carefully prepared for disposal and the murderer had successfully disposed of it. His only error had been due to a lack of knowledge of the action of the tides.

'Which inclines me to think that he is not a Venetian,' said the inspector. 'Any native of Venice knows that anything put into the lagoon will be carried in and out with the tides for days.'

'Perhaps it was not put in the water here,' said the sergeant. 'It could have been on the Lido or even further down the coast.'

'We'll see,' said the inspector. 'Would you ask the laboratory if they're ready with their report yet?'

It was the day following the discovery of the corpse and, although it was already nearly noon, no report had been received from either the police laboratory or from Dr Rosso.

The laboratory was not ready with the report, but the chief technician said that he would come over and brief the inspector verbally on what they had determined so far.

This turned out to be quite a lot.

The trunk, said the technician, had been in the water a relatively short time. According to their estimate, it had entered the water between midnight and one in the morning of the day it was found.

The cords binding it were of a type not common in Venice and probably not available in the city.

The packages of nails were untraceable as they were sold all over Italy and there were no markings on the wrappers.

Two large, comparatively expensive dolls had been stuffed into the corners of the trunk. They were in very good condition and had probably never been in the hands of a child.

The blue plastic in which the body was wrapped consisted of rubbish sacks issued by the community of Vipiteno, a small resort town in the South Tirol, a hundred and twenty miles to the north-west of Venice and a stone's throw from the Brenner Pass.

'But no identification,' said the inspector.

'None,' said the technician. 'There are a great many other small objects in the trunk. Dirt, hairs, scraps of things. It's not a new trunk. We're evaluating all of them now, but there's nothing that might lead to an identification.'

Sergeant Cristetto had already checked with the missing persons section that morning and had drawn a blank. There was no report of a missing woman answering to the description of the one found in the trunk.

'She must be from Vipiteno,' said the sergeant. 'But how she got up here . . .'

He was a cheerful-looking young man with a round face and black curly hair. Although he had not had much experience in criminal investigation work, the inspector was well pleased with him as he was intelligent, hard-working and good-natured.

'The murderer must have brought her up here in the trunk,' he said. 'Although why anybody would do such a thing is a mystery to me. Call Vipiteno and see if they have any missing reports on a woman. I'm going over to the morgue.'

He was curious as to what had been holding up the autopsy report and hopeful that whatever it was, it might be helpful to the investigation, but as it turned out it was not particularly.

'I have been running tests on the time of death and the time of entry into the water,' said the doctor, a short, barrel-shaped man with a large bald spot on the top of his head. 'She was killed at approximately eleven in the evening of November the thirtieth and she entered the water at around midnight yesterday.'

'The time of entry into the water agrees with what the lab determined for the trunk,' said the inspector. 'It was strangulation?'

The doctor nodded. 'Something soft. A scarf. A twisted towel. She was also hit over the head with something hard and it is probable that she was unconscious at the time she was strangled. In any case, there are no indications that she attempted to defend herself, no skin or hair under the fingernails and no bruises on the hands or arms from fighting.'

'I don't suppose you can determine whether she was sexually molested?' said the inspector.

'There were substantial traces of acid phosphotase in the vagina,' said the doctor.

The inspector nodded. Acid phosphotase was not proof of sexual activity, but it was a strong indication as it was a product of the normal chemical breakdown of semen.

'Otherwise,' continued the doctor, 'she was a woman in her mid-thirties, five feet one inch tall, weighing ninety-six pounds and in good health. She worked at something that required her to use her hands and arms and to walk. She had never had a major operation or born a child. Her last meal consisted of fried chicken and vegetables and she was killed before she had had time to digest it.'

Walking back to his office, the inspector found that the grey early winter day precisely matched his mood. Despite the professional detachment which any homicide investigator must develop in defence of his own mental equilibrium, the doctor's dry, clinical description of the victim had, in some strange manner, brought to life this pretty, anonymous woman whose life had been so abruptly terminated in mid-course.

'We have a tentative identification,' said the sergeant as the inspector entered the office. 'A woman named Emma Giraldo, reported missing in Vipiteno on December the first. Thirty-six years old. She's a waitress at the Alte Post tavern and she lived upstairs. When she didn't come down to work, they went up to look for her and she wasn't there. As her clothes and personal possessions were all still in the room, they thought something was funny and reported it to the police. They've found no sign of her yet.'

'And won't either,' said the inspector. 'Because she's over there in the morgue. The murderer must be a Venetian. This is about the last place anybody else would pick to get rid of a body.'

'But why would a Venetian bring a woman down here to murder her?' said the sergeant. 'Or did he murder her in Vipiteno and just bring the corpse down in the trunk?'

'Neither way makes sense,' said the inspector. 'Either we're dealing with a total madman or we're lacking information that would explain his actions.'

'Perhaps I should go up to Vipiteno,' suggested the sergeant.

'Not yet,' said the inspector. 'First of all, let's get a positive identification. The fingerprint people took prints from the corpse. Get copies sent up to Vipiteno for comparison with prints from her personal possessions. In the meantime, while we're waiting for the identification, get some people out with photographs of the woman and of the trunk. It's off-season and we should find somebody who saw one or the other.'

The task was rendered more simple by the findings of Dr Rosso regarding the time of death and the time of entry into the water.

If the victim had been murdered in Vipiteno on November the thirtieth, then she could not have been seen in Venice at any time after that and all that the sergeant's men could expect was sightings of the trunk, a conspicuous object to be transported from the railway station to the Sant' Elena landing at the extreme opposite end of the city.

On the other hand, if the woman had been murdered in Venice, she would have had to arrive with her murderer either by train at the station on the mainland or by car at the car park nearby before eleven o'clock in the evening – when she was murdered – but after seven, when she had gone off duty in the tavern.

'It's not physically impossible,' said the sergeant, 'but it's highly unlikely. He'd have had to stuff her into the car the minute she came off work and drive like a madman in order to get to Venice and murder her by eleven o'clock. I think we can safely assume that she arrived here as a corpse and probably in the trunk.'

The inspector agreed, and that same afternoon their suspicions were confirmed with the discovery of several witnesses who had seen a man trundling a large wooden trunk along the narrow streets and over the bridges in a rough sort of handcart. He had had great difficulties with the bridges, most of which were reached by stairs, and had attracted some attention. One or two persons had actually helped him out.

'Fantastic!' said the inspector. 'The man murders a woman in Vipiteno, brings her all the way down here in a trunk and then carts the trunk all the way across town to dump it into the canal. He must be insane.'

'Well, perhaps not,' said the sergeant. 'Sant' Elena's the end of the island, the last landing before the open lagoon, and, if he isn't from Venice, he might have thought that it would be carried out to sea from there.'

'True,' said the inspector. 'How are the descriptions?'

'Nothing special,' said the sergeant. 'We've taken statements from all the people who reported seeing the man and the trunk, but he was apparently not striking enough to impress anybody. Tall, fairly well-built, dark hair, dark eyes. The estimates of age run from twenty-five to fifty. He was wearing a sweater, blue or dark grey.'

'See if you can find anybody who saw him with the cart but without the trunk,' said the inspector.

'Why?' said the sergeant, puzzled.

'Because I doubt he'd have taken it away with him,' said the inspector, 'and if it's still here in Venice, maybe there would be something on it to help identify him.'

The inspector's hunch appeared to be accurate. No one could be found who had seen the man with the handcart empty.

The conclusion was obvious. After throwing the trunk containing the corpse into the water, he had pushed the cart in after it.

The only question was: had he thrown the trunk into the water at the Sant' Elena landing, or was that merely where it had ended up after being brought back in by the tide?

The question was answered with two passes of the grappling hooks from the police launch. A small but sturdy and obviously home-made cart was brought to the surface and handed over to the technicians in the police laboratory for examination.

This did not result in very much. The cart had been knocked together by someone who was handy with his hands but no carpenter. There was nothing special about it. It could have been made anywhere in Italy.

In the meantime, however, positive identification of the corpse had been received from Vipiteno. The body in the Venice police morgue was that of Emma Giraldo.

'You leave for Vipiteno tomorrow,' said the inspector. 'I've talked to the head of their criminal investigations department and they'll provide you with all the support they can. They don't have a proper homicide squad.'

'Any specific instructions?' said the sergeant.

'Catch the murderer, of course,' said the inspector, 'but, failing that, assemble everything you can on Miss Giraldo's background. If she was a waitress, she didn't have much money, so this is presumably a crime of passion and the murderer will be within her most intimate circle of contacts. I just hope that she wasn't promiscuous. Telephone me as soon as you have something.'

The sergeant went up to Vipiteno by train. As it was not possible to use a car in Venice, he, like many Venetians, did not own one.

The Vipiteno police did, of course, but they were not much needed as the community was small, with a year-around population of only about five thousand. Located in the high Alps, it owed its existence mainly to holiday skiers and, being so close to the border, was as much Austrian as Italian. It even had two names, Vipiteno in Italian and Sterzing in German.

The Alte Post was a German name and meant the Old Post tavern, but the owners were Italian and they were able to tell the sergeant a good deal about Emma Giraldo.

She had been born in Enna, Sicily, but she was not pure Italian, her mother having been a German concert pianist. Her father was a successful businessman and owned an export company, but Emma had had little contact with her family.

Although she was not precisely estranged from her parents, there had been a serious conflict over her marriage, which had been opposed by them and had turned out badly.

She had been a waitress at the Alte Post for six years and her employers had thought very highly of her. She had been serious and hard-working, and her open, friendly personality had made her popular with everyone who knew her. The owners of the Alte Post had regarded her more as a daughter than an employee.

As they had known her so well, they were able to answer two of the questions troubling the investigators in Venice. Why the two dolls in the trunk and why Venice?

Emma, it seemed, had loved dolls and collected them. The two found in the trunk with her body were her favourites.

And, as for Venice, it had been Emma's great dream. She had been there many times, but only as a visitor. What she had wanted was to live in Venice, to become a Venetian, to spend her life there, to die there.

'She didn't exactly realize even the last part,' said the sergeant, telephoning his report in to the inspector, 'but the people here say that, if the family doesn't object, it would be a nice gesture to bury her in Venice. It would be something, at least.'

'I'll see what can be done,' said the inspector. 'Anything that looks like a suspect?'

'Well, the husband,' said the sergeant. 'Supposed to be a violent type and he made threats against her at the time of the divorce.'

'You mean he's there in Vipiteno?' said the inspector. 'What's his name?'

'Luciano Muti,' said the sergeant. 'Thought to be around forty years old. Works as a waiter when he's working and, reportedly, as a pimp. Miss Giraldo divorced him because he beat the tar out of her and tried to force her into prostitution, or so she told the people here. He's been in Vipiteno a couple of times, but he hasn't been seen for months now.'

'Send me up the information you have on him and I'll put out a pick-up-and-advise request,' said the inspector. 'We thought it would be somebody close to her and this Muti sounds crazy enough to have done it.'

The inspector was exaggerating. Vast numbers of men beat their wives and not a few try to force them into prostitution. If Luciano Muti was crazy, he was not crazy enough to let himself be easily taken. The pick-up-and-advise request to all police units in the north of Italy produced nothing at all.

'Which is a good sign, in a way,' commented the

inspector. 'If he wasn't guilty of something, he wouldn't be so hard to locate.'

He had not expected that Luciano Muti would be hard to locate. The man had a criminal record for theft, breaking and entering, aggravated assault and procuring. His fingerprints were on record and so were his official police photographs. With that much information in police hands, it is usually difficult for a fugitive to stay out of sight.

'And even so, I'm not too happy with him as a suspect,' said the inspector. 'There are too many things that don't correspond to the facts.'

The sergeant, who had long since returned from Vipiteno, wanted to know what they were and the inspector told him.

To begin with, they still did not know where the murder had taken place. It had, presumably, been in Vipiteno, but in Emma's room at the Alte Post?

She was believed to have gone there directly after going off duty, but no one had actually seen her do so. Both the Vipiteno police and Sergeant Cristetto had gone over the room carefully, but no signs that a murder had taken place there were discovered.

But if not at the Alte Post, where then? Vipiteno was a small place and the real skiing season had not yet begun. There were few visitors and anyone moving around the village would be noticed. Muti's picture had been shown to practically every one of the inhabitants. None could recall seeing him on that date.

And yet, the murder had been planned in advance. The hand-made cart was exactly the size and shape to take the trunk. It had been put together before the murder took place, certainly not after. Even for someone very handy and with a full set of tools, it would have taken a day or more to make. Where had that been done? And, if the cart had not been made in Vipiteno, how had it been brought there?

Even the origin of the trunk was unknown. No one at the Alte Post had ever seen it before.

The removal of the body was easier to explain. In Vipiteno, nothing stirred after eleven o'clock at night. At one or two in the morning, a hippopotamus could have been carried out of the Alte Post and out of the town without a soul noticing it.

The sergeant thought that he had answers to most of these objections. In his opinion, he said, the murder had taken place in Emma's room at the Alte Post.

Her ex-husband had been waiting for her there and, as soon as she entered it, he hit her on the head with something hard, knocking her out.

He stripped her and put her baby doll nightdress on her in order to confuse the investigation into thinking that she had already been in bed when she was murdered.

He had sex with her while she was still unconscious and then strangled her to death with one of her own garments or a towel.

He then remained in the room until midnight, before going to fetch the cart which he had made previously. He had plenty of time, and the cart could have been in any of the villages nearby, or even in Bressanone, a much larger town but only fifteen miles to the south on the main highway to the Brenner Pass.

The trunk would have been with the cart and he had, probably, left it in the car and carried the body down to it.

'What car?' said the inspector.

'The victim's,' said the sergeant. 'I told you when I reported from Vipiteno that Miss Giraldo's old Renault was found behind the tavern with the keys in it and the fingerprint people said the steering wheel and the gear lever had been wiped.'

'So you did,' said the inspector, 'but tell me something else now. From what you know of Muti, does he strike you as a man of fine sensibilities and compassionate feelings?'

'The man's a thug and a pimp,' said the sergeant. 'There's an official report of that. He has all the emotional sensitivity of a wart-hog.'

'Good,' said the inspector. 'Then tell me why did he put those two dolls in the trunk with the corpse and why did he accept the enormous risks and difficulties of transporting Emma Giraldo's body to the city that she loved so much?'

The sergeant opened his mouth, started to say something and then stopped. He did this several times.

'No,' he said finally, 'you're right. Muti wouldn't have done that. She must have been mixed up with somebody else.'

The sergeant returned to Vipiteno. Somewhere there was a tall, well-built man, good with his hands and of an emotional nature, who had been close enough to Emma Giraldo to know her love of dolls and her dream of Venice.

Given this profile, the Vipiteno police took just under a week to find him. He was a forty-five-year-old pizza baker who came from the town of Riccione, a holiday centre on the Adriatic to the south of Venice, and his name was Roberto Festinese.

Festinese worked in a restaurant called the Wiener-wald, which is the name of a fast food chain and means the Vienna Wood, in the nearby community of Wiesen, and it was there that he was taken into custody.

He proved to be as emotional as anticipated and confessed in tears to the murder before the officers could even get him to the station.

Divorced and the father of two children, Festinese said that he and Emma had been intimate for nearly four years and he had loved her above all else in the world. She had, he said, often spent her nights at his small flat in Wiesen.

On the night of the murder, he returned from his work to find her completely drunk. She flung herself on him and attempted to scratch his face.

In a sort of automatic defence reaction, he threw an ashtray at her head and she fell down either unconscious or, as he thought, dead.

Terrified over this accident, he strangled her with a belt or perhaps a towel – he was not certain which.

As he had known of her life-long ambition to live in Venice, he did what he could to make her wish come true by taking her body there.

This last statement was undoubtedly true. As for the rest, the investigators were dubious.

It now having been established that the murder took place in Wiesen, the matter was out of the inspector's hands and the remaining investigation was carried out by the Vipiteno criminal police with assistance from the district capital of Bolzano.

Their findings were that there was no evidence Emma Giraldo had been intimate with Festinese or had spent nights in his room.

There was no evidence of where the murder had taken place, but Emma's room at the Alte Post appeared the most likely as the clothing she had been wearing that day was found there.

The cart had, despite Festinese's denials, been prepared in advance and for the purpose to which it was put. The trunk belonged to Festinese and he had purchased a supply of the plastic rubbish sacks two days before the murder took place.

According to their theory of the murder, Festinese had been romantically in love with Emma Giraldo, who perhaps rejected his advances. On the night of the murder, he attempted to obtain by force what he could not obtain by consent and, having knocked out and violated his victim, realized that he could not permit her to live as she would expose him. There was reason to believe that he had thought of this in advance for he had been prepared with the cart, the trunk and the sacks.

Roberto Festinese denied these base motives and said that the killing had been accidental. He had loved Emma and his bringing her body to her beloved Venice was proof of it.

The jury found this was a dangerous sort of love and, on 4 May 1984, sentenced him to fifteen years' imprisonment.

10

LIFE IN THE EXTENDED FAMILY

Like nearly all of the communities in the north of France, Lille, with a population of a little under two hundred thousand, is an economically depressed area.

The manufacturing and mining industries which once made the city prosperous are dead or dying and unemployment stands at record levels.

As elsewhere in post-industrial Europe, dependence on government allocations is the only possible way of life for many.

And a longed-for goal for some. Not everyone is qualified. There are people living in Lille under conditions comparable only to the Middle Ages.

In the late autumn of 1981, a number of such underprivileged people were occupying a hideous slum building off a courtyard at 180 rue des Postes, a main thoroughfare on the southern edge of the city. The exact number was not known, either by the authorities or the occupants, because it changed frequently and many of the people were only vaguely aware of their surroundings.

This uncertainty was the result of mixing two popular forms of refreshment: beer and ether.

The combination of beer and ether is not particularly healthy, but it is potent and it is cheap. Continued for any length of time, it produces such relaxation that the consumer not only does not mind being underprivileged, he or she does not even know it.

The Lille police are quite aware of the popularity of

beer and ether in some circles and of its consequences. The officer on duty in the communications centre, therefore, immediately recognized the slurred tones, long pauses and startling *non-sequiturs* and took the report seriously. People on beer and ether do not play jokes on the police.

Nor are they inclined to regard anything short of major catastrophies as serious. It takes a great deal for such a person to call the police.

The call was rather long and rambling, but the upshot of it was that an unconscious man was lying in the courtyard at 180 rue des Postes and the people there wanted him removed.

Under other circumstances, this would have meant a drunk, but, on the basis of his estimate of the condition of the caller, the communications officer took it to be something rather less innocent.

Not lending himself to the futile exercise of asking the caller's name, he threw a glance at the position chart of his patrol cars and ordered the nearest one to proceed to the address.

The patrol car did so and the mission was later described in a report submitted to the department of criminal investigations, homicide section.

Upon arrival at the courtyard situated at 180 rue des Postes, wrote the senior of the two officers from the patrol car, we found lying some six feet from the stairway leading to the entrance of the building a partially unclothed man whom we took to be a Negro because of the colour of his skin.

Upon examination, however, it appeared that the man was not a Negro, but was burned black over all the visible parts of his body and head. His hair was missing and he appeared to be blind.

The man was conscious and obviously in great pain. He was able to say several words, which included the names Kotyk and Edith Chandon.

The ambulance was immediately summoned and the

circumstances were reported to the communications centre.

In compliance with orders received, a watch was maintained over the entrance to the courtyard until the arrival of the officers from the department of criminal investigations.

The criminal investigations department's officers did not, however, arrive until the ambulance had already come and gone. They were, in any case, only a detective first class and a probationary detective who had happened to be on duty that Sunday morning. As they had not seen the victim, they did not know exactly what they were investigating and they contented themselves with determining the identities of all the people in the house. There were a great many.

In the meantime, the ambulance had completed its run and deposited the injured man at the emergency hospital. The entry in the log of the ambulance for Sunday, 29 November 1981 was terse and factual. It read:

At 08:12 on 29.11.81, duty ambulance 347 at Centre Hospitalier, Lille, was summoned to 180 rue des Postes, Lille, where adult male suffering from various injuries was found lying in the courtyard. Man was conscious and repeated several times the names Jean-Claude Kotyk and Edith Chandon. He appeared to be suffering from chemical burns over much of his body. No first-aid measures were undertaken and victim was brought immediately to emergency hospital service.

This entry into the log of the ambulance would later be transferred to the file marked 'Homicide Jules Quinart' in the homicide division of the criminal police. There it would join the report by the duty physician in the emergency service at the Centre Hospitalier.

At 08:47 on 29.11.81, an adult male, later identified as Jules Quinart, aged 49, was delivered by the emergency

ambulance to the emergency section of the Centre Hospitalier. Patient had been very severely beaten and had
suffered chemical burns over head, face and a large part
of the body. There were, additionally, relatively severe
injuries to the lower bowel, genitals and anus.

Despite all efforts of the hospital staff, the patient's
condition worsened steadily and at 14:00 on 29.11.81 he
was pronounced dead.

Quinart remained conscious up to within two hours of
his death and made a number of statements which were
tape-recorded and which accompany this report.

The body was transferred by hospital ambulance to the
police morgue at 16:30 on 29.11.81.

As might be expected from a man so severely injured
that the hospital was unable to save him from dying, the
tape-recorded statements were made up of broken scraps
of sentences, punctuated by harsh, rasping gasps for
breath and groans. They were, however, perfectly clear
on the subject of what had been done to him and by
whom. Pain and fear had swept away the cobwebs of
twenty years of alcohol, ether and worse and, as he lay
dying, Jules Quinart had never been more lucid.

'It was Edith,' he croaked. 'Edith Chandon. Had it in
for me . . . Hit me with the wood . . . Dumped the stuff
over my head . . . It burned . . . Trying to get it off . . .
she stuck something up my behind . . . hurt . . . Kotyk
too hit me with the wood . . . kicked in the crotch . . .
used his fists . . . made me eat shit . . . Couldn't get
away . . . My eyes . . . my eyes! Get the names. It was
Edith Chandon. Jean-Claude Kotyk. Others watched.'

The rest was repetition. Jules Quinart was very
anxious to identify the persons who had tortured him to
death. He need not have made such an effort. None of
the persons involved in the murder would even bother
to deny it – but only when it became clear that there
had been a murder and they were involved.

The detective first class and the probationary detective
who were the first members of the department of

criminal investigations to arrive at the scene learned nothing of what had taken place and had some difficulty in determining the identity of the people present. Their report consisted simply of a list of names and a few comments.

It was a long list. Although the house was not large, when the police arrived there were twenty-seven persons in it, of whom nine were children under the age of twelve.

None of these people had an official address and the tenant of the premises, fifty-year-old Jean-Pierre Hallouchery, was not present. A night-watchman, he had not yet come off duty.

All those present appeared to be related to one another, either by blood or by common-law marriage, but the detectives made no attempt to sort out the relationships. That would only be undertaken if the case turned out to be serious.

It was, of course, far more serious than they realized and, by the time they had completed their list and returned to headquarters, the police had already been informed by the hospital that Quinart's condition was critical and there was little chance he would survive.

The case had, therefore, been tentatively classed as homicide and assigned to the duty homicide squad officer, Inspector Jerome Marais, a squat, grumpy little man with fierce bushy eyebrows.

Although Quinart was not yet dead, the inspector proceeded at once to the house in the rue des Postes, bringing with him his assistant, Detective Sergeant Charles Dubois, and a detachment from the police laboratory.

The inspector wanted to learn what had taken place and to secure any physical evidence before it was destroyed. He did not expect to find anyone present at the scene. To his amazement, all twenty-seven of the people on the list were still in the house, most of them asleep or semi-conscious from the effects of alchohol or narcotics.

They had, in the meantime, been joined by Jean-Pierre Hallouchery, who said that he knew nothing about anything that had happened during the past eight hours as he had been on duty at the factory where he was night-watchman.

Asked if he knew a person named Jules Quinart, Hallouchery said that he was an old friend with whom he had gone to school. He had formerly been a normal person, had held a job and been married twice, but had become addicted to alcohol and drugs some twenty years earlier and was now a bum without so much as a roof over his head.

Informed that Quinart was in the hospital and not expected to live, he replied that he was sorry to hear it, but he was probably better off dead than alive.

If the questioning of Hallouchery produced no information concerning the incident, very casual interrogation of the other persons present showed that many or all of them had been witnesses to whatever had taken place. The inspector therefore sent the adults to the detention cells at police headquarters for further questioning and the children to the juvenile section of the Social Welfare Department.

The detachment from the police laboratory remained for another four hours at the scene and the following day turned in a report on their findings.

Secured and taken to the laboratory as possible evidence: one blood-stained piece of wood 81 x 12 x 4 centimetres originally forming the sill of the window to the right of the front entrance, one plumber's helper with wooden handle 2 centimetres in diameter and 62 centimetres long bearing traces of blood and human excrement over 14 centimetres of its length, one empty one-litre plastic container of Javelle water, a powerful bleach and cleaning agent containing fifteen per cent sodium hypochlorite, one empty can of caustic soda in crystal form intended for clearing drains, forty-six grams of hashish, four grams of heroin, thirty-nine grams of a not yet identified substance believed to be narcotic and one bottle containing eight centilitres of ether.

Condition of the premises was extremely dirty. Floors had not been washed or swept for many years and were encrusted with dirt to a depth of five and six centimetres in places. Toilet was clogged and had overflowed on to floor. There was an accumulation of rotting garbage several weeks old in kitchen. Floors and walls showed in many places traces of blood, excrement, urine and other human excretions. Some of these in kitchen and living room are recent and may have stemmed from victim.

By the time that this report was received, Quinart was dead and the inspector was investigating his murder.

For murder it definitely had been, and about all that remained was to determine who and how many persons had been involved, discover the motive, and fix, in so far as possible, the responsibility.

The inspector proposed doing this by interrogation of the persons present and Sergeant Dubois had been assigned a team of half a dozen detectives who were now thus engaged.

One of the first tasks was to attempt to straighten out the relationships within what amounted to a small tribe and this was not easy as the members of the tribe were, themselves, not clear on the subject.

The connection to Hallouchery had, however, been established. His mistress, forty-four-year-old Henriette Davaine, was the mother, the common-law mother-in-law or the grandmother of nearly all of the persons who had been, more or less, living in Hallouchery's house.

An attractive, if not particularly well-groomed, woman, her statement to the police displayed an innocence of spirit such as to make it unlikely that any court would ever convict her of complicity in anything.

She was, she told the sergeant proudly, the mother of eight children, six by her deceased first husband and two by her current husband, Armand Davaine. She did not live with Armand any more as he beat her and, anyway, she did not know where he was.

She had been living with Jean-Pierre Hallouchery for three or four years, but he was not always very nice to her and her family and only that summer had put them all out of the house. They had had to sleep in doorways for nearly two months before he relented and let them back in.

She did not recall having seen anyone do anything to Jules Quinart, but the young people had been frolicking around and something might have happened accidentally. She did not think that Edith would have hurt anyone. She was a gentle girl and the only one of her children who was not epileptic.

'She doesn't appear to drink excessively or take drugs,' remarked the sergeant as the inspector finished reading the statement and handed it silently back to him.

'Probably doesn't need to,' said the inspector cryptically.

Mrs Davaine and Hallouchery were released. Neither had any knowledge of the murder and the detention cells were already crowded with the rest of the family.

The sergeant continued with the interrogations, deliberately saving Edith Chandon and Jean-Claude Kotyk for the last. Quinart had incriminated both of them as he lay dying in the hospital and he wanted as much supporting testimony as he could get in order to apply the pressure necessary to obtain their confessions.

Actually, he need not have taken so many precautions. Solidarity was not a characteristic of the tribe and the members cheerfully, even gleefully, incriminated each other, whether the charges were true or not.

The sergeant was, however, a conscientious civil servant and he went patiently and methodically about sorting out the true from the false. A mild-mannered man with a high, smooth forehead and large, pale-blue eyes set rather too far apart, he was quite prepared to spend the next five years on the case, if necessary.

At times, it appeared that it would be, not because the witnesses were reticent, but because their relationships were so intermingled that care had to be taken to avoid testimony being offered against a person concerning whom it would be inadmissable by reason of consanguinity.

Henriette Davaine and Jean-Pierre Hallouchery were, for example, related in more ways than one. Hallouchery also had a number of children by other women, both legitimate and otherwise, and one of these was Jocelyne Coutsier, who was currently living with Emmanuel Lugiez, also known as Albert. Jocelyne was pregnant at the time of the murder, but, it was thought, not by Albert, but by one of Henriette's sons from her first marriage, Marcel Chandon. Albert, on the other hand, was believed to be the father of a five-year-old boy whose mother was another of Henriette's daughters.

In fact, paternity in almost all cases involving the tribe was regarded as problematical and no one appeared to be much concerned with it. It was, so to speak, all in the family and there were other preoccupations which loomed larger.

The autopsy report had long since been handed in by Dr Guy Pelletier, the department's tall, swarthy and painfully thin medical expert, and read like a script for a horror film.

The corpse is that of a man physically older than his chronological age bearing all the signs of acute alcohol and drug abuse. The subject was seriously under-nourished and there is severe deterioration of all of the internal organs, particularly the liver. Life expectancy, assuming an unchanged way of life, would be around five to six years.

The head of the corpse shows signs of violent blows with some relatively hard object such as the window sill recovered at the scene of the crime. There are minor skull fractures in three places.

The sixth and seventh ribs on the left side and the

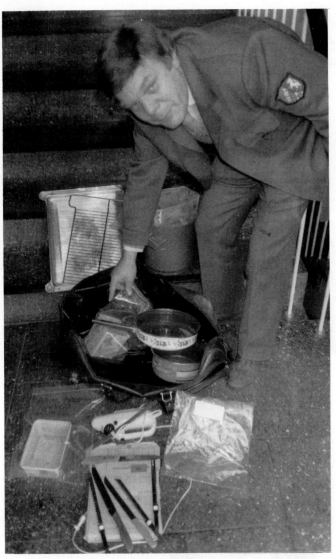

Kitchen utensils used by Martina Zimmermann on Hans Josef
Wirtz *(An Act of Love)*

(Above) Martina Zimmermann in court *(An Act of Love)*

(Left) Hans Josef Wirtz *(An Act of Love)*

(Above right) Fond son-in-law Heinrich Birzer, with Mathilde Milis and her grandchild *(Doing the Mamba)*

(Below right) Roberto Festinese in court *(To Die in Venice)*

Bernard Pesquet *(You Can't Reform an Honest Man)*

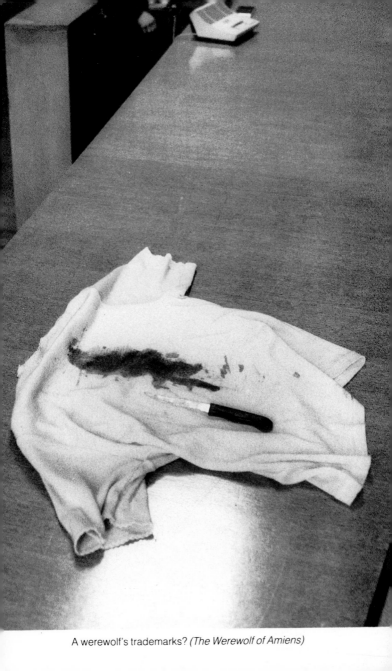

A werewolf's trademarks? *(The Werewolf of Amiens)*

A policewoman re-enacts the scene *(Strong Sex Drive)*

Hans Wilhelm Hadler *(right) (Hairbreadth Hairy)*

eighth rib on the right side are fractured, probably as the result of kicks with heavy boots.

The spleen is ruptured and there are lesions of both lungs.

The right cheek was perforated by a relatively dull object, which has left a wound over a centimetre in diameter.

Both arms and legs are severely bruised and the skin is broken in many places.

The lower bowel and the anus are deeply lacerated by the forceful insertion of a round, hard object corresponding to the handle of the plumber's friend secured at the scene by the laboratory.

The genitals are badly bruised and lacerated by what appear to have been kicks.

Face, head, genitals, buttocks and parts of the hands, arms, shoulders and torso are severely burned as the result of the application of strong chemical agents, identified as sodium hypochlorite and caustic soda. The skin has been completely eaten away in many places, all hair on the scalp is lacking and there is irreversible damage to the eyes.

Immediate cause of death is fixed as having been due to failure of vital organs and shock.

'Read it carefully,' said the inspector, handing it to the sergeant. 'You'll never see another like it if you remain in criminal investigations for the next hundred years.'

The sergeant read it, remarked that, if all the autopsy reports were like this one, he would not remain in criminal investigations another hundred minutes and went off, in a rather savage mood, to interrogate Edith Chandon and Jean-Claude Kotyk.

Kotyk, who had previously lived with Edith's half-sister, Véronique Davaine, by whom he had a little daughter, now lived with Edith. A large young man with a broken nose and his arms and hands covered with tattoos, he had worked on occasion as a plumber's assistant and as a house painter. Now twenty-four years of age, he had not worked for five years and devoted himself full time to the consumption of beer and ether. There was no explanation of where he obtained the money to pay for even these simple pleasures.

In fact, there was no explanation of anything from the young man himself. The few utterances which he made were largely incoherent and he appeared unable to grasp the meaning of the questions or the fact that he was a suspect in a murder case.

Véronique Davaine had testified that Kotyk was violent, quarrelsome and unpredictable. While they were living together, he had not only beaten her up, but her mother as well, a claim which was confirmed by Mrs Davaine.

Véronique denied, however, that she had seen Kotyk strike or otherwise injure Jules Quinart, and this was probably true as she had neither desire nor reason to protect her former common-law husband.

In fact, although all of the witnesses appeared to be more than happy to incriminate Kotyk, only Emmanuel Lugiez admitted to having actually been a witness to the torture. His imprudence and the wisdom of the others soon became apparent, for he was indicted on charges of failing to come to the assistance of a person in mortal danger.

Lugiez would, however, get off with a suspended sentence for, as he pointed out, he was a rather small man and Kotyk was large and violent. He had been afraid that, if he interfered, he would suffer the same fate as Quinart.

Anyway, he said, he had not thought that Kotyk was murdering Quinart, but only giving him a lesson because some-one said that Quinart had referred to Kotyk that same afternoon as a 'crazy'.

Asked if this had been his motive, Kotyk responded with a non-committal grunt, possibly significant as it was more of a response than he made to most questions.

Any lack of information from Kotyk or anyone else was, however, more than made up for by Edith

Chandon, who proved to be not only a loquacious, but an admitted, if somewhat improbable, murderess.

The fact was Edith did not look very much like a murderess. Although twenty years old and a mother, she looked more like a dishevelled street urchin of about fourteen. She was small, under five feet; frail, under ninety pounds; and had round, plump cheeks, a snub nose and an innocent expression.

However, what she had to say in her high, vulgar street slang turned the blood of seasoned criminal investigators cold.

'We were making the rounds of the cafés,' she said. 'Jean-Claude had got some money. I had to stay with him because he had had trouble with one of my sister's friends and I had to calm him.

'Then, we went to visit Emile Buri. I started living with Emile when I was fourteen. He's seven years older than I am and we have a little boy named Gaetan who was born last year on February the twenty-seventh. I had to leave Emile in January this year because he was put in jail.

'Emile got out in September and we went to visit him that Saturday. Then all three of us went to Hallouchery. Jules Quinart was there.'

'You knew Quinart?' asked the inspector.

'And how I knew him,' said Edith. 'When I was seven years old, he waited for me outside the school. He showed me his privates and said, "Come on. I'll give you a hundred francs." Another time, he pulled up my skirt and pushed himself against me. He didn't give me any money.'

'So you wanted to revenge yourself for what Quinart did to you when you were a little girl?' said the inspector, trying to establish motive.

Edith said that she had never wanted to revenge herself on Quinart. She did not hold what he had done against him. Everybody did things like that.

'Who was present when you arrived at Hallouchery's house?' asked the inspector, baffled.

'I don't know,' said Edith vaguely. 'Jocelyne, Hallou-chery's daughter. Albert. Jean-Pierre Davaine, my half-brother. Some other people . . . kids . . . We'd been drinking a little, you know.'

'Beer and ether?' said the inspector.

'Jean-Claude wanted some ether,' said Edith, 'but Jocelyne didn't want to give him any. I showed him where the bottle was.

'Emile left then and I wanted Quinart to leave too, so I took off my shoe and I hit him in the face with the heel.'

'Was he standing up when you did that?' said the inspector.

Edith shook her head. 'He was kneeling and drinking ether.'

'Continue,' said the inspector grimly.

'I took the window sill and hit him a few times,' said Edith. 'Then Jean-Claude came and hit him for about ten minutes. He got away and crawled up the stairs, but Jean-Claude followed him. He hit him with his fists and kicked him. Then we threw him down the stairs.

' "You're not the boss here!" he yelled and sat down on one of the steps. I took a bottle of Javelle water that was standing on the fridge and poured it over his head.

'He got up and went to the sink to try and get if off and I pulled down his pants and his underwear . . . '

'And according to the other witnesses, you said, "I'll give you back what you gave me when I was little!",' interposed the inspector, still trying for a motive.

'No,' said Edith. 'I didn't want to get even. I was drunk.'

The inspector sighed.

'I took the bottle of stuff for cleaning the drains,' continued Edith, 'and I poured it over his head and on his privates.'

The inspector handed her the empty tin of caustic soda.

'Did you see this warning on the can?' he asked. 'Where it says here in red letters that this is dangerous if it comes in contact with the skin?'

'I didn't see it,' said Edith. 'I have never used this product. I was drunk.'

'Go on,' said the inspector.

'I took the handle of the plumber's friend and I stuck it up him behind,' said Edith. 'I thought then he would leave. I just wanted him to go.'

'Did Jean-Claude Kotyk also sodomize the victim?' said the inspector.

Some of the other witnesses had testified that he did, although they denied having seen the act themselves.

'No,' said Edith, apparently not understanding the question. 'I used the plumber's helper. Jean-Claude took the poker for the stove.'

It was the first time that the police realized Quinart had been raped with the poker as well.

'And then?' said the inspector.

'Well, Albert got him dressed and threw him outside,' said Edith vaguely. 'Jean-Claude gave him some money so he could call the ambulance.'

'Did he?' asked the inspector.

'I don't know,' said Edith. 'Maybe. I didn't look to see. We'd been drinking, you know'.

The trial of Edith Chandon and Jean-Claude Kotyk lasted only two days, possibly because the jurors could not stand to listen to any more of the testimony. Kotyk said nothing, but Edith was frank as always and her language was graphic. Some spectators hurriedly left the courtroom.

As neither of the defendants denied the crime, the question before the court was mainly whether there were extenuating circumstances which might warrant a reduction in the sentences.

There was one. The murder of Jules Quinart was obviously not premeditated.

However, the details of the crime were so grisly that, on 28 June 1983, both defendants were found guilty of murder and given the relatively heavy sentence of eighteen years' imprisonment each.

I I

YOU CAN'T REFORM AN HONEST MAN

The wedding in Pierrelaye on 8 December 1968 was something of a social event. Located in the lovely valley of the Oise to the north of Paris, Pierrelaye does not have many weddings of prominent persons among its scant five thousand inhabitants.

Bernard Pesquet was, unquestionably, Pierrelaye's most prominent citizen. No one else in the village had ever attracted half the attention in the press that he had.

To an extent, he was a national symbol, a classic example of the fallibility of justice and the successful rehabilitation of one of its victims. It was to Bernard Pesquet that the libertarian left pointed in their courageous struggle to outlaw the death penalty in France.

For Bernard Pesquet had come perilously close to the razor edge of the guillotine and survived to become the respectable citizen and useful member of society that the advocates of lenient law enforcement always maintained he would be.

What had nearly cost Bernard Pesquet his head at the tender age of nineteen was a conviction for murder.

The murder took place in a grimy alley in Rouen on 4 February 1941 and the victim was Julien Quibel, a twenty-year-old electrician and Bernard Pesquet's close friend.

Quibel's head was smashed in from behind with an iron bar and there was substantial evidence that Pesquet did it. The motive was believed to be money; Quibel had been robbed.

Bernard Pesquet denied this. He admitted that he had killed Julien Quibel, but he had done so, he said, to protect the French Resistance. Quibel had been a traitor who was preparing to denounce his fellow resistance fighters to the Germans.

As France was still occupied by the Germans at that time, the defence did not go down very well. Pesquet was, however, still young and the court was inclined to mercy. Rather than the guillotine, they sentenced him to life imprisonment.

Following the end of the war and the departure of the Germans, Pesquet's claim was regarded with greater favour. Many things had happened during the Occupation that were not too well explained and, perhaps, there was something to his accusation that his judges had been collaborators who had wanted to get him out of the way.

Although the Rouen appelate court refused his request for amnesty in 1955, the pressure groups crusading for prisoners' rights continued their efforts and, seven years later, they managed to obtain his release.

Hailed as a victim of society, the law, the judicial system, and right-wing capitalist politics, Pesquet promptly and fully vindicated the faith of his supporters by settling in Pierrelaye and founding a glazing, house-painting and decorating company in which he exclusively employed former fellow prisoners. By 1963, he was already a prosperous businessman and a member of the chamber of commerce.

The sole element lacking from this success story was romance and Pesquet corrected the omission with his marriage in 1968 to Christiane Ruaux, a lovely and charming woman of thirty-two, whom he had met through the rather prosaic medium of a matrimonial agency.

The wedding was a great success and put an end to certain snide rumours in Pierrelaye to the effect that Bernard was a trifle uncertain as to his own sex.

The joy was, unfortunately, somewhat mitigated by

the expense. Although he did not come from a poor family and had enjoyed a normal, middle-class upbringing, Pesquet sometimes appeared to be obsessed with money and he did not like to part with it.

Christiane was a girl with expensive tastes and he had had to pay not only the fees of the marriage agency, but for a wedding reception, an orchestra and even a fireworks display, to say nothing of the bridal dress, his own wedding suit and the honeymoon.

It was, therefore, not surprising that he should be utterly shattered when Christiane ran away on 24 November 1974, precisely two weeks before their sixth wedding anniversary. The shock was as much to his pocket as to his emotions.

Not a man to suffer in stoic silence, he bewailed his misfortune to everyone in Pierrelaye who would listen to him.

Christiane, it seemed, had not only abandoned him for another man; she had practically cleaned him out. Missing were thirteen thousand eight hundred francs (£1400) in cash, the embroidered curtains from the living room, which had cost a fortune, two valuable stamp albums, which he had just had appraised, and two of his best suits.

These suits were the only clue to the identity of Christiane's lover. He had to be a small man or he could not have got into Pesquet's clothes. Strangely, no small man had disappeared from Pierrelaye at this time nor could anyone remember seeing Christiane with a man of any size other than her husband.

Pesquet received, of course, a great deal of sympathy. The man, after having suffered a grave injustice, had managed to pull himself up by his own bootstraps and now, just when everything was going smoothly, his wife had betrayed him.

Sympathy would not bring back Christiane, however, and she was still missing, presumably permanently, when, on the evening of 30 April 1976, a Miss Marylene Soka came to the office of a Pierrelaye estate agent named

Henri Francqui, with whom she had an appointment concerning the purchase of a property.

To her astonishment, she found attached to the front door of the house, which served as both office and home to the widowed Francqui, a card saying that he had been called away suddenly and had gone to Gabon.

That he might have been called away suddenly was possible, but the destination of Gabon struck Miss Soka as highly improbable. She knew Mr Francqui rather well. He was sixty-eight years old and neither temperamentally nor financially capable of impulsive trips to Africa.

Miss Soka rang the bell, hammered on the door, tried to peer through the windows and, when all failed, went to the police.

Pierrelaye has, of course, a very modest police force, but, because of the small size of the community, the officers knew Henri Francqui as well as did Miss Soka.

They were, therefore, in complete agreement that a sudden trip to Gabon or anywhere else in Africa was out of the question.

They could not, however, find out where Henri Francqui had gone. Armed with the necessary authorization, they entered his house. They found no indication of where he might be, but, if he had gone on a trip, it was without his toothbrush and razor.

Fearing the worst, the police searched all of Pierrelaye with great thoroughness.

Franqui was not anywhere in Pierrelaye either.

The Pierrelaye police then turned the matter over to their colleagues at the Quai des Orfevres, the headquarters of the Paris criminal police.

They would not be able to find Henri Francqui either, but they were able to determine one thing. He was not in Gabon. The Gabonese Embassy in Paris had issued no visa for a Mr Henri Francqui to visit the country.

'The commissioner has decided to open a homicide investigation on the Henri Francqui case,' said Inspector Jean Villemain, the plump, high-complexioned head of one of the suburban Paris homicide units, stroking his fine, pointed, blond moustache with the index finger of his right hand. 'We've been given it.'

His assistant, Sergeant of Detectives Claude Laroche, nodded soberly. He was not as plump as his chief and his moustache was longer and darker, but, otherwise, he was not unlike what the inspector had been twenty years earlier.

'You want me to go to Pierrelaye,' he said, making it sound like an accusation.

'Unless you think you can solve it by sitting here in the office,' said the inspector, opening the file on his desk and thus indicating the end of the conversation.

The sergeant did not think that he could solve the disappearance of Henri Francqui by sitting in the office and he was doubtful that he could solve it by going to Pierrelaye.

He was familiar with the case as they had had it for over two weeks before it was decided to make a homicide investigation out of it.

The decision was logical and inevitable. Francqui was beyond the age of impulsive adventures and he had disappeared without taking even his personal identity papers. Either he had been killed in some sort of freak accident or he had been deliberately murdered.

The theory of an accident was largely eliminated by the investigation of the Pierrelaye police. Short of falling into the Oise river and drowning, there was no accident possible where his body would not have been discovered by this time.

The Oise at Pierrelaye is not, however, such a mighty stream as to present a danger to the inhabitants and, even if Francqui had chosen such an improbable means of committing suicide, his body would, by now, have floated down to one of the many locks which make the river navigable.

The sergeant went, therefore, to Pierrelaye with a pessimistic attitude which proved to be fully justified.

The only things that he was able to determine were

that the note attached to the front door had been typed on Francqui's own typewriter and someone had gone through the house very carefully, presumably in search of money, for there was none present.

'The indications are that he was robbed and murdered,' reported the sergeant, upon his return from Pierrelaye, 'but what was done with the body is beyond me. It's definitely not on the premises.'

'Probably taken away in a car and dumped God knows where,' said the inspector. 'Well, if you can't find anything else to follow up, I suppose we'll have to class it unsolved. Take care of it, will you?'

The sergeant took care of it. From the police point of view, it was largely a matter of routine. In any large population centre such as Paris, there are always unexplained disappearances.

From the time Henri Francqui disappeared up until the police came to the conclusion that they could not find him represented a period of something more than two months, so it was now the middle of July 1976 – and Inspector Villemain was soon to be entrusted with the investigation of another and worse case.

The first indication of this came with a telephone call from a little boy to his grandmother.

The call took place at approximately eleven-thirty in the morning of July the twenty-ninth, a Thursday, and the grandmother was Mrs Elizia Bergaud, who lived in a large and luxurious flat at 54 Boulevard Maillot in the exclusive suburb of Neuilly-sur-Seine.

For Inspector Villemain and Sergeant Laroche, the address was important for it lay to the north-west of the city and fell, therefore, within their possible assignment territory.

The little boy, however, knew nothing of inspectors or sergeants and was merely concerned that, instead of his grandmother's familiar voice, a strange, raucous sort of quacking was issuing from the telephone.

Assuming logically that he had dialled a wrong number, he dropped the instrument back into the cradle and went to ask his mother to dial the number for him. He was, after all, a very small boy.

His mother obliged, but with precisely the same result. The noises coming over the telephone were, she thought, human, but she could make nothing out of them.

Oddly, perhaps, she was not concerned. The French telephone system is not the best in the world and, in Paris in 1976, it was sometimes chaotic. Strange electronic *mésalliances* could result in a connection to North African purveyors of goats' milk or a West Indian practitioner of voodoo speaking with the voice of the spirits.

At three-thirty that same afternoon the little boy's father received a telephone call at his office which did cause him great concern.

Actually, it was his secretary and not he, personally, who received the call, but the content was immediately passed on to him. It was purportedly a message from his parents, Emile and Elizia Bergaud.

Said the caller, 'I have been asked to call and tell you that Mr and Mrs Bergaud are leaving immediately for Mégève and from there will go to the Côte d'Azur. It is not, therefore, necessary for the chauffeur to pick them up at their home.'

In one respect, this was a reasonable message. Emile and Elizia Bergaud were to have dined with their son and daughter-in-law that evening and would normally have been picked up by their son's chauffeur.

In another respect, it was totally senseless. Mégève is a winter holiday centre in the Haute Savoie and July was certainly no time of the year for skiing. Besides, Emile was seventy-three years old and Elizia sixty-six. Neither had been on skis for twenty years.

The Côte d'Azur was hardly more probable. It was the height of the summer season, when every typist and clerk in France who had been saving desperately all year for those glorious weeks of holiday would be crowding the beaches, the hotels, the restaurants and even the streets of every town along the coast from Menton to Marseille. Like most of the wealthy French, the

Bergauds did not go to the Côte d'Azur in July or August.

Bergaud immediately telephoned his parents' flat and, when he received no reply, the police. Then, unwilling to wait for his chauffeur, who was absent on an errand, he summoned a taxi and headed for the Boulevard Maillot as fast as traffic conditions would permit.

He did not get into the flat, although he had keys to it. The police had arrived before him and, having been let in by the concierge, had already seen enough not to allow anyone in, relative or not.

This initial police party consisted of no more than the officers from two patrol cars, who confined their efforts to determining that there was no one alive in the flat and notifying the police central that they were at the scene of a triple murder.

They did not tell Bergaud that his parents were dead, but, considering the circumstances and their refusal to let him enter, they did not need to.

As it chanced, Inspector Villemain and Sergeant Laroche were on duty that afternoon and they left immediately for the scene, bringing with them a short, dark and harassed-looking medical expert, whose name was Dr Marcel Prevoste, and half a dozen specialists from the police laboratory.

The crime was, as had been reported, a triple murder. Emile and Elizia Bergaud lay on the floor of their bedroom, his body stretched over hers as if he had been trying to protect her.

In the toilet, separate from the bathroom, a young woman, later identified as twenty-four-year-old Alfia Borgioni, the Bergauds' maid, was seated on the toilet, her skirts tucked up and her panties down. Like the Bergauds, she was dead.

'Thirty-eight calibre revolver or pistol,' said Dr Prevoste, beginning his examinations with the two bodies in the bedroom. 'Fatal head wounds in both cases, plus other bullet wounds in the torsos. I'll get you something more precise when I perform the autopsies. They haven't been dead long. Some time around noon, I should say.'

The technicians had scattered through the flat and now began calling the inspector's attention to such indications and potential clues as they thought important.

In the dining room they found a sheet of plastic wrapping material covered in dried blood. In the second bedroom a woman's purse lay open on the floor with its contents strewn around it. In a closet off the bathroom, a cleverly concealed safe had been pried out of the wall and opened. Nearby lay seven empty jewel cases.

'Well, no question of the motive,' commented the inspector. 'They were robbed.'

'Unusual for them to be murdered like that though, don't you think?' said the sergeant. 'Couldn't have been professionals.'

The inspector agreed. Professional robbers or burglars rarely killed anyone unless they had to. They were basically businessmen, interested in making the maximum profit for the minimum risk. Murder carried a far heavier penalty than did robbery or burglary, and when a burglar was in prison, he was not earning. For the same reason, burglars rarely carried firearms. Sentences for armed robbery were longer.

This robber had not only carried a gun; he had used it ruthlessly and needlessly. The Bergauds were too old to defend themselves against even the feeblest robber. All that would have been necessary would be to tie them up. As for the maid, she was a simple, easily frightened woman who would hardly have resisted, particularly as she was not being robbed.

'No,' said the inspector, 'It was not a normal robbery. He knew them and they knew him. He had to kill them to avoid being exposed.'

'I'll get some people tracing their connections as soon as we have the reports from the lab and the morgue,' said the sergeant.

He and the inspector returned to their office after only a short inspection of the scene of the murders. There was nothing more that they could do and they were only in the technicians' way.

The technicians would be in the flat for the better part of the night. They had now been joined by fingerprint men, photographers, weapons experts and specialists in the detection of clues. The case was major and no effort was being spared.

The bodies were taken to the police morgue after having been photographed as found, and Dr Prevoste was now beginning the autopsies. As he had no intention of working all night, they would not be finished until the following day, but there were certain factors which had to be determined as early as possible.

Inspector Villemain and Sergeant Laroche could also have gone home, but they had found it useful in the past to discuss a case under investigation before sleeping on it. The morning following sometimes brought valuable deductions and ideas.

In this case, the morning following brought nothing other than a strengthened conviction that the murders had been committed by someone known to the Bergauds.

'And known rather well,' said the inspector. 'That safe was very cleverly hidden. I doubt that even a professional would have found it if he didn't know where it was.'

'And there's the telephone call to the son,' added the sergeant. 'A stranger would not have known that the Bergauds had a son, let alone where to find his telephone number.'

He had just returned from taking statements from the Bergauds' son and their daughter-in-law, who reported the strange response she and her son had received when they rang the Bergauds' flat on the preceding day.

'Let me hear the tape on the secretary's statement again,' said the inspector. 'There was something there . . .'

The sergeant ran the tape again.

'That's what I thought,' said the inspector. 'He said, 'Don't send the chauffeur.' That means he knew the Bergauds so well that he knew they were dining with their son and daughter-in-law that evening, and the son would be sending his car to pick them up. As far as I'm concerned, that means family or such a good friend he was practically family.'

'Looks like it, doesn't it?' said the sergeant. 'Well, that shouldn't be hard to trace. There couldn't be more than a few potential suspects.'

There were none at all. Apart from their son, the Berguads had not had many close relatives in the Paris area and the ones they did have were all far too rich to be interested in burglary.

'And no intimate friends at all,' said the sergeant. 'they were not young people and the friends they had had were mostly dead or moved away. There's no one who corresponds to our theory.'

The inspector was not surprised. He had by now received the autopsy reports and he knew that the killer was no ordinary person who might be a member or friend of the Bergaud family. According to Dr Prevoste, he was a dangerous psychopath who killed at least as much from inclination as necessity.

The autopsy reports were, of course, dry and factual. Mrs Bergaud had been shot once through the head, once in the back and once through the liver. Mr Bergaud had been shot in the left temple and in the left armpit. Alfia Borgioni had been strangled unconscious and, while in that condition, had been shot once through the head and once in the chest. Several cuts had been inflicted on her jaw with a kitchen knife, probably after death. Of the seven bullets fired, six had been recovered and sent to the ballistics section, which reported them to be thirty-eight calibre, all fired from the same gun. Time of death was fixed at eleven o'clock in the morning of 29 July 1976, plus or minus twenty minutes.

To this, the doctor had added his opinions and comments, which were not part of the official autopsy report, but which were frequently more valuable as far as the investigation of the case was concerned.

'The murderer,' he wrote, 'is, in my opinion, a person

with dangerous mental problems and will, probably, have been at one time or another under psychiatric treatment.

'He is strongly attracted to money and regards murder as a legitimate means of obtaining it. He is probably very careful with money and may be known to the people around him as a miser. Considering the ruthlessness and savagery of the crimes, it is more than probable that he will be found to have a criminal record.'

This was useful information, but it provided no indication of the killer's physical characteristics.

The laboratory technicians' report did. The murderer, they said, was a small man, not small enough to be classed a dwarf, but under the average height and weight. He was accustomed to using his hands and was skilled with tools. He could be a locksmith or in some related profession. A person with no knowledge of safes would have found it extremely difficult to remove from the wall and open the one in the Bergauds' bathroom.

'If you can't identify him with a profile like that, I'll have you transferred to traffic duty on the Champs-Elysées,' said the inspector.

Traffic on the Champs-Elysées is very heavy. The sergeant took less than twenty-four hours to identify and take into custody model rehabilitated prisoner and successful businessman Bernard Pesquet.

Pesquet was neither a relative nor a close friend of the Berguads. He had merely painted and wall-papered their flat.

And had kept his eyes and ears open.

And, as far as the police were concerned, his mouth shut.

Pesquet vigorously denied any connection with the murders and protested piteously that the police were once again persecuting him because of his past record. He demanded the presence of a newspaper reporter.

Before the press could rush to his rescue, however, the sergeant obtained a warrant and seached his house in Pierrelaye.

There was found a modest sum of French money, sixty-eight gold Swiss, English, Belgian and Italian coins and an American Express credit card in the name of Emile Bergaud.

Pesquet said these things were easily explained. The coins were from his savings. The credit card had been in a book of wall paper samples which he had left with the Bergauds so that they could choose a new paper for the maid's room. He had not got around to giving it back before they were murdered.

This was a reasonable explanation, but the sergeant's men had by now extended the search to the outbuildings and there they found hidden in a barn a yellow leather case containing forty-four pounds of gold bars, three hundred and forty-seven gold coins, Mrs Bergaud's jewelry and the keys to the Bergaud's flat.

This would have been quite enough to satisfy the inspector, but the sergeant uncovered still more. Hidden together with the other objects were a personal identity card, a cheque book and a driving licence in the name of Christiane Pesquet, wnd the cheque book and personal identity card of Henri Francqui.

As Christiane had never been reported missing, the police did not know that she existed, but the sergeant remembered very well Henri Francqui and his mysterious, unsolved disappearance.

Questioning of Bernard Pesquet produced only the customary glib explanation. Christiane and Francqui had been lovers, he said. They had run off together.

The sergeant, who was aware the estate agent had been thirty years older than Mrs Pesquet and in poor health, found this hard to believe, and huge numbers of police armed with picks and shovels descended upon the house in Pierrelaye and began digging up the garden.

Bernard Pesquet, wearing handcuffs, watched them with an amused smile, which vanished only when they transferred their attentions to the basement of the house.

'You may run across two bodies there,' he said.

His prediction was remarkably accurate and the detectives found, not buried but wrapped in plastic and stored at the back of a deep, low niche in the wall, the bodies of Henri Francqui and Christiane Pesquet. Both had been shot, and ballistics tests would later show that it had been with the same weapon that had killed the Bergauds and Alfia Borgioni.

Bernard Pesquet was, consequently, indicted on five counts of homicide and ordered to be held for trial.

This took place in the autumn of 1982 and Pesquet was able to explain everything.

Christiane, he said, had been killed accidentally. She told him, 'I am sick of you. I am going away with Henri. But first I want you to sign me an IOU for all my debts.' Pesquet refused to sign and she drew a pistol and threatened him with it. He tried to get the gun away from her and she accidentally shot herself.

'In the back?' said the dumbfounded judge.

'In the back,' said Pesquest calmly.

'And Francqui?' said the judge.

'We were fighting over Christiane,' said Pesquet. 'I knocked him down and, as he started to get up, I saw something shiny like a gun in his hand so I fired to defend myself.'

'And hit him in the back,' said the judge, who had the results of the autopsies before him.

'In the back,' confirmed Pesquet.

As for the Bergauds and their servant, he was, he protested, simply innocent. The gold bars and other things found on his property had been planted there by the police.

On 8 October 1982, Pesquet was found guilty on all counts and sentenced to life imprisonment.

The verdict was appealed on technical grounds and a new trial was ordered.

This took place on 17 and 18 April of 1984 and Pesquet was, once again, found guilty and sentenced to life imprisonment.

Not discouraged by this latest error of justice, he expressed his approval of the socialist party, which had, by this time, succeeded in doing away with the death penalty, and said that he was looking forward to clemency and an early release.

He is probably not too optimistic.

12

THE WEREWOLF OF AMIENS

He could feel it beginning to happen again!

Something deep down inside him was swelling, raging, howling to be released.

The pressure was unbearable!

The girl beside him, trendy, modern, in her jeans and trainers, her blonde hair clipped short, seemed to sense the danger. Perhaps it was his suddenly staring eyes, the rigid contraction of his muscles, the trickle of saliva from the corners of his mouth.

Her hand crept to the handle of the car door, but his was quicker. Diving as a hawk to that familiar spot beneath the seat, it rose gripping its prey, the long, narrow-bladed, razor-sharp boning knife.

The girl squeaked, too frightened to scream, and the knife went in to the hilt, just under the adolescent left breast and through the heart, which contracted about the cold steel like a fist.

He left it there, got out, walked around to the passenger side and lifted the corpse effortlessly out of the car. She was no small girl, but, in the Other state, his strength was quadrupled.

Dragging the body under the fence, he drew out the knife and plunged it fifteen times more into the corpse.

Release. Something within him had burst, letting out all the hate and the hurt and the crazy festering thoughts.

He knew now. This was not she. It was only a schoolgirl. He did not even know her name.

He started the car and drove away. He felt suddenly very tired.

'Well, it was only a question of when and which unlucky girl would draw the short straw,' said Inspector Jerome Vitry wearily. 'The miracles couldn't go on forever.'

So far, to the knowledge of the police, there had been three miracles. Three times the Werewolf had struck and three times the victims had survived. Sixteen-year-old Dominique Crete had been the unlucky fourth.

And all this within seven weeks. It was now 11 May 1983 and the first reported attack had taken place on March the twenty-second.

It was as pointless and as mysterious as the murder of Dominique Crete. Eighteen-year-old Véronique Dubois was coming home to her parents' flat in the straight, grey streets near the north railway station in Amiens.

The time was nine o'clock in the evening and, the day being cloudy, it was completely dark except for the pools of light cast by the widely spaced street lamps.

Véronique did not feel nervous. In Paris, a hundred miles to the south, a girl alone in such dark, deserted streets would have been close to hysteria, but this was Amiens, with a population of under a hundred and forty thousand and a low crime rate. Here there was nothing to fear.

Or was there?

Véronique, still over a hundred yards from home, became aware of the sound of footsteps on the street behind her. Not the hard rap of leather soles, but the soft padding sounds of rubber.

Turning her head, she saw a tall, lean figure advancing through the darkness between the street lamps. The man was moving rapidly and she estimated that he would catch up with her before she could reach home.

Well, so what? Simply because there was a man walking in the same direction as she was meant nothing. He had as much right to walk the streets as anyone else. Probably someone going home, as she was.

But something inside her told her that it was not true. The man was not a harmless pedestrian. There was a sort of terrible urgency in that wolf-like lope. He was overhauling her rapidly . . .

Panic clutched at her heart and, in a purely involuntary reaction, she broke into a run.

Instantly, she heard the quick thud of the rubber soles striking the pavement in great bounds, closing on her with terrifying swiftness.

How many doors yet to the house? She was running as fast as she could, her breath coming in great gasps. Would she have time to open the door?

A terrible pain shot through her back. He was upon her! She fell to the pavement, her legs still moving in a running reflex. The man bent over her, the knife swinging down and slicing into her neck. She felt the gush of blood. The man struck again at her throat. There was a terrific impact and a sharp snapping noise. Somewhere far away some one was screaming, screaming, screaming. Véronique did not realize that it was she.

When she recovered consciousness, she was in the white-walled room of the hospital, in a clean, white bed and her mother was sitting beside her, no longer weeping but radiant with the knowledge that her daughter would retain no more than minor scars to remind her of her experience.

'A miracle!' she said. 'When he stabbed at your throat the point of the knife struck right on your St Joseph's medallion and the blade broke.'

Véronique nodded and tried to smile. She was unable to speak and her throat was very sore.

The police were unwilling to wait until she could speak again and, the following day, a sergeant of detectives called François Lejeune came round and asked her to write out a description of her attacker on a pad which he had brought along for the purpose.

Véronique wrote that he was tall and thin and had worn shoes with rubber soles. Otherwise, she knew nothing about him. It had been dark and everything had happened very quickly.

The sergeant, an earnest young man with a long sympathetic face and a fine, drooping blond moustache, was disappointed. He had already taken statements from Véronique's parents and the others who ran to the rescue in response to her screams, and no one had been able to report even that much. All that had been seen was a tall, lean figure sprinting away down the street. The blade of the broken knife lay beside the bleeding girl. The handle he had taken with him.

Inspector Vitry, the sergeant's immediate superior and the investigations officer to whom the case had been assigned, had some hopes that the knife blade could be traced.

A tall, dour-faced, swarthy man with a permanent expression of glum sorrow, he was, in reality, an incurable optimist and invariably believed that something would turn up to solve even the most difficult case.

He was, of course, usually wrong and he was wrong in the case of the attempted murder of Véronique Dubois. The knife was untraceable.

The case was classified as attempted murder as there was no indication that the attacker had had any other intentions. He had simply run down the girl and started stabbing her with the knife. Had it not been for the miracle of the medallion, he would almost certainly have killed her on the spot.

Seated at his regular table in the place where he took all his meals, the Werewolf sipped his morning coffee and smiled over the newspaper account of the attack on Véronique Dubois. It was only from the newspaper that he had learned her name.

The press, he noted, had already christened him the Vampire of Amiens. It was a foolish name. Vampires drank the blood of their victims, sometimes without killing them. He did not want to drink blood. It would turn his stomach. What he wanted was to kill that shadowy figure which danced and smiled, short-haired, in jeans and trainers, in his mind.

Véronique Dubois's blonde hair had been cut short and she had been wearing jeans and tennis shoes.

'The only good thing about this,' remarked the inspector, 'is that he's certain to do it again.'

'You call that good?' said the sergeant, mildly shocked.

'I mean it will give us another chance to identify him,' said the inspector.

It was March the twenty-fourth and, although only two days had passed since the attack on Véronique Dubois, the police investigation was already terminated. The only hope of identifying the attempted murderer had been to look for an embittered lover, but the investigation quickly showed that Véronique had none. Being an attractive girl, she had gone out with boys, but with no one regularly and always in a group.

The inspector put the Véronique Dubois file where he could easily lay hands on it again and he and the sergeant went home to have their dinners. The time was six-thirty in the evening.

Two and a half hours later, a Miss Liette Sauteret was taking a late walk in the streets around Notre Dame Cathedral, roughly a quarter of a mile to the north-west of the railway station.

As the bells in the tower high above struck nine, a tall, slender form crossed the open square and was swallowed up in the darkness between two of the great buttresses supporting the cathedral wall.

The pressure had been building up all afternoon and evening. The Werewolf had eaten, but had not been able to digest his supper. His entire system was in a turmoil. The Other state was coming over him.

Fortunately, he was prepared. He had bought a new knife that same morning, a better, stronger, sharper knife, a butcher's boning knife that would slice into female flesh like butter.

It was thrust through the waistband of his trousers now as he waited, silent in the darkness, in ambush, hunting.

Like the inspector, he was optimistic. She, the one with the short blonde hair, the jeans, the tennis shoes, would come. She would come and he would . . .

Liette Sauteret turned the corner of the cathedral and started across the square. She was wearing jeans, a short jacket and tennis shoes. Her blonde hair was cropped short.

The Werewolf came out of his lair like a shadow in the night. His rubber soles made only the slightest whisper on the cobbles.

But it was enough!

Liette Sauteret tensed, half turned and, as the form bore down on her with knife raised, seized an arm, turned, twisted and, suddenly, the Werewolf was flying through the air to land painfully on his face!

Liette was a black belt judoka and her training had stood her in good stead. The reaction had been purely automatic and it undoubtedly saved her life.

Unfortunately, surprise led her to a dangerous under-estimation. Instead of taking to her heels before the Werewolf could regain his feet, she stood motionless, her mouth gaping in disbelief, partially at the attack and partially at her own riposte to it.

She could not know, of course, that, in the Other state, the Werewolf was possessed of the strength of four and the resilience of a tennis ball.

In an instant, he scrambled to his feet and, as she belatedly realized the danger and turned to run, he drove the knife into the small of her back.

Liette screamed blood-curdlingly and stumbled forward as, from somewhere nearby, there came the sounds of answering shouts and running feet.

The man followed for a few steps, but people were running across the square and he slanted away to disappear in the shadows.

'Less injured than the first one,' said the sergeant, who had just returned from the hospital where he had taken a statement from Liette Sauteret. 'And less information. Tall and thin. That's the sum of it.'

'Damn!' said the inspector. 'I was sure we'd get a better description this time. What are the girls thinking of? They should keep their eyes open.'

'She said it happened very fast,' replied the sergeant non-committally. 'Nothing from the files, I suppose?'

The inspector shook his head. 'Not enough points of reference for the computer. It could be anybody in Amiens.'

He had been attempting to find some precedent for the attacks in the police files, but he was unsuccessful. There had been attacks enough on girls and women, but all by men who wanted sex in some form or other. There had been none where the only motive was murder.

This lack of a lead in the cases left the inspector in an uncomfortable position. The women and girls of the city had to be alerted to the danger of being out alone after dark, but, if no one went out in the evening, there would be no more attacks and no new opportunity to trace the psychopath.

For it was a psychopath. That much was certain. Given an utterly wild coincidence, Véronique Dubois and Liette Sauteret could have a common acquaintance who had developed a grudge against both of them. The possibility needed to be investigated and it had been. There was no coincidence. The girls did not know each other and they had not had a single contact in common.

In the end, the inspector decided that the safety of the public was more important than trying for a quick solution to the case. The newspapers and the local television station were fed with what he judged to be enough lurid details, not all entirely true, so that no female in her right mind would dream of setting foot outside after sundown.

Of course, it did not work. In a community the size of Amiens, there were thousands who did not read the newspapers and other thousands who believed not a word of what they did read in them. Statistically, there were, perhaps, fewer women and girls on the streets after dark, but the difference was not perceptible to the casual observer.

The Werewolf sipped his morning coffee and read his newspaper expressionlessly. The news was not good. Liette Sauteret had been only superficially wounded. He was hoping that he had carved out her kidneys. His face was still sore, although the swelling had gone down quickly. No one had noticed anything at work.

More gratifyingly, if the newspaper could be believed, she had not been able to provide any precise description of him. He was safe.

Or was it a police trick? Perhaps it would be better to hold off for a while.

He lasted for five days before he was literally forced to seek relief. The Other was taking over even while he was at work, and his colleagues were beginning to notice.

'Aren't you feeling well?' they asked. 'Why don't you take a day off and go to see the doctor? Don't worry about the work. We'll take care of it.'

They were good friends, good comrades on the job. He realized with a warm glow of satisfaction that he was popular, attractive to others . . .

But not to her!

Blonde heads, jeans, scuffed trainers spun and danced in his brain. On the night of March the twenty-ninth, he slid the boning knife into his waistband and quietly left the bed-sit which held so many bitter memories. The time was nine o'clock.

Jacqueline Croiset was twenty years old and married. She lived with her husband of eight months in a small flat at 8 rue de la Contrescarpe. From her kitchen window, she could see the roof of the railway station. When she went to do her shopping, she passed by the cathedral.

Jacqueline Croiset read the newspapers and, in so far as the reports of the so-called Vampire of Amiens were concerned, she believed them. She knew that Liette Sauteret and Véronique Dubois had been stabbed within a few hundred yards of her home, but she was a logically minded woman and she reasoned that the Vampire would not risk yet another attack in the same area.

It did not occur to her that the thought processes of a psychopath might not be logical.

She was not, therefore, nervous as she hurried down the shadow-filled rue de la Contrescarpe for she had no inkling that the Werewolf was trailing silently almost at her heels.

He had seen the short blonde hair and the jeans and trainers as she passed under the lamp in front of the cathedral and had followed her.

Jacqueline Croiset laid the parcels from her shopping on the doorstep and fumbled in her bag for the key. Hercule, her husband, was probably watching television and she did not want to disturb him by ringing the bell.

Without the slighest warning, an incredible pain tore through her body. She had been stabbed in the back, but the agony was such that she thought her whole body was on fire.

She was paralysed with the pain, unable to hold herself up, unable to speak, and she toppled silently forward on to the parcels, her helpless body turning and twisting so that she was looking upward into the werewolf's face.

It was only a darker mask against the blackness of the night. All she could see was that he was not wearing a hat and that his ears stood out from the sides of his head.

He was jabbing the knife into her chest and belly, again and again, but it did not hurt. She was already in such pain that her brain could register no further hurt.

Dimly, she thought, 'Why, he's killing me!' and then she was slipping down, down and the darkness was closing over her head.

Hercule found her in a welter of blood on the doorstep. He had not been watching television after all, but pacing up and down the little hall, worrying over his new bride who had stayed out late shopping and would be coming home in the darkness when everyone knew that a killer was abroad.

It would later be theorized that it was the gasping

breaths of the wildly excited Vampire which had brought him to the door. Jacqueline had not made a sound for she was mercifully unconscious.

Hercule Croiset was not able to say whether the Vampire had still been in sight when he opened the door or not. His entire attention had been concentrated on the blood spurting from his wife's body and the urgency of obtaining medical help before it was too late.

He had been certain that it was too late, but Jacqueline was still breathing and the emergency ambulance responded swiftly. She arrived at the hospital alive, survived the operation and, three days later, was able to reassure her husband, who had spent the first night at the hospital under sedation himself, that he was not yet a widower.

The third attempt had failed and there was still no worthwhile description of the Vampire.

This time not only the police but a large segment of the public was scared and alarmed. Jacqueline Croiset had been very seriously injured. It was obvious that if she had survived, it was not because of any lack of murderous intent on the part of the Vampire. He was out to kill and it was only a question of who would be the victim.

It would be Dominique Crete, the youngest victim of all, a sixteen-year-old schoolgirl who had missed the four-thirty train to her home in Fouencamps, five miles to the south-east of Amiens.

Dominique was a responsible girl who might dress according to the trend but always came home when she was supposed to. When she failed to come home that afternoon, her mother was immediately worried. Having telephoned one of her school mates to determine that she had left school at the usual time, she called the police.

The police were as concerned as she. Where would Dominique have gone after school? The railway station. How was she dressed? Jeans and trainers. Her hair? Short, blonde.

'Good God!' exclaimed Inspector Vitry. 'Do you realize that every gril who's been attacked was near the railway station and looked just like that!'

It was the first time that anyone had noticed the remarkable uniformity in the appearance of the victims.

'It can't be a coincidence,' said the sergeant. 'The fellow has a fixation on girls with short blonde hair who wear trainers and jeans. If we'd only realized before . . .'

The sergeant thought that, with such pronounced preferences in victims, it might be possible to trace the identity of the Vampire through his non-fatal involvement with females of similar appearance.

As a matter of fact, he was wrong. The Werewolf knew only one girl with short blonde hair who habitually wore jeans and trainers. She was at the root of his problems, the creator of the Other, the splinter at the heart of the festering sore.

The realization of the striking uniformity in the victims' appearance and dress lent an even more frightening significance to the disappearance of Dominique Crete, and search-parties of off-duty police and firemen moved out immediately.

As she had obviously not been attacked at the railway station in the middle of the afternoon, the search began in Fouencamps, with the result that her body was found in less than two hours, only a quarter mile from her home.

Inspector Vitry and Sergeant Lejeune were notified and hurried to the scene, bringing with them the department's top medical expert and a detachment of technicians from the police laboratory.

The technicians were able to determine only one thing. Dominique had been brought to the scene in a car and dragged, dead or unconscious, under the fence.

Dr Michel Parmentier, a rather beefy young man, with plump red cheeks and metal-rimmed glasses, was able to say more.

He had had an opportunity to examine the wounds of Jacqueline Croiset at the hospital and, in his opinion, these were identical to them, deep stab wounds made by a sharp, narrow, single-edged blade.

The immediate cause of death had been a single stab-wound through the heart and, considering the circumstances, it appeared probable that this had been the first wound inflicted.

There had been no sexual tampering. The girl's underwear was in place and she had died an intact virgin.

The time of death he estimated to be around five o'clock that afternoon.

The examination at the scene completed, the body was removed to the police morgue, where, because of the importance of the case, the doctor completed the autopsy that night.

The only information that he was able to add was that Dominique had known she was in danger. Her bloodstream had been full of adrenaline at the time of death.

The police still had no indication as to the identity of the murderer, but they knew where Dominique must have encountered him and the route which would have been taken.

Armed with this information, they were eventually able to obtain witness sightings of a young girl with short blonde hair riding in the front seat of a red Volkswagen, and even a sketchy description of the driver.

He was young, slender, had long hair and wore an earring in his right ear.

The inspector, on the basis of the sergeant's theory concerning the Vampire's preferences in women, broadcast an appeal to the public. Any girls with short blonde hair who sometimes wore jeans and trainers were urged to contact the police.

The results were modest. A single response was received, and this not from a girl, but from the counterman in a fast-food restaurant called the J.J. La Frite. One of his customers had been a girl with short blonde hair who invariably wore jeans and trainers. He had not seen her since the preceding autumn and thought she might have been murdered.

The inspector did not know whether this was a lead or not until the counterman mentioned that the girl, whose name, he said, was Brigitte Parque or Pacque, had usually been in the company of a tall, slender young man who wore his hair long and had a gold earring in his right ear.

The restaurant the J.J. La Frite was located at 21 rue de l'Ecole, only a few yards from the railway station, and the street was soon swarming with detectives. The young woman was identified as Brigitte Pacque, born Brigitte Adams, and the man as Philippe Pacque, a storeroom clerk at the CO-OP, a retail store located at 13 rue de l'Ecole.

Pacque, who lived at 17 rue de l'Ecole and took all his meals at the J.J. La Frite, had received an eighteen-month suspended sentence on 20 October 1981 as the result of a strange incident which had taken place on 9 October 1980.

On that date, Pacque had picked up an eighteen-year-old girl hitch-hiker in his red Volkswagen. A student at the local university, she was on her way there.

Pacque told her that that was where he was going too. His wife worked in the university restaurant and he was going to pick her up.

Before reaching the university, however, Pacque had suddenly put his hand under her skirt and tried to touch her genitals.

The girl protested and he abruptly swung the car around and raced off in another direction.

Terrified, the girl opened the door and flung herself out of the car, which was moving at an estimated speed of fifty miles an hour. She was severely injured, but Pacque drove away without stopping. Discovered lying unconscious beside the road, she was taken to the hospital and was able to identify her attacker through a description of him and his car, and the information that his wife worked at the university restaurant.

The police record tended to throw the investigators off. It was true that Pacque had attacked a woman, but it was a very different sort of attack to those carried out by the Vampire of Amiens. The motive was obviously sex and he had had no knife nor had he actually harmed the girl. Her injuries were due to her attempt to escape. It was possible that his intentions had been largely innocent.

He was, however, the only suspect that the police had, which guaranteed that he would be thoroughly investigated. As it turned out, there was not much to investigate.

Philippe Pacque was twenty-six years old and had been working at the CO-OP, living in the rue de l'Ecole and eating at the J.J. La Frite since early 1977. He was well-known and popular in the street and was highly regarded by his employers.

Up until his marriage on 1 April 1980, he had been what is known to non-squares as 'square', meaning that he wore his hair short, dressed conventionally and did not use drugs.

Following the marriage to Brigitte Adams, aged sixteen at the time, he had changed his image, letting his hair grow and having his ear pierced for an earring. He still did not use drugs.

Brigitte was an abandoned child who had grown up in state institutions and, although she wore her blonde hair cut very short and dressed exclusively in jeans and trainers, she was apparently not very hip either.

Brigitte and Philippe lived in the tiny studio at 17 rue de l'Ecole for roughly one year and she then ran away to the city of Lille.

Philippe persuaded her to return, but she ran away again in September of 1982 and filed for divorce, stating as grounds that Philippe was pathologically jealous and that he beat her.

The divorce was granted and she was now living in Turcoing, a city near Lille, and working as a waitress in a roller-skating rink.

The inspector went to Turcoing to interview her personally. He was hoping she would be able to provide some information useful to the case, and, for once, his optimism was justified and she practically solved it for him.

Philippe, she said, had been one of the nicest, most gentle people in the world when she married him and he remained that way for nearly a year.

At the end of that time and after his attack on the girl student, he began to suffer from strange fits. His eyes would take on a glassy, staring look, his muscles would become tense and rigid and he would drool slightly. He was abnormally strong while in this state and he would beat her so violently that she feared for her life.

Neither he nor she could guess what was wrong with him, but she privately thought he was going crazy.

Inexplicably, the psychologists did not agree with her. Philippe, they said, had seizures which affected his personality and even his physical capacity, but he knew what he was doing and was capable of controlling his actions.

Arrested, charged and interrogated, he confessed to the crimes, and the boning knife, still bearing traces of his victims' blood, was found in his studio. Although unable to offer any explanation of his acts or suggest any motive other than that Brigitte had had a powerful effect on him, he appeared to be sincerely repentant.

It was not enough for the jury. On 10 June 1984, they found him guilty of murder with no extenuating circumstances and sentenced him to life imprisonment.

13

NEVER TRUST AN FBI AGENT

Humans are hunters. They like to hunt animals, birds, fish, insects, plants, microbes and humans. In the city of West Berlin, only the last two are in generous supply, but the hunting is good.

Like all predators, the human hunter tends to prey on the old, the infirm and the weak, and, because of a demographic distortion, West Berlin has a large reservoir of such game.

A lost island of capitalism drowning in the red sea of socialist East Germany, its two million population is maintained only through massive infusions of money by the West German government. As these subsidies tend to benefit the young and the old, the two groups are disproportionately larger than the working-family age group.

The young are, generally, physically superior to the old and often have expensive habits. The old are often isolated, alone, defenceless. It is logical that the one should prey on the other.

They do, and so frequently that it is not difficult to reconstruct a typical hunt from the court records and police files.

The game begins with the quarry. She is trotting briskly or, perhaps, limping slowly down the street with her shopping bag. It contains mainly vegetables and bread. If she stops at the butcher's at all, it is for a few slices of sausage. Perhaps she is so poor that she cannot afford to eat meat.

She is spotted by the hunter. He is not deceived by

the modest purchases. People in their eighties often eat little meat by choice. The saving habits of a lifetime are not easily changed. The little hoard hidden under the bed or at the back of the closet must be added to painful pfennig by pfennig so that there will be a proper burial, and, perhaps, a little something for the grandchildren who would come to visit if they were not so busy.

She does not notice him. He is conventionally dressed, inconspicuous, a pedestrian like thousands of others.

They pass down the street, joined by an invisible bond, the wolf and the deer, the fox and the rabbit, and, presently, the doomed victim goes to earth in the dark entrance of a block of flats.

It is not an expensive building, but it is respectable. An encouraging sign. She can pay a normal rent.

The hunter must hurry now. He wants to know which floor and which flat. Silent as a ghost, he slides through the entrance and cocks his head up the stairwell, listening for the sound of the closing door.

Right. Second floor, to the left of the stairs. The hunter goes up in great cat bounds, two steps at a time. The shorter the interval spent in the building, the better.

She is surprised, but his credentials impress her and she slips the chain lock to let him in.

'Where is the money?' he hisses, pushing the door shut and reaching for her.

She begins to scream, the hopeless, frail screaming of an old woman who knows that the hunter is upon her and death or worse is instants away.

Mercifully, it is not worse. His hands close over her throat. There is a sense of suffocation, the feeling of horror that comes with the knowledge that a fellow human is deliberately taking your life, then darkness descends. Perhaps the last sensation is one of gratitude that she was not tortured.

'He's no sadist,' said Inspector Karl Heiden, officer in charge of the commission that had been formed to investigate the latest series of killings of old persons.

'Very businesslike. He wants the money and he kills them simply to avoid leaving a witness.'

The inspector and his assistant, Detective Sergeant Franz Wagner, were in a flat at 27 Borussia Strasse in the Tempelhof area. The corpse of the occupant, Mrs Erna Hoedicke, was being examined by the medical expert attached to the squad.

'Identical to the others,' said Dr Morris Scheidel. 'Manual strangulation. Quick and thorough. She's been dead at least forty-eight hours.'

It was Saturday 31 March 1984, and Mrs Hoedicke's body had been discovered at approximately ten o'clock in the morning by a social worker named Petra Haarmann.

It was part of Mrs Haarmann's job to look in at regular intervals on persons as old as Mrs Hoedicke and, there being a great number of them, she normally worked on Saturday mornings, although she was not required to.

Mrs Hoedicke and the other old people looked forward to these visits and, when she did not answer the door, Mrs Haarmann went to look for the building superintendent who had a pass key. Mrs Hoedicke, she thought, had perhaps died. At eighty-seven, it would not have been entirely unexpected.

Mrs Hoedicke had indeed died, but in an unexpected manner. She lay in the small entrance hall of the flat, her clothing neatly arranged. Apart from the bruises on her throat, she could have been sleeping.

Mrs Haarmann promptly called the police. Although this was the first murder victim that she had found, she was aware that there had been a number of such murders in recent months.

One a month, in fact, since December of the preceding year. On the twentieth of that month, five days before Christmas, Mrs Hedda Buekow had become what was believed to be the first victim of the Doorbell Killer, as the newspapers christened him.

He was called the Doorbell Killer because it was thought that he simply rang the doorbell of his victims' flats and, when they opened the door, strangled them.

The bodies of all the known victims had been found near their front doors.

Inspector Heiden did not think it was that simple. A bluff, fair-haired man with round red cheeks and innocent-appearing blue eyes, he had had extensive experience of crimes against old people and he knew that they did not, as a rule, open their doors to strangers.

In every one of the four murders which had taken place so far, the front door had been equipped with a chain lock so that the occupant could see who was at the door before letting anyone in.

'Which could mean that they knew him, if the murders weren't scattered all over town,' said Sergeant Wagner.

They had, indeed, been scattered all over town. No two of the crimes had taken place in the same area.

Hedda Buekow, the first in the series, had lived in the Tiergarten district, at 14 Birken Strasse, which was a good deal to the north of Tempelhof.

It had not then been recognized as a series, and the murder was investigated by the Tiergarten precinct police, who were unable to develop any lead to the identity of the murderer.

Mrs Buekow was eighty-two, but she had a male admirer a year younger than herself. His name was Otto Ploeck and it was he who discovered her body as he had a key to her flat.

Ploeck nearly went with her, for the shock caused him to suffer a heart attack. Interviewed at the hospital, he told the police that Mrs Buekow had been an exceedingly cautious woman. She had regarded Berlin as a sort of jungle filled with dangerous beasts and she would not let even a delivery man into her flat.

'They had to put the parcel on the floor in front of the door and she only came out to get it when they'd gone back down the stairs,' said Ploeck. 'It has to be someone she knew very well.'

But the only person that Mrs Buekow had known very well was Ploeck himself so, despite his age, he was investigated.

The result was proof positive that Ploeck had had nothing to do with the murder. The autopsy determined the time of death within half an hour, and he had been elsewhere at the time.

There was, however, confirmation of what Ploeck said. Mrs Buekow had been extremely cautious.

The motive of the crime was clear. The flat had been ransacked and Mrs Buekow's savings were gone. Ploeck, who knew a good deal about her private affairs, believed that the sum would have amounted to approximately three thousand six hundred marks (£1200) – no fortune, but worth the trouble. Like many older people on the Continent, Mrs Buekow had not trusted banks.

'Which is what makes them such perfect targets, of course,' said the inspector.

'Probably better than being tortured to death because they can't tell where their savings are hidden when they don't have any,' said the sergeant.

He was a short, stocky, cheerful sort of man with a rough, squarish face and light brown hair cut high on the sides.

He and the inspector had only come to review the Hedda Buekow case when a special commission was formed following the murder of Elli Grybek.

Mrs Grybek had lived at 44 Detmold Strasse in the Wilmersdorf area, which was to the south-west of Tiergarten.

The circumstances of the eighty-four-year-old woman's death were fed into the police computer, which reported that a nearly identical case had taken place in the Tiergarten area only a little more than a month earlier. The probability of a series was then recognized and the commission was set up to deal with it.

Mrs Grybek's body had been discovered by a grand-niece called Karin Franck, who told police that she thought there would have been around one thousand six hundred marks (£550) in the flat. It was, of course, not there now.

The formation of the commission was a more or less

routine response to similar murders taking place over the entire city and it was not the first such series that the officers had had to investigate.

But, in some ways, it was the most difficult. In other cases where older persons had been killed there were more indications. The killer had been a sadist who tortured his victims unmercifully. Or he had mutilated the bodies. Or he had been sexually deranged. The rape of women in their eighties was not at all uncommon.

The Doorbell Killer was, however, neither sadist nor sexually interested in his victims. Indeed, there was reason to believe that he took some pains to arrange their clothing in a decent manner. What he wanted was money or jewelery, and he went about getting it with the passionless efficiency of a machine.

In some unknown manner, he persuaded each victim to let him into her flat, strangled her immediately, searched the flat, took whatever he found and departed. He left no fingerprints or any other clue to his identity and, so far, no witnesses who claimed to have seen him had been found.

'He's got some kind of a gimmick,' said the inspector. 'The old people here are super-cautious. Some of them won't let their own relatives into their flats, but they let this fellow in, even when the newspapers are full of the Doorbell Killer.'

'Well I've got the print-out here on past cases,' said the sergeant. 'There were people who pretended to be meter readers, people who claimed to be repairmen sent by the landlord, people in phony police uniforms, phony postmen and one real postman. There's quite a selection.'

'Publicize all of them,' said the inspector. 'We have to reduce his targets as much as possible. Then, he may get desperate and make a mistake.'

Off-hand, the inspector did not think that he would. If the Doorbell Killer were on drugs, he might become so hard pressed for money to buy the stuff that he would do something foolish, but the cold efficiency with which he operated was not typical of an addict. However, publicizing the tricks that had been used to gain entrance to victims' flats in the past could save the life of some old person now.

'It's apparently nothing that's been used before,' said the sergeant. 'We've had warnings plastered all over the newspapers and on television and there's a new one just reported. Eighty-one-year-old woman named Sigurd Bessener.'

Mrs Bessener had lived in a block of flats at 37 Naumann Strasse in the Schoeneberg area, which was about halfway between Tiergarten and Templehof, and the inspector went out to take a look at the scene.

The body had been discovered by a friend, Mrs Marta Bauer, who was in her late seventies herself, and Dr Scheidel, who had just arrived, was still examining it.

'Astonishing uniformity,' he said. 'It's practically a trade mark. I don't think he got much here though.'

The flat was very small and shabby and there was nothing in it that a second-hand shop would have accepted. Mrs Bauer confirmed that her friend had been very poor and had had only the minimum pension. She doubted that her total saving would have amounted to more than three hundred marks (£100).

Whatever there was, the Doorbell Killer had found it and had left his signature, the decently arranged body of an old woman who had been strangled to death.

Perhaps it was because she had been so poor, or perhaps it was because she had been an unusually small, frail woman, but the murder of Sigurd Bessener enraged the inspector, who, as an experienced investigations officer, was rarely enraged by anything.

'The poor woman was hardly able to feed herself,' he growled, 'but she was still trying to keep up appearances when she went out, and he took it for money.'

He had seen it often enough before. Proud old women who had but one good dress for going out, with which they vainly hoped to convince the neighbours that they were not as poor as everybody knew they were.

There is no more materialistic society in the world than Germany. If you have nothing, you are nothing.

Sigurd Bessener had had one good dress and she had died wearing it.

'Meaning that she had just come in,' said the inspector. 'See if she had time to put her shopping bag in the kitchen.'

The sergeant went to look.

'Cabbage, potatoes, a litre of milk and a loaf of bread,' he reported. 'She hadn't taken it out of the bag yet.'

'Give me a time, Morris,' said the inspector.

The doctor squinted at him with short-sighted brown eyes behind thick-lensed glasses. He had a heavy beard and he did not shave as frequently as he should have.

'How exact?' he said.

'Half an hour, forty-five minutes,' said the inspector.

'Two-thirty to three-fifteen yesterday afternoon,' said the doctor.

'All right, Franz. Get your people out into the street,' said the inspector. 'Find out where she shopped and question the shop assistants along the route to the flat. See if anybody noticed when he started following her.'

It was what had been done in all the preceding cases, and no witnesses had been found.

This time was different. Perhaps it was because of the publicity that the Doorbell Killer had been receiving. Perhaps it was because February the seventeenth had been a day of particularly harsh weather, with a savage little gale drifting down from across the Baltic to lash Berlin with snow, hail and freezing rain. In any case, there had been fewer shoppers than usual on the street.

No less than two witnesses, both shop assistants, had noticed a tall, strongly built young man, with the faint beginnings of a moustache and dark wavy hair worn down to the collar, strolling casually along not far behind Sigurd Bessener.

They had not realized that he was following Sigurd and they had not thought that he looked like a murderer.

'Nobody looks like a murderer,' commented the

inspector. 'With the possible exception of people who are not. Murderers look like just anybody because murderers are just anybody.'

'Well, it's something at least. What does the computer say?'

The computer had been searching the records for a match to the description of the young man and turned up a number of candidates. There are a good many large young men with skimpy moustaches and dark hair worn down to the collar in Berlin.

All those noted by the computer had, of course, police records, mainly for narcotics offences, and all had to be individually checked out by the sergeant's detectives.

The result was, as the inspector had feared, a blank. None of the men from the police files could have been in the street behind Sigurd Bessener on the afternoon that she was murdered.

'They're mostly addicts,' said the sergeant glumly, 'and you never did think he was an addict.'

'I still don't,' said the inspector. 'This is no fuzzy-minded, brain-damaged junkie. It's a man who's thinking clearly and logically.'

'And feloniously,' added the sergeant. 'A few more like him and there'd be no senior citizens left in Berlin.'

The inspector and the sergeant were becoming frustrated and impatient. So far, there had been three murders of old women, in all probability by the same man, and they still had no clue as to his identity other than the rather vague description garnered in this latest killing.

The knowledge that this was still a modest series as compared to ones that had run to ten, fifteen and more victims was of no comfort. Old women were dying at the rate of one a month and there was nothing that they had been able to do about it.

March was almost an exception, but Erna Hoedicke died on the thirty-first to keep the string of once a month intact. No clues were found at the scene. No witnesses reported seeing the young man with the incipient moustache. It was estimated that he had got approximately eight hundred marks and a small amount of jewelery.

'Who and when in April?' said the sergeant. 'Is there anything we can do to warn them that we haven't done?'

'No,' said the inspector. 'There's no old woman in Berlin who doesn't know that a series is going on. He has some compelling argument for being let into their flats. If we knew what it was, we could stop him, but we don't. As for when, after the fifteenth. He's never struck before the middle of the month.'

Nor did he this time. It was the afternoon of Friday, 20 April 1984 when Caecili Hidde died at the age of eighty-three, although her body was not discovered until the following day.

Eighty-year-old Mrs Julia Keppler told the police, 'I had a feeling that the Doorbell Killer had got Caecili. That's why I went to her flat.'

She had rung the bell, knocked on the door and, when the building superintendent refused to open it with his pass key, called the police.

Mrs Hidde lay in the front hall, her clothing decently arranged. She had been strangled to death.

'He hit a good one this time,' said the inspector.

An examination of Mrs Hidde's finances indicated that she would have had close to twenty thousand marks in the flat.

'Do you think her friend really had a presentiment?' asked the sergeant curiously.

'I think a few thousand elderly women are having presentiments twenty-four hours a day,' said the inspector. 'Have you seen the record of calls to the police?'

The police emergency numbers had been almost continually blocked for weeks on end with frantic calls from old women who thought that they were being attacked by the Doorbell Killer.

'They really have nothing to worrry about,' said the sergeant. 'If they're still alive, it wasn't him.'

It was one of the most outstanding of the killer's characteristics. He was invariably lethal. Once his hands closed over the victim's throat, she was lost. There was no instance of a victim who had survived.

Which, of course, made the task of the police harder. Survivors would have been able to describe the killer and, above all, explain how he had persuaded them to open their flat doors.

The inspector had gradually come to the conclusion that his means of entrance was the key to the solution of the cases. Someone had come up with something new and it was working like a charm.

'It's not a uniform,' he mused. 'We'd have witness reports of somebody in uniform in or near the building and we don't. So it's credentials . . . papers . . . a badge . . .'

'But we've warned against false credentials and false badges and even uniforms, and it hasn't had any effect,' said the sergeant. 'Or is it simply that there is a certain percentage of elderly ladies who are foolish about such things?'

'There probably is,' said the inspector, 'but that's not it. How could he pick out the foolish ones? It's virtually certain that he's had no previous contact with them.'

It had been their original hope that the strangler had no trick for getting into old women's flats – he simply knew the victims personally.

The hope diminished with each murder and had now utterly vanished. Mrs Hidde, the last victim in the series, had lived in a rather expensive building at 61 Thomas Strasse in the Neu Koelln area, which was by the Berlin Wall separating East and West Berlin. As in all the preceding cases, no connection to any of the other victims could be traced.

The Hidde case was, however, different from the others in two respects. Mrs Hidde had been financially much better off; and what was thought to be a clue had been found at the scene.

It was not immediately recognized as a clue for it was

only a sales receipt from a nearby clothes shop and it was assumed that it represented a purchase made by Mrs Hidde.

It was investigated, and within an hour the inspector had the break for which he had been waiting so long.

Mrs Hidde had, indeed, been an old customer of the shop and she was known to the staff.

She had not, however, made any purchases in the shop on the day for which the sales receipt was issued. As it was coded, it was possible to determine what had been sold and which assistant had handled the sale.

The item had been a pair of men's gloves and the customer, according to the assistant had been a large, young man with the beginning of a moustache and dark wavy hair down to his collar.

Incredibly, she knew his name. When he had taken out his wallet to pay, he had accidentally dropped his personal identity card on the counter and she had picked it up and handed it back to him. Without really intending to, she had noted the name Waldemar Stepinski and found it unusual and interesting.

Actually, it was not all that unusual. The Berlin Residents' Registry listed no less than nine Waldemar Stepinskis, but only one was large, young, had a faint moustache and wore his dark wavy hair down to the collar.

He was a twenty-two-year-old married factory worker who had lost his job in September of the preceding year and was living on unemployment compensation.

Except for a few witness sightings, there was nothing to connect Stepinski to the crimes, but he was buying an expensive flat in a new building in the Mariendorf area, one of the few places where no murders had taken place, and, although his income had stopped in September, the heavy payments on the flat continued unabated.

The inspector wanted to know where he had got the money.

Stepinski was unable to answer the question and, after

extended interrogation, broke down and confessed to the murders of Erna Hoedicke and Caecili Hidde, even adding one of which the police knew nothing.

This last victim's name was Kaethe Deichfuss and her corpse was found by the police in her flat at 10 Stulpnagel Strasse in the Charlottenberg district. Her murder had brought Stepinski a thousand Swiss francs (£500) and a small amount in marks.

According to Stepinski, his operation had been simple in the extreme.

He had chosen his victims purely at random from the street, followed them inconspicuously home and rung their doorbell immediately they were inside. He tried to avoid being in the corridors and stairwells as much as possible.

All this was logical and corresponded to what the police knew, but the trick which had got him into his victims' flats was so childishly simple that the inspector could not, at first, believe it.

Stepinski had had a tin badge such as is sold in novelty shops in the United States and intended to deceive no one. It read: *New York. FBI. Special Agent.*

'I told them that I had been called over specially from the United States to help in solving the Doorbell Killer murders,' said Stepinski.

Perhaps, elderly German ladies could be forgiven for not knowing that the FBI is not a New York organization or even for believing that American law officials would be operating in Berlin. The city is, after all, still under the control of the Allied forces and officially not a part of West Germany.

But how could Stepinski have told Hedda Buekow and Elli Grybek that he was investigating the Doorbell Killer series when, at the time they were murdered, the name had not even been coined?

Stepinski's answer to this was not conducive to peace of mind among the old ladies of Berlin.

He had not, he said, had anything to do with the

murders of Hedda Buekow, Elli Grybek and Sigurd Bessener.

As a consequence, although Stepinski was found guilty of the murders of Erna Hoedicke, Caecili Hidde and Kaethe Deichfuss and, on 7 June 1985, sentenced to life imprisonment, there are still a great many very worried old ladies in West Berlin.

The inspector is not worried. In his opinion, Stepinski's signature on the first three cases was as clear as on the last three. Moreover, there have been no other such cases since Stepinski was taken into custody.

14

MURDER IN THE MOORS

The land in the north of West Germany is flat and there is astonishingly little of it. The great city of Hamburg on the estuary of the Elbe river lies less than twenty-five miles from the North Sea to the west and fifteen miles from the East German border to the east. Luebeck on the Baltic is a scant forty miles to the north-east.

It is, generally, good agricultural land, but wet. There are many swamps and moors, some of which have been turned into nature parks and recreation areas.

One such recreation area, which is, however, neither swamp nor moor, is the Saxon Forest ten miles due east of Hamburg. A favourite walking place for city dwellers, it numbers among its other attractions the ruins of Castle Friedrichsruh.

On a sunny, Saturday afternoon, 12 May 1979, a Miss Renate Schliemann went for a walk in the Saxon Forest and did not return.

Although she was twenty years old and not due to resume work until Monday, her unexplained absence frightened her parents very much.

And yet, the disappearance of a daughter was a common enough occurrence in Germany at that time. Indeed, many parents would have been puzzled, albeit gratified, if their daughters did not make off to develop their personalities through indiscriminate sex, drugs and a spurning of personal hygiene in some revolutionary commune.

Germany follows closely the periodic fads which, beginning in California, sweep across the United States and traverse the Atlantic to fog the spirits of European youth unwilling to accept that the basic purpose of a fad is commercial profit.

Germans, and particularly young Germans, are a serious people and when they set out to destroy the system, they put their hearts into it.

They are also a tenacious people and, long after it becomes apparent that destruction of the system is impractical, they continue their efforts. A trend that will generate publicity and profit for a scant six months in the United States may well be going strong after ten years in Germany.

In 1979, Germany was, therefore, still suffering under the 1960s' ideology of boundless liberation. Youth was in, revolution was in, protest was in, primitive music was in, drugs were in, sex was in, while, in America, all were long since out and the riders of the trend had gone thundering off on other quests.

Most of the suffering was, of course, being done by parents. The suffering of the children would only begin later when they sought to compete in the market place and found that revolutionary activity or group sex experiences were regarded by prospective employers as less desirable qualifications than educational certificates and degrees.

The Schliemanns had not, however, been suffering. Members of a happy, perhaps minority group, they were the parents of a daughter who was hard-working, beautiful, too strong of character to be affected by self-destructive tendencies within her peer group and, incredibly for the time and place, chaste.

Alas! The happiness was ephemeral. The Schliemanns were going to suffer now – and more than others.

Once it had begun to get dark and it was obvious that Renate was not going to be home in time for dinner, her father called the police.

All that he could tell them was that Renate had gone for a walk in the Saxon Forest at around two in the afternoon and had not returned. He and his wife were now leaving for the forest to look for her.

The police took this report seriously. Hamburg is a city of nearly two million and Renate was not the first young girl to go for a walk and not return. By ten o'clock that evening, there were already half a dozen parties of off-duty police and firemen systematically combing the forest.

Fortunately, it was one of the police parties and not her parents that found her, for she was not a pretty sight. All her clothing had been torn away and she lay, bloody and mauled, face down, at the edge of a small stream, her head in the water.

'It was a human being,' said Dr Hartmut Weissmueller, 'but he savaged her like an animal. Badly beaten and, undoubtedly, internal injuries, but the immediate cause of death seems to be strangulation.'

A small, quick man with short dark hair parted on the side and black, penetrating, deep-set eyes, he was the duty medical officer for the eastern suburbs homicide unit, which had been called out immediately following discovery of the body.

His remarks were addressed to the unit's officer-in-charge, Inspector Walter Reinecke, a lean, sandy-haired man with a narrow face, a sharp nose and startlingly blue eyes.

'Not drowning?' said the inspector. 'Her face is in the water.'

'I don't think so,' said the doctor. 'I'll check when I perform the autopsy. Motive was, of course, aberrant sex. She's been raped very brutally. He probably cut himself as well. Time would be around four or five o'clock yesterday afternoon.'

It was now three in the morning and the forest was full of police officers, some uniform branch from the search-parties, some plainclothes from the department of criminal investigations and some in the white smocks which Germans invariably don when they think they are doing something technical.

Many of them were doing something technical: photographing the corpse and the scene, examining the ground and even the trees and bushes for potential clues to the identity of the murderer and marking on graph paper the location of the torn items of the victim's clothing.

The inspector stood watching them silently. He was presently joined by a stockily built man in his late thirties who wore his medium blond hair combed straight back from his forehead and gave an impression of open, honest sincerity very useful in his work.

This was Detective Sergeant Albert Schumann, the inspector's assistant, and he had just returned from taking the Schliemanns to the hospital where they were to spend the night under observation. Although they had been told nothing of the circumstances, they had taken their daughter's death very badly.

'I thought it best not to question her,' said the sergeant. 'He made a statement, but there's nothing in it. The girl went for a walk alone. Didn't come back.'

The inspector nodded.

'There's nothing they could know,' he assented. 'This was nobody she knew. Sex psychopath out here in the woods. She came past. He got her. Do you agree, Hartmut?'

'That's about what I would say,' said the doctor. 'He should be in the files. I doubt it's his first performance.'

In this, the doctor was mistaken. There was no shortage of potential suspects in the police files, but, for one reason or another, all eventually had to be discarded. If the murderer of Renate Schliemann had a record of sex offences, they were minor. He was not among the known killers.

To the naïve it might seem that any known sex killers would not be at liberty and mingling with the general public, but West Germany is a progressive country with an enlightened attitude toward murderers in general.

This can be summed up concisely: there are no murderers, there are only sick people.

But modern psychology can cure sick people.

The solution to sex crimes then is to cure the sick people and return them to society as useful members.

This the Germans do, sometimes curing the same subjects half a dozen times or more. The result is that there are a great many known sex criminals at liberty in West Germany and not a few of them are murderers.

The police, of course, keep files on these known sex offenders so that, when they rape or kill someone else, they can be arrested and sent to be cured.

There is no question of persons with such records being sent to prison. They are officially certified mentally ill and are not, therefore, responsible for their actions.

Inspector Reinecke was disappointed that the murderer of Renate Schliemann appeared not to be one of the department's regular customers, so to speak, as this meant there would be more work to the case and, indeed, as it turned out, there was going to be a great deal more.

Only very meagre clues were found at the scene: a few textile fibres stuck in blood to the corpse, a human hair, a chip from a fingernail and a little of the murderer's blood.

The autopsy did not provide more.

As the doctor suggested, Renate had been strangled rather than drowned and she did have severe internal injuries resulting from kicks and blows. The murderer had also bitten her savagely in a number of places and dug his fingernails into her flesh. Some of her hair had been torn out. The time of death was fixed at four o'clock in the afternoon of May the twelfth, plus or minus twenty minutes.

This last item was actually the most important for it established when the murderer was in the Saxon Forest and, as there were other strollers then, it was possible that someone had seen him.

It might seem a difficult task to identify the people taking a stroll in a sizeable forest near a large city on a Saturday afternoon, but there is considerable public spirit in the country and, when the police ran appeals for information in the local newspapers and over the local television station, a number of people reported in.

From these, it was possible to identify still others and, in the end, the inspector was able to assemble a comparatively complete list of those who had been in the Saxon Forest between the hours of three and five.

There was little doubt some of these people would have seen the murderer either arriving at or leaving the scene of the crime.

The problem was that they had not known that he was a murderer, and the only way for the police to distinguish between sightings of the murderer and sightings of other strollers was by cross-checking statements, eliminating impossible suspects, such as women or children, and, finally, organizing viewings of photographs from the files of minor sex offenders.

This proved successful and three witnesses positively identified twenty-one-year-old Reinhard Hecker as the person they had seen in the Saxon Forest near the scene of the murder at the time in question.

Hecker, a hard-muscled, athletic labourer with thick black eyebrows and a strangely shaped mouth, had a modest record of attacks on women and adolescent girls. Although he had only been charged with attempted rape, it was believed that he had gone further in cases that were not reported.

Taken into custody, Hecker admitted he was in the Saxon Forest on the day in question, but said that he had been merely taking a walk like everyone else. He had not raped or murdered anybody.

There was no direct evidence that he had. None of the witnesses had actually seen him together with the victim. The textile fibres could have come from a pair of trousers found in his wardrobe, but they could also have come from other garments. The human hair was similar to his, but the experts could not swear that it was his. And the traces of blood left by the murderer were of the same group as his, but so was the blood group of perhaps a third of a million residents of Hamburg. All things considered, it was a miracle that the examining magistrate even indicted him.

He was indicted, however, and eventually came to trial.

The result was that the sergeant had to buy the inspector's lunch for a week. He had incautiously bet that the court would find Hecker too dangerous to go free.

Reinhard Hecker took his acquittal as impassively as he took everything else. He was not an emotional man or one who displayed very much interest in his surroundings, even when he was being tried for murder.

Even so, the events had made enough impression on Reinhard Hecker for him to abandon his native city and go to Luebeck, where, a year or so later, he was arrested in connection with rape, attempted rape, assault, grievious bodily harm and other assorted charges. On 6 March 1981, he was sentenced to seven years in prison.

The sentence was, naturally, a mistake. Hecker was a sick man and the court, recognizing this, put aside the jury's decision and sent him to be cured at the Ochsenzoll psychiatric institute for the criminally insane. There he was placed in house 18, a closed facility harbouring some thirty other psychopaths considered to be too dangerous for immediate release.

Ochsenzoll is in the suburb of Longenhorn, ten miles to the north of Hamburg. A short distance further to the north and to the east are two nature parks, Kiwitts Moor and Raak Moor. Both have fitness trails for joggers. Both are scenically attractive with ponds, streams, groves of trees and bushes.

Both are, however, a little lonely.

On Wednesday, 29 February 1984, a sixteen-year-old girl named Maja Kellner went jogging in Kiwitts Moor. She was a very pretty girl, but a trifle plump and slim was in. Hence the jogging in weather which would have made a polar bear cringe.

Located on such a flat strip of land between two bodies of water as chilly as the North Sea and the Baltic, Hamburg seldom exposes its residents to danger of heat stroke, but the end of February is widely accepted as one of the worst times of the year.

Maja wanted to lose weight very badly.

Instead, she lost her life.

Maja, although perhaps marginally less virtuous than Renate Schliemann had been, was still greatly loved by her parents and, when she failed to return home by nightfall, they immediately called the police.

Nightfall was, of course, early. Hamburg lies further to the north than Nova Scotia and, at the end of February, the days are short.

The Hamburg police responded with their usual alacrity and set about searching the Kiwitts Moor in a slashing mixture of freezing rain, snow and hail, the tail end of a North Sea gale which was sweeping inland from the Deutsche Bucht. It was dark as a coal cellar in hell, and even the powerful electric lanterns used by the police seemed no brighter than the fretful sparks of giant fireflies.

Under such conditions, it was a wonder that they found her that night, but they did.

She lay face down with her head resting in the freezing water of a small stream, naked, battered, bloody, dead.

The corpse was examined not by Dr Weissmueller, who had handled the Renate Schliemann case, but by the duty medical officer for the northern suburbs homicide unit. His findings were, however, fed routinely into the police computer system, with the result that on the following day Dr Weissmueller was summoned to the morgue to view the body. The computer had reported that the circumstances of the crime were nearly identical to those of the Renate Schliemann case, which was, of course, classed as unsolved, Reinhard Hecker having been found not guilty of it.

Having examined the corpse and discussed the matter with his colleague, the doctor went to inform Inspector Reinecke that there was a new development in the Schliemann case. Renate Schliemann's murderer was apparently not who the police thought he was.

Despite the findings of the court, the police thought that Reinhard Hecker was guilty, but, as he was in the closed section of the psychiatric institute, he could not have murdered Maja Kellner.

'And it is ninety-nine per cent certain that it was the same man in both cases,' said the doctor. 'The injuries, the manner in which they were made, the position and location of the bodies, everything corresponds so exactly as to rule out coincidence. She was also raped. He cut himself again. The blood group is the same.'

'Al,' said the inspector. 'Call Ochsenzoll and see if Hecker is till there.'

The sergeant reported Reinhard Hecker was still in Ochsenzoll.

'The next time you see him, offer him my apologies,' said the inspector. 'I suspected him wrongly. I'm going to see the commissioner about reopening the Schliemann case.'

The commissioner not only wanted the Renate Schliemann case reopened; he wanted the inspector's team to take over the Maja Kellner case as well.

'This is apparently a series of sorts,' he said, 'and you've already done all the background on the Schliemann murder. No point in someone else starting from the beginning again.'

The inspector returned to his office and called for copies of the findings of the investigation at the scene of the Kellner murder and the autopsy report. There was no need to go to Kiwitts Moor to view the scene as the investigations there had been long since completed.

The reports from the Schliemann murder were still in the computer files and, compared to the new case, corresponded as precisely as the autopsy findings.

There were, however, fewer clues in the Maja Kellner murder, possibly because the weather had been so violent, and the only new element was a white nylon glove for the right hand. It had been found within a yard of the body and bore six small blood stains.

The laboratory had examined the glove and reported

that it was a special type of man's glove worn by surgeons under their rubber gloves when operating. The blood on it was from Maja Kellner.

'The murderer is a surgeon?' said the sergeant in surprise, reading the report.

'I don't think that follows,' said the inspector. 'Granted, surgeons can be as crazy as anybody else, but this fellow is more than crazy. You know what the weather was like out there that day. Can you imagine anybody other than a complete, raving madman who would be capable of sex in a howling sleet storm with the temperature ten degrees below freezing?'

'Not an erotic atmosphere, I admit,' said the sergeant. 'Just somebody who had some contact with a place where surgery is performed then?'

The inspector nodded.

'We'll begin by checking out maintenance personnel at the hospitals,' he said. 'Some of them are pretty low-grade labour.'

It took the sergeant and his men a long time to investigate all of them. There are a great many hospitals and clinics in Hamburg and a great many people employed in them. As might be expected in any such large group, some of the people turned out to have criminal records and some even had criminal records for sex-related offences. However, none could be regarded as a valid suspect in both the Renate Schliemann and the Maja Kellner murders.

'I think we've exhausted the possibilities,' said the sergeant, wiping the sweat from his forehead.

It was the first week of July and the weather was, by Hamburg standards, warm.

The inspector frowned.

'I'm afraid you're right,' he said. 'I've been following your reports and I haven't seen a thing that would warrant further investigation. I'll put in a request to the commissioner to send both cases to the inactive file.'

Inactive was not quite so definite as unsolved. It meant

that the police had not definitely abandoned the case, but that they had run out of things to investigate.

The inspector could have sent the Schliemann and Kellner cases to the inactive file without requesting permission from his superiors, but the prudent civil servant does not assume responsibility that he can shift elsewhere.

He therefore sent the request through channels, but, before he had received an answer from the commissioner, he found himself confronted with a third murder, which took place on the afternoon of July the twelfth, a Thursday, in Raak Moor, north-east of and contiguous to Kiwitts Moor.

The victim was another jogger, a twenty-one-year-old woman named Silkie Westphalen. She had apparently accomplished roughly half of the five-thousand-metre jogging circuit when she was fallen upon, stripped, raped, battered, bitten, scratched, strangled and left lying with her head partially submerged in a brook. Her body was found by other joggers.

Inspector Reinecke and his detachment were immediately summoned to the scene and both nature parks were searched. No suspects were detained and the sole clue to the identity of the murderer was a sample of blue textile fibre.

Otherwise, the condition of the body was identical to that of the bodies in the Schliemann and Kellner cases, and traces of blood of a different group to Miss Westphalen's indicated that the murderer had, once again, cut himself.

'Always does,' remarked Dr Weissmueller, who had been summoned to examine the body. 'He's too impulsive.'

'In a frenzy is more like it,' said the inspector. 'You only have to look at the body and the scene to realize that he must lose all control of himself.'

'And that's what the court will say, if we ever catch him,' said Sergeant Schumann. 'He has no control over himself so he's not responsible. The least they could do would be to stick him into Ochsenzoll permanently.'

'Nobody stays in Ochsenzoll permanently,' said the inspector. 'That would mean they were incurable.'

'Is Hecker still there?' asked the doctor.

'I suppose so,' said the inspector. 'He was when the Kellner girl was murdered.'

'You're sure he was?' said the doctor. 'He wasn't just sleeping there and let out during the day?'

'Oh, I don't think so,' said the inspector. 'He's in house 18. That's top security.'

'I'd check it,' said the doctor.

The inspector looked at the sergeant.

'Do,' he said.

'Well, no,' said the psychiatrist who was in charge of Hecker's treatment. 'Reinhard has made great progress since he's been with us and it's the institute's policy to begin the reinsertion into society as early as possible. He really only has to spend the nights here.'

'And where does he spend his days?' asked the sergeant, the hair rising slightly on the nape of his neck.

'Oh, various places,' said the doctor. 'He often borrows one of the institute's bicycles and goes for rides in Kiwitts Moor or Raak Moor. He's very interested in ecology and nature.'

The sergeant had one last question.

'When did Hecker start going out for rides in the nature parks?' he asked.

'Early last autumn,' said the doctor. 'It's actually a sort of therapy. Does him a world of good. He really enjoys it.'

'I don't doubt it,' commented the inspector dryly when the sergeant repeated the conversation. 'Put everyone in the unit on it and bring him. He can't be tried on the Schliemann case, but we'll charge him with Kellner and Westphalen. I want an all-out effort to locate witnesses.'

The police operation worked out perfectly. A left-hand glove identical to the right-hand glove found at the scene of Maja Kellner's murder was found in Hecker's room at the institute and he admitted having stolen the gloves from a cabinet of surgical supplies. A blue shirt matching the textile fibres found on the body of Silkie Westphalen was recovered from his room and traces of blood matching her group were found on his clothing. Witnesses were located who had seen Hecker, a man with a distinctive appearance, near the scenes of both murders at the times in question.

The only thing lacking was a confession. Impassive as ever, Hecker's only response to interrogation was a flat statement that he had never raped or killed anyone and he did not know what the police wanted of him.

However, the case went to trial. The prosecution believed there was enough physical evidence to obtain a conviction.

There was not. Hecker's court-appointed defence counsel skilfully demolished the prosecution case point by point and, on 14 June 1985, after twenty-seven days of hearings, Reinhard Hecker was acquitted of all charges.

But he did not leave the court a free man. In Germany, the prosecution can also appeal a sentence and the prosecution did. The result was a compromise.

Although Reinhard Hecker is completely innocent of any wrong-doing in connection with the murders of Renate Schliemann, Maja Kellner and Silkie Westphalen, having been so declared by the court, he has been returned for an indefinite period to the Ochsenzoll security section, where certain changes in the regulations have been made.

His situation is not hopeless. Psychiatrists are optimists and if, at some day in the future, a jogger in Kiwitts Moor or Raak Moor should encounter a muscular young man with heavy black eyebrows and a strangely shaped mouth, she will know that Reinhard Hecker has, once again, been making progress with his emotional problems.

15

STRONG SEX DRIVE

During the period from 8 May 1980 to 3 November 1983, in a ten-square-mile area around Frankfurt am Main, West Germany, a man murdered eight young women.

The police had not the slightest clue to his identity.

They did not even suspect that the murder in Langen on Thursday, 8 May 1980 was only the first of a long series.

The town is less than five miles to the south of Frankfurt and the police thought the murderer of Gabriele Roesner was, probably, a sex criminal from the larger city. As Langen has a population of under forty thousand, it was possible to rule out any local sex offenders.

This having been done, the findings of the investigation and the autopsy report were sent to the department of criminal investigations in Frankfurt, as was the usual practice with felonies committed in the smaller communities around the city.

There was not a great deal in the reports. Gabriele was twenty-three years old, unmarried, an office employee. She had gone for a walk after work in the spring woods near Langen. She had not returned. Her parents, with whom she lived, reported her missing to the police, who searched the woods and found her.

She lay near a footpath, fully dressed, but with her skirt turned up and her underwear torn away. According to the findings of the autopsy, she had been strangled manually and raped by a man with blood group B.

It was the sole indication. Nothing else was found.

Gabriele was not a virgin, but she had resisted the rape for the insides of her thighs were bruised.

The Frankfurt department of criminal investigations could not do a great deal with this. A sergeant of detectives named Max Busch, who was attached to the southern suburban sector homicide squad, came down, looked at the scene, talked to the dead girl's parents, went over the case with the local CID and filed a report.

He was a heavy, slow-moving man with a massive head and a rather glum expression which corresponded largely to his conclusions.

The murderer, he suggested, should be in the police files because this was probably not his first offence, but there were not enough indications to identify him.

His chief, Detective Inspector Karl Dorner, read the report, together with a number of others, marked it 'unsolved' and sent it to the files. There was nothing more to investigate.

The inspector had, however, an excellent memory and when, a little over a month later, a second girl was murdered within a mile of the Langen woods, he remembered the Roesner case and had the file brought back for comparison.

There were a good many points in common. Fourteen-year-old Regina Barthel, a secondary-school pupil from the village of Dietzenbach, had gone for a walk in Heusenstamm Forest on the afternoon of Saturday, June the fourteenth and had not returned.

As Dietzenbach is nearly within sight of Langen, her parents were very conscious of the murder of Gabriele Roesner only a little more than a month earlier and they not only called the police, but rushed out to the woods themselves.

There they were joined by numbers of neighbours, relatives, friends and the entire Dietzenbach police force, which, Dietzenbach being a relatively small village, is modest.

Actually, such a massive search operation was not necessary. Regina lay in open view near one of the paths through the forest, her jeans and underwear ripped away and the little bouquet of wild flowers that she had picked scattered around her head.

She had been raped and murdered.

The murder had been messier than that of Gabriele Roesner.

To begin with, Regina had been a virgin and she had bled badly. Secondly, she had not been strangled, but stabbed with what was later thought to be a hunting knife.

'Single stab wound, apparently,' said the sergeant, reporting to the inspector on the result of his telephone call to the Dietzenbach police. 'The body's being transferred up here for the autopsy.'

'Good,' said the inspector. 'Keep me posted. Those two cases are rather too close together for comfort, both in time and place.'

He was a handsome man with a fine sweeping brown moustache and soft brown dachshund eyes, but he did not look happy and, indeed, he was not. A criminal investigations officer's job in central West Germany is not easy.

The inspector was still not aware that a series of murders was beginning, and the third murder did nothing to bolster his suspicions.

The only knowledge he had of it was from the routine reports passing over his desk and the newspapers, as it took place in Offenbach. Although contiguous to Frankfurt and less than ten miles from Langen and Dietzenbach, Offenbach is a city in its own right and has its own department of criminal investigations.

Moreover, the circumstances were very different. The victims in Langen and Dietzenbach were respectable young girls. The victim in Offenbach was a twenty-eight-year-old prostitute called Annedore Ligeika.

Like Gabriele Roesner, Miss Ligeika had been strangled, but in her own bed and, if she had been raped, there was no evidence that she had resisted.

The case was puzzling in that the victim had been

neither robbed nor mutilated, the most common motives for murdering a prostitute.

It was, therefore, only tentatively classified as a prostitute murder, a general term covering crimes involving the profession. Prostitution is a high-risk business and enough prostitutes are murdered to form a crime group of their own.

Miss Ligeika had been diligent and, on the basis of her file of regular customers, skilled and talented. She had consequently made a lot of money and some of it had been in her flat.

It was still there. The murderer had not even bothered to look for it. He had had intercourse with her, with consent or not, strangled her with her stockings and departed leaving no trace of his identity other than the fact that his blood group was B.

There are approximately two hundred and forty thousand people in the Frankfurt area who have blood group B.

The Offenbach department of criminal investigations was, therefore, forced to deal with the Ligeika case in the manner in which Inspector Dorner had been forced to deal with the Roesner and Barthel cases. They sent it to the Unsolved section.

If the murder of Annedore Ligeika had aroused no suspicions of a series, the murder of Fatima Sonnenberg on 7 February 1981, did.

However, only the Ligeika and Sonnenberg murders were taken into consideration. There was no reason to connect either of them to the murders of Gabriele Roesner and Regina Barthel.

The Ligeika and Sonnenberg murders were, however, nearly identical. Fatima, a forty-two-year-old Algerian who made up in exotic charm any excess in age, was also a prostitute, albeit a slightly less prosperous one than Annedore.

She had engaged in sexual relations with a man possessing the blood group B and she had been strangled, presumably by him, in the entrance hall of her flat in the Rodgau suburb of Frankfurt. The murderer had taken nothing and had, apparently, looked for nothing.

These details having been run routinely into the records section computer, the machine pointed out the similarity of the two crimes and they were investigated as two incidents of a possible series.

But without success. There were no more clues in the Sonnenberg case than in the Ligeika one.

The police waited warily for another prostitute to be brought down in the line of duty, but it turned out to be a sixteen-year-old virgin.

Beatrix Scheible was, like Regina Barthel, a secondary-school pupil and, five days before Christmas of 1981, she went for a walk in the Frankfurt city park, which is nearly as extensive as the Heusenstamm Forest.

When Beatrix failed to return home in time for dinner, her parents notified the police.

Fortunately, Beatrix had mentioned that she was going to the park and no time was wasted looking elsewhere.

As it turned out, however, the time made little difference as Beatrix had been dead for close to two hours when her parents reported her missing. Like Regina Barthel, she had been stabbed and, like all of her predecessors, raped.

The computer, of course, called the investigators' attention to the similarities between this and the Barthel case and included the Gabriele Roesner murder on the grounds that it had taken place in the same general area, within the past two years and was unsolved. The victim was older and she had been strangled rather than stabbed, but the other details corresponded.

As Inspector Dorner had been handling the Roesner and Barthel cases, he was also given the Scheible one, although the park was in the north-west corner of the city and not within his normal territory.

The new development was of little help to him. Although the possibility of a series now appeared stronger, he had no more indications of the identity of the killer than before.

However, as he pointed out to the sergeant, the total lack of clues in all three cases was a sort of indication in itself. Few murderers were so deft – or so lucky.

The murders had, of course, received a certain amount of publicity in the press, but the journalists, for once, had been unable to come up with a suitable name for the murderer and were reduced to scare headlines on the order of 'Mysterious Sex Psychopath Sows Panic in Frankfurt Area'.

This was not utterly accurate. Sex murders of women are no novelty in modern society and so little panic was sown that no reduction in the number of girls and young women going for walks in parks and forests could be determined. Which made sense in a way as, statistically, crossing the street was more dangerous.

Statistics apply to groups, however, and Regina Spielmann was an individual. The seventeen-year-old daughter of an Offenbach professor, she was also a secondary-school pupil. On Sunday morning, 9 May 1982, she set off for a hike in the Heusenstamm Forest.

If Regina knew that a younger namesake had been murdered there less than two years earlier, she undoubtedly did not expect to meet the same fate.

She did, however, and was even stabbed to death with what appeared to be the same or an identical hunting knife. A cast made of the wound in Regina Barthel's body matched perfectly a cast of the wound in Regina Spielmann's.

Inspector Dorner was now quite certain that he was dealing with a series killer, although he did not realize just how long the series already was.

In his series he included the Barthel, the Scheible, the Spielmann and, possibly, the Roesner cases. The Ligeika and Sonnenberg murders were considered to be something quite different.

The Barthel, Scheible and Spielmann cases showed remarkable correspondence. All three victims had been secondary-school girls. All three had been intact virgins. All three had been raped. And two, at least, had been killed in the same forest. The murder weapon had been the same or identical in all cases and the murderer had had blood group B.

'There's no question but what it's a series,' said the inspector, looking worried, 'and, considering the lack of leads, I'm afraid it's going to be a long one. Has the records section completed the check of past similar offences?'

Sergeant Busch nodded. 'Nothing,' he said. 'If this is a series, Roesner was the first in it. We have nothing in the past ten years that's so featureless.'

A lack of features was the strongest feature of the murders. The murderer had had no sadistic tendencies. He had not mutilated his victims. He had not robbed them. He had kept no parts of their bodies or clothing as souvenirs. He had subjected them to no perverted sex acts.

He did exactly two things to the victims and two things only.

He raped them and he killed them. In that order.

'As sex murderers go, he's practically boring,' said the sergeant. 'The man has no imagination.'

He was, however, efficient. He apparently never failed and he apparently never spared a victim. Appeals had been run in all the media for women or girls who had been raped or had escaped rape to contact the police anonymously. Only a small percentage of sex offences are ever reported and it was hoped that there might be a survivor who could provide at least a description.

If there was, she did not come forward. There were a few dozen responses to the appeal, but, upon investigation, none turned out to have any connection to the crimes concerned.

Putting out a wider net, the inspector set up a list of every unsolved sex murder or attempted murder in the Frankfurt area within the preceding five years.

Frankfurt is a dangerous city. The list was long and it included, of course, Annedore Ligeika and Fatima Sonnenberg, but the inspector still had no reason to connect them to the other murders. He thought that he was investigating a series of four.

Which, on 3 November 1983, became a series of five.

On that date, a twenty-two-year-old chemistry student named Simone Newin went jogging in the Offenbach city park. An athletic girl, she went jogging every day.

She was not athletic enough to outrun or outfight the killer and other joggers found her strangled with her own trousers.

A typically efficient operation. He had had to remove the trousers to rape her anyway.

As the Offenbach city park is almost within sight of the scenes of several of the other murders, notably Heusenstamm Forest, the case was recognized as forming a part of the series under investigation by Inspector Dorner and he was immediately alerted.

Although he, the sergeant and an enormous detail of technicians and experts of every kind quickly arrived at the scene and spent the best part of the night there, the case turned out to be typical. There were no clues at all.

'Can't you offer any conclusion, Walter?' pleaded the inspector desperately. 'She's not been dead four hours.'

Dr Walter Oberle shook his head. A short, barrel-shaped man with a bullet head and scanty blond hair parted on the side, he was considered the top medical expert with the Frankfurt police. He had joined the inspector's team following the murder of Beatrix Scheible.

'He's strong,' he said. 'The girl was in perfect physical condition and he apparently had no more trouble in overpowering her than he would in overpowering a rabbit.'

'You mean unnaturally strong, a body builder or a wrestler or something like that?' said Sergeant Busch.

'No,' said the doctor. 'Just a normal, healthy, probably above average size man. He may not even go in for sports at all, but he's almost surely young, under thirty, I should think. Strong sex drive.'

'Yes,' said the inspector with a touch of irony. 'A

strong sex drive. A very, very strong sex drive. Does this park strike you as an erotic place? The sort of place that would lead you to think of having sex here?'

The doctor looked thoughtful, but did not answer.

The park was about as far from erotic as it was possible to get. The temperature was two degrees above freezing and a nasty little early winter wind was whining and snarling through the leafless black limbs of the trees. The sky was the colour of dirty lead and even the lights of the city in the distance looked cold and cheerless. An occasional stronger gust lifted gritty showers of dirt and dead leaves from the gravel path.

'He must be obsessed,' muttered the sergeant. 'I wouldn't even be able to jog here.'

Technically, there was no reason for the inspector and the sergeant to remain at the scene until the technicians had completed their work. Indeed, they were somewhat in the way.

The inspector, however, felt uncomfortable about leaving others in the dark and cold, and he and the sergeant were among the last to return to headquarters.

There, things were decidedly better. The office was warm and bright and there was hot coffee in the coffee maker and sandwiches in the canteen refrigerator.

'Do you think they'll find anything this time?' asked the sergeant, swallowing convulsively the better part of a cheese sandwich and stirring sugar into his coffee.

'I know they won't,' said the inspector. 'I talked to the chief technician before we left. They picked up a couple of hundred items – cigarette butts and so on – but there's no tie-in to the murder and it's all just the sort of stuff you'd expect to find in a public park.'

'City woods, really,' said the sergeant absently. 'So, what do we do?'

'What can we do?' said the inspector bitterly. 'Wait for the next one.'

He was angry and frustrated. The series had now begun to attract a great deal of publicity and his failure to solve the crimes was not doing his career any good.

There would probably be no further chances for a solution this year and, during the winter, he was liable to be quietly relieved of his assignment.

Tragically, there was another chance for the investigation only twenty-three days later.

On November the twenty-sixth, a Saturday, twenty-one-year-old Ilke Rutsch was stabbed to death in the forest outside her native village of Babenhausen.

What she had been doing there could not be precisely determined, but Babenhausen is within a stone's throw of Langen, Dietzenbach and the Heusenstamm Forest.

The inspector's detachment was promptly called away.

And, almost as promptly, returned. There were no more clues to the identity of the murderer of Ilke Rutsch than there had been for any of the others.

The autopsy determined that she had been raped by a man with blood group B and stabbed with a knife having the same shaped blade as the one that killed Regina Barthel, Beatrix Scheible and Regina Spielmann.

'He's got to make a mistake some time,' said the sergeant grimly.

The inspector remained silent. It was three-thirty in the afternoon of November the twenty-ninth and, on the Bockenheim road leading from the centre of the city to the north-western suburb of Bockenheim, motorists and pedestrians were witnessing a strange event.

A large young man with a little moustache had suddenly seized an adolescent schoolgirl and was dragging her into the bushes.

In general, residents of large communities are disinclined to become involved, but this was too much and half a dozen people converged on the point where the man and girl had vanished into the shrubbery.

They were barely in time. The girl, helpless as a kitten in her attacker's powerful hands, was down on the ground with her skirt up around her waist and he was in the act of ripping out the crotch of her panties when he was fallen upon in his turn, dragged off his victim and pinned to the ground.

A taxi-driver had alerted the police over the radio and the young man was taken into custody, brought to police headquarters, charged with attempted rape and released with instructions not to leave the city until his case had been heard.

Pre-trial detention or bail were not thought necessary. The accused was married, the father of a three-year-old daughter and held a steady job. It was not, however, his first sex offence.

The matter was routine, one of the few dozen minor sex crimes committed almost daily, and it was scheduled for pre-trial interrogation of the accused on 1 February 1984.

In the meantime, Inspector Dorner and Sergeant Busch spent an uncomfortable winter. Neither had, of course, heard anything of the incident on the Bockenheim road.

It was an uncomfortable winter because both were hoping that there would be no further murders, but simultaneously aware that, unless there were, they had little hope of solving their cases.

There were no further murders and there was no further progress in the cases. Almost to the inspector's surprise, he was not relieved of responsibility for the investigation. The press, with its short attention span, was gradually letting the affair die out.

The inspector had not, however, forgotten that somewhere out there in the city was a man who had raped and murdered at least six girls and women and, unless something fatal had happened to him, could be depended upon to continue. He did not think that he would stop voluntarily.

He was, therefore, immediately interested when he received a telephone call from one of the other sections of the criminal police to the effect that they had a man in custody who appeared to know more about the series killings than he should.

It was Friday, 3 February 1984, and the inspector at

once sent Sergeant Busch to bring back the suspect and the tapes of his statements so far.

Twenty-five-year-old Michael Wolpert, an electrician who lived in the suburb of Neu-Isenburg, had appeared for interrogation in the Bockenheim road case on the first. He would have been released again with an hour or two, had he not begun making references to 'girls in the woods' and mentioned specifically the Heusenstamm Forest.

The interrogators knew, of course, what had happened at least twice in the Heusenstamm Forest and they altered the direction of the questioning away from the incident in the Bockenheim road to the forests outside the city.

Wolpert was evasive, but he was dealing with professionals and what he did not say was nearly as significant as what he did. Their suspicions strengthened, the investigators contacted Inspector Dorner.

The inspector continued the questioning and assigned the sergeant to an in-depth investigation of the suspect's background, which, it turned out, was somewhat unusual, even for the time and place.

Wolpert, it seemed, was indeed married and the father of a three-year-old daughter, but he was living with another woman and child. They were twenty-two-year-old Heidrun Mahler and her daughter, Sonja.

Wolpert's own wife, Ilonka, also twenty-two, and their daughter, Jessica, were living with his old school friend and fellow electrician, twenty-six-year-old Detlev Mahler.

'A straight swap,' said the sergeant. 'Took place in June of 1982 and everybody has been happy ever since. No hard feelings. They're all as thick as thieves and everybody has it off with everybody as the spirit moves. Otherwise, completely normal families. Both men are hard workers and highly regarded by their employers.'

The inspector was puzzled. With two beautiful young and reportedly active women at his disposal, it seemed scarcely likely that Wolpert would need to rape other women.

On the other hand, there was the matter of his two previous offences. Both had been for exhibiting himself obscenely to young girls, the first in 1979 and the second in 1982. He had been fined the first time and given a six-month suspended sentence the second.

Obviously, there was something wrong with Michael Wolpert and, although the inspector could not believe that this engaging open-faced young man was the killer he had sought for so long, he could not let the matter drop until he had got to the bottom of it.

The bottom was a long way down and it was 5 March 1984 before the interrogation finally ceased.

The inspector had known long before that, however, with whom he was dealing. As was the usual practice, the police had withheld details concerning the scenes of the murders. Wolpert knew them all.

And more. In addition to his confession to the murders of Gabriele Roesner, Regina Barthel, Beatrix Scheible, Regina Spielmann, Simone Newin and Ilke Rutsch, Wolpert added the names of Annedore Ligeika and Fatima Sonnenberg which he had read in the newspapers. He had, of course, not known the names of any of his victims when he murdered them.

The psychologists were unable to agree as to what was wrong with Michael Wolpert. He was obviously over-sexed, and both his wife and Heidrun Mahler described him as being a fabulous lover.

However, they also described him as gentle, tender and never rough or violent. Even after he had confessed, they could not believe that he had raped and murdered women.

Wolpert himself was unable to explain his actions and made no real attempt to.

On one point, the psychologists were in agreement. Wolpert was too dangerous to be allowed his freedom and there was no certainty that psychiatric treatment would ever cause him to be less so.

Wolpert was, therefore, sentenced to life imprisonment on 24 May 1985.

He is receiving psychiatric therapy while in prison and several of the organizations concerned with prisoners' rights have expressed an interest in his case.

16

AN ATTACHMENT TO THE PROFESSION

By Friday of the week ending 21 January, 1983, the mailbox in the entrance hall of the block of flats at 67 Calle Benimenette in the San Cristobal de los Angeles district of the city of Madrid was overflowing with uncollected mail.

Something had to be done. Building superintendent Julio Garcia was proud of his new, modern building. He could not tolerate such a mess. The tenants of flat number 467 would have to be spoken to firmly.

It was probably nothing more than carelessness. Perhaps they had gone off on a trip and forgotten to tell him to keep the mail in the office.

He was not worried that they might have skipped. Like everyone else in the building, they had paid a three months' deposit before moving in and the rent had been paid promptly and in advance ever since.

Not for long, to be sure. The woman had moved in on December the first and the man had followed on January the first. Definitely not married, but that was not his business. His job was to maintain the building and collect the rents.

And maintaining the building included keeping the mail boxes tidy.

But he could not simply empty the mail box and take the mail into the office. That was illegal. He could be charged with mail robbery and, if anything was missing or claimed to be missing . . .

Perhaps if he took a look at the flat he could find some

indication of where they had gone. He was certain that they were not there. Although it was possible for tenants to come and go without him seeing them, an entire week was unusual and there was, of course, the overflowing mail box.

The name on the mail box and on the printed card inserted into the metal clips on the front door was Carmen Esposa with 'Antonio Molina' written beneath it in pencil.

That was the man, a big fellow, blond, handsome, slightly too elegantly dressed. Garcia thought he might be in some branch of the entertainment business.

The woman too, no doubt, although she was hardly attractive enough to be in the theatre.

They kept odd hours, apparently sleeping all morning and only going out in the late afternoon or early evening. He had no idea when they came home. He was always asleep by that time.

Nobody answered the bell and Garcia inserted his pass key and opened the door. There was nothing illegal about that. Right of inspection at any time was written right into the rent contract.

'Hello?' called Garcia, stepping into the entrance hall of the flat. 'Is anybody . . .'

The words died in his throat.

Directly opposite him was the open door to the living room, and lying on the floor was a man whom he took to be Antonio Molina. He was curled almost into a ball with his hands clasped over his stomach and, surrounding him, was an enormous irregular dark spot on the light-coloured carpet.

Mystified and alarmed, Garcia moved forward through the living room door.

He could now see the man's face and his alarm turned to horror. It *was* Molina, and his head was turned backward and upward toward the ceiling in the most ghastly grimace that Garcia had ever seen, the eyes wide open and bulging from their sockets and the lips drawn back from the teeth in an expression of agony. Two broad black bands crossed his cheeks from the corners of the mouth to the ears like Indian war paint.

Abruptly, the significance of the black bands and of the great dark stain on the carpet dawned upon the building superintendent.

It was blood! Blackened, dried blood!

The appalled Garcia began to back instinctively out of the door, but came to a halt as his gaze fell upon the living room sofa and what was lying on it.

It was, he thought, the body of Carmen Esposa, but it was so covered with dried blood that it looked barely human.

Shaking with nervous tension, he backed hurriedly out of the flat, locking the door behind him, and descended to his office, where he dialled the telephone number of the police.

He then got out the brandy kept for emergencies and drank a third of it straight from the bottle.

It had not occurred to him to check the bodies for signs of life. Possibly because the blood was dry, he assumed that the couple were dead, and had been dead for some time.

So too did the officers from the patrol car which answered Garcia's call, but regulations required that they attempt first aid and summon the ambulance.

The ambulance was summoned, but the first aid consisted of nothing more than a cautious approach to the man's body and a finger laid on the artery in the cold, lifeless neck.

There was, of course, no pulse and they withdrew to join Garcia, who was waiting in the hall.

While one of the officers remained guarding the flat door, the other went with Garcia down to the office and phoned in confirmation of the murder report.

At police headquarters, the full homicide squad, which had been waiting for this confirmation, left immediately.

In charge of the unit of detectives, technicians, identification specialists, weapons experts, photographer and medical officer was a tall, thin-faced, dark-blond man with a leathery complexion and a receding hairline. This was Chief Inspector Gerardo Sansana, a senior investigations officer with very extensive experience in homicide cases.

Second in command was a sergeant of detectives named Basilio Fernandez, a handsome, muscular man in his mid-thirties with a very fine head of blue-black hair and coal-black eyes. A seasoned criminal investigations officer, he was being groomed as a replacement to Inspector Sansana, who was due for promotion to commissioner.

The investigation began with an examination of the bodies by Dr Fidel Aguiar while the other members of the unit remained outside in the hall.

It did not take long. The doctor, a small, dark man with quick, deft movements, spent only a few moments with each corpse and then came out to report while the technicians poured into rooms and began setting up their equipment.

'They've been dead four or five days,' said the doctor. 'Stab wounds. Apparently only one for the man. Several for the woman. There is what looks to be a knife embedded in the woman's genitals.'

'The murder weapon?' said the inspector.

'I presume so,' said the doctor. 'No indications of resistance by the man, but she had a defence cut across the palm of the right hand.'

'Meaning that he was probably killed first,' said the inspector. 'Could you tell what kind of knife it is?'

'Kitchen butchering knife,' said the doctor. 'Not new.'

The photographer was now engaged in shooting pictures of the bodies and the scene from various angles, and the inspector waited until he had finished before going to inspect the corpses.

He was looking thoughtfully at the dead woman's face, which bore a startled but not agonized expression, when the sergeant entered the flat and came to join him.

'The building superintendent discovered the bodies,' he said. 'I've taken a statement from him, but he knows nothing about the murders and hardly anything about the people. They haven't been living here long.'

'A couple of lovers, probably,' said the inspector. 'They ran away together and the husband caught up with them.'

There was support for this theory in the laboratory and autopsy reports turned in the following day. Robbery had definitely not been a motive. There was a surprising amount of money in the flat, some of it lying exposed, but nothing had been taken.

The identification section had been unable to recover any finger prints other than those of Molina and Esposa and the building superintendent, who had left his prints on the door handle.

The murderer had, therefore, either been wearing gloves or he had touched nothing other than the handle of the knife.

The knife driven to the hilt in Carmen Esposa's genitals was the murder weapon in both cases, but the handle was too worn and rough from frequent immersion in water to hold a print. It apparently came from the flat, as no other large knife could be found in the kitchen.

It had a sharp, single-edged blade eight inches long and it had entered Molina's upper abdomen, edge upward and at an angle, slicing through the left lung and penetrating the heart. Death had followed within a minute to a minute and a half.

Carmen Esposa had been stabbed four times with the same knife, not counting the slash wound across the palm of her hand where she had grasped the blade in an attempt to save herself. Three of the wounds were in the stomach and chest. The stab wound in the genitals had been inflicted after death.

The times of death had been fixed by the doctor as roughly simultaneous and at five in the afternoon of 17 January 1983.

'The anger and intent of the murder was directed primarily against the woman,' wrote Dr Aguiar in the autopsy report. 'The murders were an act of vengeance and the identity of the murderer can be sought among the victims' most intimate contacts.'

This agreed precisely with what the inspector was thinking, but there was a problem. The most intimate contacts of the victims could not be identified until the victims themselves were and, so far, this had not been possible.

Carmen Esposa was not an uncommon name and a search for Carmen Esposas had turned up no less than twenty-four of them.

All alive and well.

'Her name is almost surely not Carmen Esposa,' said the sergeant, 'but there's nothing in the flat to indicate what it is other than the "Dear Elvira" letters.'

The Dear Elvira letters were practically the only papers that had been found in the flat. The only places that the names Antonio Molina and Carmen Esposa appeared were on the front door and the mailbox.

The mail box had been emptied and found to contain nothing but advertising and an electricity bill in the name of Carmen Esposa. Neither the electricity company nor Garcia had seen any official identification at the time that the flat was first rented.

There were seven of the letters, none dated and all signed simply 'Sara'.

'The vice squad says that Sara is a whore and so is Elvira,' said the sergeant. 'The language used is red-light slang.'

'I gathered as much,' said the inspector, 'but the question is: Was Carmen Esposa Elvira? Or did the letters belong to Molina? Any identification on him yet?'

'Yes,' said the sergeant. 'According to vice, he's a pimp. He was twenty-eight years old and, when last heard of, operating a stable of three girls in the Puerto del Sol area.'

The Puerto del Sol was Madrid's notorious red-light district.

'Doesn't make sense,' observed the inspector. 'If Molina was a pimp, the woman, whatever her name was,

was a whore. But what was she doing living anonymously in a high-class block of flats? She wasn't bringing customers back there. The building manager would never have stood for it.'

The sergeant nodded in agreement.

'And, on top of it, who would have such strong feelings about a whore as to commit two murders because of her?' he said. 'She wasn't any great beauty and Aguiar estimates that she was thirty years old or more. If she was making any money, it was on sheer volume. She couldn't command a high price.'

'We'll have to work with the vice squad,' said the inspector. 'They have contacts and sources of information. Tell them we want a run-down on Molina. Maybe if we can identify the girls in his stable, they'll know something about who Elvira and Sara were or are and what Esposa and Molina were doing in San Cristobal de los Angeles.'

The vice squad did have contacts and sources of information within the world of prostitutes and procurers who inhabited the Puerto del Sol and other entertainment districts, but the reports received on Carmen Esposa and Antonio Molina were more puzzling than useful.

Carmen Esposa was, indeed, a prostitute and had been one for close to ten years. Her real name was not Carmen Esposa, although it was the only name she was ever known to have used.

What her real name was or where she came from, no one knew.

'Country girl,' observed the inspector sagely. 'They always change their names because they don't want to risk somebody from the village finding out what they're doing.'

'A hard worker, in any case,' said the sergeant. 'Her going rate was around three hundred and fifty pesetas and the rent on the flat was fifty thousand without the charges. Vice contacted some of her clientele. She didn't have many regulars, but they said she was honest and clean. Her biggest attraction was that she was cheap.'

'Doesn't sound like a girl who would be the victim of a crime of passion,' said the inspector. 'What about Molina? Why was he living with a cheap whore when he could have had better?'

The sergeant shrugged. 'A great mystery,' he said. 'They've only been together for about six months. Before that, she had another pimp. Fellow named Fernando Nunez.'

'Ah!' said the inspector.

'Well, maybe,' said the sergeant, 'but vice doesn't think that Nunez has the guts for murder. They're trying to locate him now.'

'And Molina's other girls?' said the inspector.

'They're trying to locate them too,' said the sergeant.

The search for the two business associates of the late Antonio Molina and for his competitor, Fernando Nunez, soon ceased to be a matter for the vice squad and became the primary objective of the department of criminal investigations.

The vice squad's inquiries had produced the information that Nunez and the girls had not only left at the same time; they had apparently left together.

'Now we're making some progress,' said the inspector. 'The motive is clear. Nunez simply wanted to take over Molina's stable so he killed him.'

'And one of his girls?' said the sergeant.

'Miss Esposa was a witness to the murder,' said the inspector. 'She had to be eliminated.'

'It still doesn't explain why Molina was living with his oldest and least desirable employee,' said the sergeant. 'The other two were younger and better looking. One was eighteen, the other twenty-one.'

'Who can look into the hearts of pimps?' said the inspector. 'Maybe he loved her. Maybe she reminded him of his old mother.'

'I think I'll try to locate Sara,' said the sergeant. 'Any objections?'

The inspector had none.

As it turned out, the sergeant had plenty of time to

look for the authoress of the Dear Elvira letters as the search for Fernando Nunez and the girls tended to mark time.

Reports were received that he had been seen in Barcelona and Granada, and across the French border in Montpellier. How accurate these reports were could not be determined for no arrest was made and Nunez remained missing.

As for the two girls who had formerly worked for Antonio Molina, no reports of sightings were received at all.

'Not surprising,' said the inspector, 'considering the number of prostitutes there are in the country. How are things going with Sara?'

Things were going well with Sara or, rather, they were going well with the sergeant's attempt to identify her. He had already learned that she and Carmen Esposa had been close friends and that they had sometimes used a hot-bed hotel called El Conejo as a processing location for their customers.

He was now trying to persuade the employees of the hotel to tell him what Sara's full name was and where she could be found.

The sergeant being very persuasive, he was eventually able to learn that Sara was Sara Alonzo, a twenty-six-year-old prostitute who came from a small village in Andalucia and who could often be found standing on a certain street corner in Puerto del Sol.

Which was where the sergeant found her and took her off for a glass of wine and a little talk.

A practical girl, she accepted the wine, but showed little inclination to cooperate otherwise.

'Elvira's dead,' she said, 'and maybe it's for the best. Her people think she died back in 1974, the year after she came to Madrid.'

'And they can continue to believe that,' said the sergeant, 'if you answer a few questions for me.'

Sara hesitated.

'Otherwise, I'll have to contact her family in the

village,' said the sergeant, naming the place that Sara came from.

It was only a guess. He did not know that Carmen Esposa – or Elvira – came from the same village as Sara, but she obviously did, for Sara immediately became much more cooperative and asked what he wanted to know.

'What was Carmen Esposa's real name?' said the sergeant.

'Elvira Abenogar,' said Sara, 'or Elvira Alarcon. You have a choice. Abenogar was her maiden name.'

'She was married?' said the sergeant in astonishment. It was something that had not occurred to anyone connected with the investigation.

Sara nodded. 'On 13 June 1981', she said. 'Church, bridesmaids, white wedding gown, the works.' Her voice took on a wistful tone. 'I was a bridesmaid.'

'And who was the bridegroom?' asked the sergeant, not sure where this was leading, but aware that new aspects of the case were in the process of being revealed.

'Rufino Alarcon,' said Sara.

'A pimp?' said the sergeant.

'Works at the slaughterhouse,' said Sara. 'He was a client.'

The explanation made sense. The sergeant knew that a surprising number of prostitutes married former clients. Sometimes it worked out well, other times less so. It depended upon the reasons the woman had had for being a prostitute in the first place.

'It should have worked,' said Sara, as if she was reading his mind. 'She never wanted to get into the business. There wasn't any work in the village so she came up here looking for a job, but at every place she worked, they wanted to put her on her back. Finally she thought, "If I have to do it anyway, I might as well get paid for it." So she went commercial.'

'She told you that?' said the sergeant.

Sara nodded.

'Then why did she leave her husband?' said the sergeant.

'It was too late,' said Sara. 'She couldn't get used to sitting around all day in that little flat waiting for Rufino to come home. She started going out, turning a trick or two while Rufino was working, and then she ran away altogether. She was staying with me for a while until she could get enough together to pay the deposit on a flat.'

The sergeant continued his questioning, discovering that Fernando Nunez was originally Elvira's protector, but he had been bought off by her husband before the marriage. Molina had taken her over some time during the autumn of the preceding year.

'I guess it was because she was quiet and not much on sex,' said Sara. 'They say his other girls were running him ragged.'

There was apparently aspects of the procurer's profession which the sergeant had never considered.

'Pretty big, tough type, this Rufino Alarcon?' he asked.

It had become apparent that the dead woman's husband was a far more promising suspect in the murders than Fernando Nunez. He not only had an obvious motive but, as a slaughterhouse worker, could be expected to be handy with a butchering knife.

'A mouse,' said Sara. 'He's barely five feet tall and skinny. A nice guy, but he's so shy he won't look at you. Elvira told me it took him half an hour to work up the courage to ask her the price the first time.'

'Three hundred and fifty,' said the sergeant.

'He gave her four hundred,' said Sara, who had apparently heard the details of this love story more than once and found it charming. 'Then he came back the next night and gave her five hundred. When he gave her six hundred the third time, she knew it was love.'

'A reasonable conclusion,' said the sergeant. 'And Fernando?'

'He was willing to sell her contract,' said Sara, 'but Rufino didn't have the money. They had to wait for a year until he'd saved up enough. Even then, he had to borrow everything he could lay his hands on.'

'Following which, she ran off with Molina,' said the sergeant, establishing an extenuating circumstance which would, undoubtedly, weigh heavily at the trial.

'Not like that,' said Sara. 'She loved him. She just couldn't stand sitting around doing nothing. It was partly my fault. I told her, "Go out in the afternoons. Have a drink in a café. Have a little fun." '

'Like in El Conejo,' said the sergeant.

'That wasn't fun for her,' said Sara. 'That was business. She started again because Rufino couldn't give her any money to even sit in a café. He was in debt up to his ears.'

'You think he killed her,' said the sergeant, making it half statement, half question.

Sara remained silent, staring at her wine glass. 'He was going all over town with her picture looking for her,' she said finally.

The sergeant arrested Rufino Alarcon at his little, two-room flat in the working-class district of Vallecas that evening. It was not an arrest that he enjoyed making. True, it had been murder, a double murder even, but it had also been a tragedy.

A rather plain country girl and a shy slaughterhouse worker had met, fallen in love, married – with the prostitute bride in white surrounded by her prostitute bridesmaids – and hoped for a future in which neither would ever be again alone.

The marriage had failed. Not for any of the reasons usually cited as grounds for divorce, but because there was not enough money for a cup of coffee in a café.

The little, poorly furnished flat was still filled with poignant souvenirs of Elvira, her wedding pictures, her white veil, a carefully preserved piece of the wedding cake. Her pillow lay beside his on the bed.

'I didn't want to kill anybody,' said the little man with the full beard and the sorrowful brown eyes. 'I just wanted my wife back.'

In his statement, made later at police headquarters, Alarcon said that he had finally learned where Elvira was living and went to bring her home.

He had not known that she was living with Molina or even who Molina was, and he simply ignored him, taking Elvira by the hand and saying that she was to come home with him now.

Molina intervened and said something about Alarcon not being 'man enough' for a woman like Elvira. He caught hold of Alarcon and tried to force him out of the flat. Alarcon seized the knife, which was lying on the table near the sofa, and stabbed him in the chest.

'After that, I don't remember what happened,' said Rufino Alarcon. 'I think I killed Elvira, but I don't remember it. I don't remember anything.

'I must have been crazy. I love her.'

The court believed him and, on 11 May, 1984, sentenced him to the modest term of five years' imprisonment for unintentional homicide with extenuating circumstances.

17

HAIRBREADTH HAIRY

During the weekend of 27 and 28 August 1983, a strange disappearance took place in the city of Flensburg, West Germany.

Flensburg is directly on the border with Denmark and about as far north as it is possible to go in Germany.

A not unattractive, if chilly, city of some hundred thousand inhabitants, it lies at the tip of the Flensburg Fjord and is an important Baltic naval base and seaport. A scant thirty-five miles to the west is the North Sea.

Although Flensburg is German, many of its residents are Danes and the city has no less than seven schools for Danish children.

The woman who disappeared was Danish and a teacher in one of these schools, the Jorgensby Skolen, where she taught mathematics, Danish and sports.

As might be expected of a sports instructor, Liss Ostergaard was athletic and, although forty-six years old, in perfect physical condition except for a tendon in her left leg which she had pulled jogging a few weeks earlier and which was not yet completely healed.

A large, slightly forbidding woman, she was extremely conscientious and, in the twelve years that she had been attached to the staff of Jorgensby Skolen, she had not once been late, sick or absent for any reason.

School Director Olaf Svensson was, therefore, surprised and alarmed when Liss Ostergaard failed to appear for her first class on Monday morning and, having telephoned her flat and received no reply, notified the police.

A detective from the department of criminal investigations went to the flat, but was unable to obtain any response to his knocks on the door.

He next called at the school, where he asked for the address of Miss Ostergaard's family as he thought she might have gone home for the weekend and been prevented, for some reason or other, from returning in time for work.

However, the only member of her family whom she was known to visit was her father, who lived in Denmark, not far from the border.

He was contacted by telephone and said that he had not seen Liss for weeks. As far as he knew, she had not been planning to visit him the preceding weekend.

Having been unable to uncover any trace of the woman, the detective returned to headquarters, reported the lack of results from the steps taken and asked for further instructions.

The matter was beginning to take on a more serious aspect and Detective Sergeant Juergen Bolger was assigned to investigate.

He began by bringing a locksmith to the flat to open the door, but this the locksmith was unable to do and he and the sergeant were forced to break it down.

Miss Ostergaard was not there, but there were indications that she had not expected to remain away long.

A slice of buttered bread lay on a plate on the table with a glass of milk beside it. A pair of slacks, a blouse, a brassière, white pants and stockings lay over the back of a chair as if she had been planning to change upon her return. Otherwise, the flat was in perfect order.

The sergeant returned to headquarters and reported that, in his opinion, something unexpected had happened to Miss Ostergaard and a criminal act could not be ruled out.

It had, in the meantime, already been determined by the first detective that she was not in any of the city's hospitals or clinics.

The case, the sergeant and the detective were all taken

over by Inspector Walter Trapp, a burly, red-faced senior investigations officer with a great, booming voice and a deceptively clumsy manner.

The inspector promptly sent the sergeant back to the flat with a team from the police laboratory. He wanted to know if they could determine from the milk and the slice of bread or by other means how long it had been since Miss Ostergaard had left her flat.

The conclusion of the technicians was that the bread and milk had been set out at some time in the afternoon of Sunday. She had, therefore, been missing for nearly twenty hours before her disappearance was reported to the police.

The technicians then went through Miss Ostergaard's private papers in the hope of finding correspondence with a friend, a relative or a lover whom she might be visiting.

They found nothing. Her only close relative was her father. Her friends were mainly her colleagues at the school and the members of a jogging club to which she belonged. And, if she had had a lover, they had either not corresponded or she had not kept his letters.

Her friends and colleagues said that she had had no lover nor even a boy friend. She had not been terribly interested in romantic contacts with the opposite sex, although her colleagues, male or female, all testified that she was a warm, friendly and helpful person. She was very popular at the school and in the jogging club.

She had, however, not gone jogging with the club since pulling the tendon in her leg as she did not want to slow down the others. Instead, she had gone for shorter and slower runs all by herself.

'And it appears probable that that was where she went on Sunday afternoon after putting out her clothing and her snack,' said the sergeant. 'We've checked her wardrobe and she was apparently wearing her track suit when she left.'

He was a sturdy, broad-shouldered man with light blond hair, little facial expression and a methodical manner of speaking which extended to his thinking as well.

'As they say she always did her jogging in the Volkspark, I think that's where we must look for her,' he concluded.

The Volkspark is a huge expanse of partially wooded open country on the eastern side of the fjord. It is popular with joggers and sports people of all kinds.

It proved a very difficult place to search, wild and overgrown with brush and high grass. A thorough examination would have required a larger force than was at the disposal of the police.

None the less, the police did what they could and they were joined by off-duty firemen, colleagues of the missing woman and, eventually, sailors from the naval base.

They did not find Liss Ostergaard.

At least, not right away. It was Thursday, September the fifteenth before one of the search-parties finally stumbled upon a track suit top in a heavily wooded area, not far from one of the jogging trails.

The sector was immediately cordoned off and members of the jogging club were brought to view the garment.

They tentatively identified it as resembling one that had belonged to Liss Ostergaard, and police technicians began an inch by inch examination of the entire area surrounding it.

A pair of track suit trousers was soon found, twenty feet away, and, fifteen feet beyond that, a woman's torn underclothing.

The garments lay in a straight line and at the end of the line was the corpse of Liss Ostergaard.

Not very much remained. The summer in such high latitudes is short, but it can be warm and this was the end of August. Decomposition was very advanced.

'Plus a good deal of damage by birds, insects and small animals,' said Dr Johann Schmidt, the short, swarthy, black-haired and black-eyed medical officer. 'A little longer and it would have been nothing but a skeleton.'

'But we will be able to identify, won't we?' said the inspector, who had been summoned to the scene. 'What about the motive?'

'Well, it certainly looks like sex,' said the doctor, 'but I don't know whether we'll be able to confirm that or not. I think we'll be all right on identification. There seems to be enough left of the finger tips for prints.'

There was enough. Although the face of the corpse was unrecognizable to the point that neither friends nor relatives were permitted to view it, the tips of several of the fingers were intact and adequate prints to make a positive identification were obtained.

Despite the doctor's misgivings, evidence of the sexual motive of the murder was also established at the autopsy. Miss Ostergaard, it seemed, had been an intact virgin at the time that she was raped and murdered.

'The lab seems to have built up a fairly clear picture of what took place,' said the sergeant, holding out the file he had been reading to the inspector. 'They recovered a lot of potential clues at the scene and they apparently think some of them, at least, are significant.'

The report was actually a combination of the laboratory and autopsy findings and, as the sergeant had remarked, offered a logically deduced theory of the course of the crime.

Miss Ostergaard was attacked while jogging along the path near where the body was found.

She fought with her attacker and then tried to escape by running.

He ran after her, knocked her down and succeeded in tearing off some of her clothing.

She managed to break free and run again, but was quickly brought down for a second time and more of her clothing was stripped away.

The process continued up to the point where the rape took place, followed or accompanied by the murder, at which time she was totally naked.

The actual cause of death appeared to be manual strangulation, but the victim had been badly beaten on the face and head and would, undoubtedly, have bled copiously. The murderer would have had extensive blood stains on his clothing.

All told, a hundred and forty-two potential clues had been recovered, of which lots one, six, eight, forty-eight, sixty-six and one hundred and seven were considered to be significant.

Lots one and eight were textile fibres. The rest were human hairs. All had been recovered from the clothing of the victim.

The time of death was fixed at approximately five in the afternoon of 28 August 1983.

'But no indication of the identity of the person from whom these hairs and textile fibres stem,' said the inspector.

'No,' said the sergeant. 'The clues will only be valuable when we find a suspect.'

It was an indication of his faith in the ultimate triumph of justice that he said 'when' rather than 'if'.

In fact, the prospects for a solution of the case were poor. It was the most difficult of crimes to solve, a sexually motivated crime in which there had, in all probability, been no prior contact between murderer and victim. The sexual aspects lacked the abnormality to permit identification from other cases on record. And far too much time had elapsed between the murder and the discovery of the body. Witnesses' memories, if there had been any witnesses, would have grown dim.

None the less, if any progress in the case was to be made at all, it would have to be through witnesses. The clues were important, but they needed a suspect to match them to.

The inspector went to the public, publishing appeals in the newspapers and over the local radio and television station for people who had been in the Volkspark on the afternoon of August the twenty-eighth to report in to the police, whether they had any information or not. It was possible that someone had seen something which they regarded as completely innocent, but which the police might regard differently.

The response was massive. Although on the border of permissive Denmark and the site of the largest manufacturer of sex gadgets and soft pornography in Europe, Flensburg is in some respects conservative, and the community spirit is stronger than in some other parts of the world.

This community spirit gave the investigators a great deal of work, for all of the reports, however improbable, had to be checked and evaluated.

It took a long time and, in the end, it turned out that none of the testimony of the witnesses from the Volkspark was of any value.

A number of people had seen Liss Ostergaard jogging slowly along on that day and some of them had known her by sight or even by name. No one, however, had seen her in the company of a man or with a man anywhere near her.

There were also, of course, countless reports of sightings of strange men, of sinister figures lurking in the bushes and even of extra-terrestrials descending from flying saucers or otherwise. Imagination is a powerful force and a case such as the Liss Ostergaard murder stimulates it most wonderfully.

The less spectacular of these reports were checked, but with the same results. None appeared to have any connection to the murder.

Reports from people who had been in the park on that afternoon were not, however, the only ones received. There were numerous crank calls, generally anonymous, from people sincerely convinced that they knew the identify of the murderer, or maliciously trying to get someone into trouble. They did not take up much of the investigators' time as they could not be checked in any case.

But not all of the calls were anonymous and one proved to be of vital importance.

It was from a sailor at the naval base who identified himself as Hospital Corpsman Second Class Mark Peters. He said that he had information which he thought might have a bearing on the murder. Should he come to police headquarters or would the police send someone to take his statement?

The inspector thought it best that he come to police headquarters. If the corpsman really had information on the murder, it was probably in connection with someone at the base. Sending a police officer there, even in plain-clothes, might put a potential suspect on his guard.

Peters, therefore, came to headquarters, where he made a significant and, for the investigations officers, exciting statement.

On the evening of August the twenty-eighth he said, he was on duty in the naval sick bay.

At approximately ten o'clock, a seaman was brought to the sick bay by the duty sentry on watch at the base entrance.

The man was suffering from numerous scratches and cuts on his face and hands and his clothing was soiled and blood-stained.

While the corpsman was treating the scratches, he said in a joking manner, 'I must have been with a woman.' And, later, 'If they find a body, it was me.'

The corpsman had not thought anything of the incident at the time, but, having read the appeals from the police in the newspapers, came to the conclusion that he should report it.

'The man's name?' said the inspector.

'Hans Wilhelm Hadler,' said the corpsman.

Hadler was immediately taken into custody and placed under interrogation. He denied all knowledge of the crime and said that, if he had made such remarks to the corpsman, it was because he was drunk. His scratches came from a brawl in a bar.

The sentry on duty that evening was also interrogated and made a statement confirming that he arrested Hadler while he was trying to climb over the perimeter fence from outside.

He was dirty, dishevelled and stained with blood. Asked why he had tried to climb the fence instead of coming in through the gate normally, he did not reply. He was not, however, in possession of his military identification card and the sentry assumed that he was trying to conceal the fact that he had lost it. An account of the incident was entered in the guard room log.

Any scratches that Hadler had had were by now healed and the inspector had little hope that any traces of blood could be recovered from his clothing. None the less, it was brought to the police laboratory and, unexpectedly, traces of two different types of blood were recovered from a pair of olive green corduroy trousers and a light grey shirt.

According to the statements of the sentry and the corpsman, these were the clothes that Hadler was wearing on the evening of August the twenty-eighth.

Although the two different types of blood found on Hadler's clothing corresponded to the blood groups of Liss Ostergaard and Hadler himself, this was still not concrete proof of his guilt. There were thousands of persons in Flensburg with the same blood group as that of Liss Ostergaard and, if Hadler had actually been in a fight in a bar, as he claimed, the blood could stem from his opponent.

No evidence could be found of a fight in a bar involving Hadler but, again, this was not proof that he was lying. The bar in which he said he had had the fight was popular and crowded, and so much time had now passed that the employees could not remember whether there had been a fight there that evening or not.

Hadler, for his part, said that had been the first time he ever visited that particular bar, and this appeared to be true as no one there knew him.

Likewise, the man with whom he had had the fight was a total stranger. He did not think that he was a sailor.

'He's sharp,' said the inspector. 'We're not going to get any confession out of him.'

'Then it doesn't seem to me that we'll get any conviction either,' said the sergeant. 'The statement by the sentry and the corpsman aren't enough and the lab admits that the textile fibres could have come from any of a thousand garments.'

Lot one of the clues recovered by the technicians at the scene consisted of fourteen olive green textile fibres which were identical to the fibres of Hadler's olive green corduroy trousers.

Unfortunately, such corduroy trousers in the identical colour were on sale all over Flensburg, and the same held true for the grey shirt. Lot eight consisted of fibres from a blouse of that colour, but there were many such shirts. There was no proof that the fibres came from Hadler's clothing.

'We still have the hairs,' said the inspector. 'We'll be bringing up an expert on hair from Kiel. If anybody can identify them, she can.'

The expert in question, a young and attractive woman, enjoyed an international reputation for forensic identification of body substances, particularly hair. Lots six, forty-eight, sixty-six and one hundred and seven of the clues recovered at the scene had been sent down to Kiel, where she was studying them, together with hairs taken from the body and head of the victim and the suspect. A great deal would depend upon her findings.

As the inspector had anticipated, the case came to trial without a confession. Hans Wilhelm Hadler still insisted that he had nothing to do with the murder, but admitted that he had been in the Volkspark on the afternoon in question.

He did not admit to that much until witnesses had been found who identified him positively as the man they had seen in the park, although not in the company of Liss Ostergaard.

He also still clung to his story of a fight in a bar and

now added the detail that his opponent had stolen his military identification card.

This was a hard blow for the investigation as the identification card had been considered the sole physical evidence tying Hadler to the crime.

Following the statement by the sentry that Hadler had not had his identification card, the inspector rushed every man at his disposal to the Volkspark in a search for it.

The search was successful. The card and the victim's brassière, which had also been missing, were found together under a pile of dead leaves, apparently kicked over them unintentionally.

Confident that this evidence would break Hadler's resistance, the inspector made a mistake and confronted him with it directly.

Hadler was not shaken, and came up with the story of the card being stolen by the man with whom he had had the fight.

'Too pat by a long shot,' said the inspector in disgust, 'but the court is required to give him the benefit of the doubt and his story could be true.'

'Maybe it is true,' said the sergeant. 'Maybe the man he had the fight with is the one who murdered Miss Ostergaard. After all, Hadler doesn't have any police record.'

The inspector placed the tip of his index finger on the lower lid of his right eye and pulled it downward in the time-honoured Continental expression of scepticism, but he too was forced to admit that the chances of a conviction were slim.

They were no better when the case came to trial at the beginning of September 1984. Hadler's counsel was able to challenge successfully every piece of evidence offered by the prosecution, and improved the position of the defence by maintaining that his client had been roaring drunk the entire afternoon and evening of the murder and thus incapable of running down, raping and murdering such an athletic victim as Liss Ostergaard.

This was a particularly sly defence because it accounted for any lapses or inconsistencies in Hadler's statements and, in addition, was liable to get him off even if he was convicted.

West German courts have the curious habit of excusing even the most vicious crimes if the perpetrator was drunk or on drugs at the time.

This being well known, the defence move immediately prompted protest demonstrations by every feminist organization in Flensburg and, during the entire time the court was in session, pickets were parading in the street outside the courthouse bearing signs proclaiming, 'Murder is Murder – Drunk or Sober!'

The ladies apparently had no doubts concerning Hadler's guilt, although there was nothing so far to confirm it.

The counsel for the defence having demolished all the other evidence for the prosecution, the expert from Kiel was finally called to the witness stand and gave her testimony in a detached, matter-of-fact manner.

She had, she said, examined from among the potential clues found at the scene of the discovery of Ostergaard's body, lots marked six, forty-eight, sixty-six and one hundred and seven.

All four lots consisted of human hairs, and she had compared them with samples taken from the body and scalp of the victim and from the body and scalp of the accused.

Lot six, said the expert, consisted of nine human hairs ranging in length from half an inch to three inches. They had been found on the track suit top worn by the victim.

All these hairs were from the victim herself.

'There is no possibility that any of these hairs could stem from the accused?' asked the prosecutor.

'None,' said the expert.

Lot sixty-six, she continued, consisted of two hairs, one four and the other four and a half inches long. They too were from the victim or, at least, from a woman. They were not hairs belonging to the defendant.

Lot one hundred and seven comprised three hairs, two were four inches in length and one was six inches long. Two of these could be hairs from the scalp of the defendant. She could not state under oath that they were.

'And lot forty-eight?' said the prosecutor, who knew very well what he was doing.

'Lot forty-eight is a single pubic hair slightly less than one and a half inches long,' said the expert. 'It was recovered from one of the victim's socks. The hair is from the body of the accused.'

. The Counsel for the defence immediately objected, on the grounds that the expert could not identify with certainty the person from whom a single pubic hair came.

'In most cases not,' agreed the expert calmly, 'but in the case of Hans Wilhelm Hadler, there is an aberration in the pigmentation of his pubic hair which causes the pigment to form little islands at the ends of the hairs. The formation is unique and can be easily seen under the microscope.'

Although severely cross-examined by the counsel for the defence, the expert stuck to her guns. The hair came from Hadler; she could swear it under oath.

The defence then fell back on a lack of responsibility by reason of drunkenness, but this time the ploy did not work. The hospital corpsman and the sentry both testified that Hadler had shown no signs of drunkenness that night, and the jury, therefore, found him guilty of rape and murder without extenuating circumstances.

Convicted by a hair, Hans Wilhem Hadler was sentenced to life imprisonment on 14 September, 1984 and led away, still protesting his innocence.

18

THE RELUCTANT DISCIPLE

Rising in the north-east corner of France, the Ardennes mountains sweep in a great arc across Belgium, cover the northern half of Luxemburg and pass into West Germany where they are known as the Eifel.

An old mountain chain, worn down to rounded hills only occasionally higher than two thousand feet, cut by ravines and heavily wooded, the sparsely populated Ardennes are scenically beautiful but faintly sinister.

This vague impression of evil has nothing to do with the landscape. It is due to the beliefs and practices of the rather strange people who have lived for generations in their hidden isolated little communities, drowned in the great green sea of forest.

In many places in the Ardennes, sorcery, witchcraft and evil spells are not superstition, but practical aspects of everyday life.

Members of the many modern sects now replacing Christianity are not, however, concerned with witchcraft. Being in direct communication with God, they have nothing to fear from such manifestations of evil. Moreover, property is cheap in the Ardennes.

It is, therefore, not strange that an oriental sect should come to purchase the castle of Petite Somme in the Belgian Ardennes. It was inexpensive, large enough to house the members of the sect and, if it was nowhere near any large community, so much the better. The sect was self-sufficient.

As, of course, is any organization with ample funds.

The few dozen residents of Petite Somme were

pleased. If the sect employed anyone locally at all, it would be the biggest employer in the region.

And, indeed, the sect did employ a number of people – cleaning women, gardeners, handymen.

Few remained long, however. The pay was modest and the working conditions were unacceptable. If you worked for the sect, you were bound by the same rules as the sect members, which included a great deal of prayer, very early rising, a sparse diet, plenty of hard work and utter chastity other than for the purposes of procreation.

It is only possible to hire people under such conditions in a country without unemployment compensation or welfare. Belgium has both.

The sect was not, therefore, quite as popular as it might otherwise have been. When the shaven-headed disciples went through the village with their begging bowls, they received, rather than money, curious signs behind their backs, which, had they not been under the personal protection of God, might have made them nervous.

Many of them knew what the signs meant. With one or two exceptions, the members of the sect were not orientals but Belgians and, for Petite Somme, the wrong kind of Belgians.

Belgium is, like ancient Gaul, divided into three parts: Flanders, Wallonia and a tiny German enclave in the north-east corner. The Flemings speak Flemish. The Walloons speak French. And the Germans speak German. The Flemings are Protestant. The Walloons are Catholic. The Germans are undecided. As a rule, they heartily detest each other.

The majority of the residents of Petite Somme were Walloons. The majority of the sect members were Flemings. The villagers were Christian, even if, in some cases, on the wrong side of the fence. The sect members were worshippers of exotic oriental deities. It was not the best population mix in the world.

However, all went as well as things usually go in this

era of forced integration until 10 March 1984, at which time someone noticed the glare and smoke of a fire near the castle and turned out the local voluntary fire department.

It being before six o'clock of a Sunday morning, the response was none too rapid, but it did not matter for the fire was not serious. A red Lada estate was tipped over in the ditch five hundred yards from the castle and already burned to a shell.

The Lada, a Russian copy of the Italian Fiat distinguished by its robust construction and startlingly low price, was the property of the sect, the members of which were all engaged in their morning rituals.

Informed of their loss, they came out, looked at the remains of the Lada and telephoned the gendarmerie station in Bastogne to report that someone had torched their car.

Bastogne, with a population of under twelve thousand, is not a very busy place either, and there was no one on duty at the station except a junior patrolman who was a little nervous about turning out his superiors.

The sect leader was, however, insistent and, at a little after ten o'clock, a party consisting of two gendarmes under the command of a fierce-looking sergeant with a huge, sweeping moustache, a hooked nose and a prominent chin arrived in Petite Somme.

They were engaged in questioning the sect members about how the car came to be five hundred yards from the parking space in front of the castle when there was a great outcry from one of the sect members, a Mr Diederik Vandenheiden, who said that he had lost his wife.

This provoked a certain confusion in the sergeant's mind as he had understood that the members of the sect practised chastity. They were, in fact, perhaps more famous in the region on this count than on any other.

Explanations were offered and it turned out that there were varying degrees of chastity. The members who lived in the castle itself were segregated in men's and women's dormitories, but some of the equally faithful but less chaste lived as couples in nearby houses owned by the sect.

The Vandenheidens were among the less chaste and occupied a two-storey brick house set back from a narrow lane leading from the west side of the castle.

According to Vandenheiden, he rose at the usual hour of four in the morning and made off to the castle for the prescribed dancing, chanting and prostrations. His thirty-one-year-old wife, Godelieve Dobbeleers, chose to remain in bed. Although devout, she had, he said, not been feeling well of late.

The religious services was still going on when the fire alarm sounded, and he went with the others to look at the burnt-out car. He had only just now returned home to find that Godelieve was not there.

The sergeant suggested that she might be in the castle or even at the scene of the fire, where there was still quite a crowd.

Vandenheiden replied that if she was, she was in her nightdress, for it was the only garment belonging to her that was missing.

The reply alarmed the sergeant. He did not know what was going on in Petite Somme, but the car had apparently been set on fire deliberately for there was no explanation of how it had got five hundred yards from the car park. It was not impossible that there was a connection between the fire and the disappearance of Godelieve Dobbeleers and, being a local man himself, the sergeant was frightened by what it might be.

He therefore organized all the residents of Petite Somme capable of movement into search-parties under the direction of his gendarmes and began looking in the usual places for missing persons. The members of the sect did not need to be organized. They were all searching already.

However, because he began his search at the house, it was Vandenheiden himself who found her.

He simply rounded the corner of the house and started

along a narrow path overgrown with high weeds and bushes, when he came upon her body less than fifty feet from the front door.

Godelieve was still wearing her nightdress, but it was bunched up under her armpits, leaving her almost naked. She lay face down on the path and, for a moment, he had the wild hope that she was merely unconscious.

She was, however, dead, although her body was still pliable and not yet completely cold. There was no trace of a heart beat and no respiration, and the black marks of strangling fingers were all too clear on her throat.

The thirty-two-year-old Vandenheiden went to report his find to the sergeant and then returned to weep beside his wife's body. He had loved Godelieve very much.

The sergeant, his worst fears materialized, telephoned headquarters in Bastogne, asked to be connected with Captain Armand Dunoyer and reported that he was at the scene of a murder. The department of criminal investigations would have to turn out.

Captain Dunoyer was the chief of the department of criminal investigations. A plump, sleek man with his dark hair parted neatly on one side, he had achieved his position through length of service and not through any brilliance as an investigations officer.

This was not to say that the captain would not have been as brilliant as anyone else if he had anything to investigate, but, as a rule, he did not. There has been little happening in Bastogne since General McAuliffe confused the attacking Germans there with his defiant cry of 'Nuts!'

Being francophone, Captain Dunoyer did not cry 'Nuts!' but 'Merde alors!' and set off immediately for Petite Somme, leaving orders for the medical examiner, the staff of the gendarmerie laboratory and as much of the department of criminal investigations as could be rounded up to follow him as expeditiously as possible.

Shortly before noon, the gendarmes outnumbered both villagers and sect members in Petite Somme.

Considering the state of the corpse, it was assumed

that Godelieve had fallen victim to a sex criminal. Not, perhaps, one of the sex psychopaths that make life in the bigger cities perilous for girls, boys and women, but a simple prowler who had encountered Godelieve in her very transparent nightie and been carried away.

The theory was, however, quickly discredited by Dr Jerome Jacquin, the blond, red-faced, grossly overweight medical officer, who arrived, puffing and blowing like a porpoise, examined the body and reported that Godelieve had been strangled to death manually and nothing else. The disarranged clothing was, probably, the result of the murderer catching hold of it as he brought the fleeing woman down.

The captain, who had been waiting to hear the report, promptly made off inside the house, where the sergeant with the moustache and Vandenheiden were trying to determine whether anything had been stolen.

'Nothing,' said the sergeant. 'Mr Vandenheiden says that nothing's been touched.'

The captain looked embarrassed.

'You'll have to question him about his domestic arrangements,' he said. 'If it wasn't money and it wasn't sex, it must be some personal motive. Maybe this isn't his wife.'

But it was and, although Godelieve had been an extremely attractive woman, she had had no admirers. She had mixed with no one other than members of the sect, and they were not permitted to admire women, married or not, let alone strangle them.

'There's got to be some motive,' said the captain. 'The woman didn't commit suicide. What about the husband? The book says that the spouse is always the first suspect.'

'No known motive,' said the sergeant, whose name was Paul Villemain. 'And he was jumping around in the castle with all the rest of them from four in the morning until the fire started. There are a couple of dozen witnesses.'

'Well, that takes care of the husband, I suppose,' said the captain, baffled. 'I don't know what to think.'

'If I may make a suggestion,' said the sergeant. 'I come from this part of the world and there can be motives here that have nothing to do with money or sex or domestic problems.'

'You're talking occult,' said the captain, looking at him obliquely out of the corner of his eye. 'I don't come from here, but I've lived here for eighteen years. But why? Because of the sect?'

'What else?' said the sergeant. 'We don't know what these people are doing here. Who or what do they worship, exactly? Maybe it's something that conflicts with some of the local beliefs. There have been cult murders and sect murders too before.'

The captain considered the idea.

'It's possible,' he admitted, 'but there's a lot I don't understand about it. To begin with, why this particular woman? She wasn't a sect leader and, from what I've been told, not even one of the more fanatic. If she had been, she'd have slept in the dormitory and wouldn't have got murdered.'

'Maybe that was the reason,' said the sergeant. 'Whoever it was couldn't get at the ones in the castle so he took what he could get.'

'Logical,' said the captain, 'but, from what I know of the people here, they're more liable to be sitting around sticking pins into dolls than strangling somebody. Not that that can't be effective, mind you, but . . .'

The captain had, indeed, been a long time in the Ardennes.

'That's true,' said the sergeant thoughtfully. 'It isn't the way people go about things here. Poison, maybe, or an accident, but strangling is too direct. It must have been somebody who's completely insane.'

If it was, he had been invisible. In a place like Petite Somme, a stranger stood out like a cow in church. There had been no strangers in Petite Somme and, if the residents could be believed, there was no one among them crazy enough to murder without reason.

'It must have some connection with the car being set

on fire,' said the captain. 'Find out what the car was used for, who owned it before the sect if it was second hand and, above all, find out who has keys to it. The place where it was set on fire is uphill from the castle. It had to be driven there.'

This did not strike the sergeant as a particularly promising lead, but he did as he was told and soon learned that the Lada estate had been bought new and that the keys were still hanging in the castle kitchen.

'Could someone have picked up the keys and put them back after setting fire to the car?' asked the sergeant.

The sect member in charge of such matters said no. To begin with, the keys were in a locked cabinet in the kitchen and, secondly, the castle doors were barred during the night and only opened at four-thirty for the morning ceremonies.

'I don't know about the murder,' the sergeant told the captain, 'but the car must have been set on fire by this fellow who has the keys to the key cabinet. There's no one else who could have moved the car.'

'Good,' said the captain. 'Bring him in for questioning.'

Unfortunately, things did not work out quite so simply. The man with the keys to the key cabinet had spent the morning at services with the other sect members. As the time that the car had begun to burn could be estimated fairly accurately, it was impossible that he had set it on fire.

'And you're sure this is the only set of keys?' said the disappointed sergeant.

He did not like this murder. He did not like the investigation. And he did not like Petite Somme. He was anxious to conclude the operation and get back to Bastogne.

'Not to my knowledge,' said the sect member, 'but I haven't been in charge of the keys very long. Maybe the person who did it before me knows of other keys.'

To the sergeant's surprise and gratification, the other person did.

'The car was loaned to one of the gardeners to move his furniture,' said the man. 'After he returned the car, he was asked for the keys and he said he'd lost them.'

The sergeant spent the next few hours interrogating members of the sect and local villagers and then went to report his findings to the captain.

'I don't know whether this is a suspect or not,' he said. 'He's one of the four local people who have a criminal record. It dates back over ten years now, but he was convicted of rape once and of attempted rape once. Got four years on the first conviction and served three. Got eighteen months and served ten on the second. No entries since.'

'The woman wasn't raped,' said the captain.

'No, but there are other considerations,' said the sergeant. 'Here's the background on it.'

Thirty-eight-year-old Wielfried Vander Heyden was a Fleming, like the sect members, but a native of Petite Somme.

The details of his life were well known in the village and regarded with a certain amusement.

Never over-ambitious, he left school at as early an age as legally possible and worked very rarely at various unskilled jobs.

He had not, however, lived any the worse for this as he was entitled to unemployment compensation and his wife, Mildred, four years younger than himself, was partially handicapped and received a pension.

They married following Vander Heyden's release from prison after the second conviction and, as he committed no further such offences, it was generally thought that he had been moved to his act by an exaggerated virility which had now found a legitimate outlet.

In any case, Wielfried and Mildred lived peacefully, comfortably and idly up until July 1983, when he ran into some members of the sect begging in the village market-place.

They asked him if he would like a job as gardener at

the castle and offered to employ his wife as a cleaning woman.

The Vander Heydens accepted, apparently for the sheer novelty of holding a job, but they lasted less than three months.

Their employment was terminated in September by mutual agreement and Wielfried, highly indignant over the working conditions, filled the ears of the delighted villagers with his complaints about his former employers.

The Vander Heydens had apparently not been told that they would have to follow the rules of the sect when they went to work at the castle and were horror-struck when they were pulled out of bed at four in the morning and put to hard praying before a meagre breakfast.

This was, however, nothing compared to their horror when they learned that they would be sleeping in separate dormitories and could engage in sex only if they planned to have children.

For the over-sexed Vander Heyden, this condition was totally unacceptable, but, for some reason or other, he and his wife stayed on and began to engage in sex secretly in the woods.

They were caught in the act by the vigilant sect members and severely reprimanded, but this had no effect, the lusting Vander Heyden continuing to fall upon his far from reluctant spouse whenever the occasion presented itself.

Faced with this uncontrollable weakness for the sins of the flesh, the sect compromised. Under special dispensation, the Vander Heydens were to be allowed to live in one of the sect's houses near the castle, where they would, it was hoped, restrict their sexual activities to the bedroom and the night.

This took care of the sexual problems, but it was still necessary to get up at four in the morning and pray fervently in a foreign tongue. Dissatisfied with the food, the amount of work and holding a job in general, the Vander Heydens still did not quit, but simply stopped working.

In return, the sect stopped paying them. They were a religious organization, but their bookkeeping was extremely exact. The Vander Heydens were not a profitable venture.

The result of these actions was a termination of employment by mutual agreement, the sect lending Vander Heyden the Lada estate so that he could move his furniture out of their house.

The house was the one later occupied by Diederik Vandenheiden and his murdered wife, Godelieve.

'This has got to mean something,' said the captain, 'but, for the life of me, I can't see what it is. Did Vander Heyden know the Vandenheidens?'

'Apparently not,' said the sergeant. 'They only joined the group here after Vander Heyden had left. Vanderheiden says he's never laid eyes on him and doesn't know who he is.'

The captain pondered the matter.

'I don't think he's a suspect,' he said finally. 'The business with the house is just a coincidence. Besides . . .'

'Besides?' said the sergeant when the captain showed no inclination to continue.

'You saw the corpse as it was found,' said the captain. 'She was completely exposed, but she hadn't been raped.'

'Yes,' assented the sergeant, puzzled.

'Well, Vander Heyden had two convictions for sex offences, and got into trouble in his job for unauthorized sex with his wife,' said the captain. 'There's no doubt he has a very strong sex drive. What would a man like that do when confronted with an attractive, naked woman?'

'I see,' said the sergeant slowly. 'You're right, of course. He'd rape her, dead or alive. He wouldn't be able to control himself.'

Wielfried Vander Heyden was removed from the top of the suspect list and the sergeant resumed his investigations, but soon found himself back to Vander Heyden.

'There's something about that house and Vander Heyden,' he reported. 'After the Vander Heydens moved out, a sect member named Raymond Notta moved in. Vander Heyden no longer had the use of the Lada and he wanted a car, so Notta sold him a second-hand one.'

'That might be motive for murdering Notta,' said the captain, smiling. 'If the car was a lemon. Is Notta dead?'

'He's in India,' said the sergeant. 'One of the gods is having a birthday and he went there for the celebrations. That left the house empty so the Vandenheidens moved in.'

The captain looked intrigued.

'Could it be mistaken identity?' he murmured. 'But no. He must have known Notta because he bought the car off him. What happened to the car?'

'Vander Heyden wrote it off,' said the sergeant. 'He and his wife were coming down a hill on the Neufchateau road and the brakes failed. They went off into the trees and the car was wrecked. Didn't hurt either one of them, but Vander Heyden was mad as hell and tried to get his money back from Notta. Notta wouldn't give it to him.'

'That's the motive!' exclaimed the captain. 'It has to be. Bring Vander Heyden in.'

'But it's a motive to murder Notta,' objected the sergeant. 'And it was Mrs Vandenheiden, who had nothing to do with the car and whom Vander Heyden didn't even know, that was murdered.'

'Maybe so,' said the captain, 'but it was Vander Heyden. I'm certain of it. It's just that there are things about the murder that we don't know.'

'And I don't see how we'll ever find them out,' said the sergeant.

'We'll interrogate them out of Vander Heyden,' said the captain.

And rather to his own surprise, he did.

Taken into custody, Wielfried Vander Heyden began by denying all connection with either the burning of the car or the murder of Godelieve Vandenheiden.

The captain responded by intensifying the interrogation and Vander Heyden, whose memory was apparently not particularly good, soon began to involve himself in contradictory statements and patently false explanations.

After some ten hours of this, he broke down completely and confessed to setting the car on fire and to murdering Godelieve, whom he really had never seen before in his life.

'I never lost the keys to the Lada,' he said. 'I kept them because I thought one day when everybody'd forgotten about them, I'd take the car out and junk it. I decided to burn it up instead because I thought I might get hurt cracking it up.'

'And Mrs Vandenheiden?' said the captain.

'I thought Notta was still living in the house,' said Vander Heyden, 'and I knew he went to jump around and pray every morning, so I thought I'd go in the house and tear everything up to get even with him for selling me that car.

'I went in and this woman came down the stairs in her nightdress and asked me what I was doing there. I tried to grab her, but she gave me the slip and ran out of the house. She didn't get far.'

'But why did you kill a total stranger?' said the captain. 'Were you afraid she'd expose you?'

'No,' said Vander Heyden. 'I reckoned she belonged to the sect and I hate all of them. I didn't care which one I killed.'

This turned out to be a good motive as far as Wielfried Vander Heyden was concerned, for it impressed the jury as being so weird that they doubted his sanity.

Rather than finding him guilty of murder, they convicted him of unintentional homicide and, on 4 April 1986, sentenced him to the comparatively modest term of twenty years' imprisonment.

19

REHABILITATION CHALLENGE

It was a strange sort of murder on 24 December 1974. The victim, fifty-eight-year-old Ernst Dorf, was neither rich nor had he any enemies. A quiet man attached to the outdoors, he had been taking a walk in the great moor to the north of the town of Gifhorn when someone smashed in his skull with a stone.

He was found that same afternoon by other walkers and the police were summoned. They found no indication of a struggle. What money Dorf had had on him was still in his pockets. The stone with which he had been murdered lay nearby.

The police investigation concentrated on finding witnesses who might have seen Dorf with another person.

They found none. The case was classed unsolved and filed. There was nothing more to investigate. The motive for the crime remained a mystery.

Gifhorn is in central West Germany, approximately fifteen miles to the north of Braunschweig. Willich is a hundred miles to the south and on the opposite side of the country, west of Duesseldorf.

There was, therefore, no reason to connect the murder which took place there on 24 December 1978 with the Dorf murder.

In fact, there was no similarity between the two murders at all. The victim was a thirteen-year-old schoolboy called Andrew Robinson and he was not even German, but the son of an English soldier serving with NATO troops in West Germany. Moreover, the crime had taken place in an abandoned railway building rather than the countryside and Andrew had been stabbed and not killed with a stone.

He had not been robbed, but he had had scarcely enough money to be worth robbing.

The sole common factor in the murders of Ernst Dorf and Andrew Robinson was that no motive could be found for either of them.

Andrew had been an attractive boy and, at first, a sexual motive was suspected. The autopsy showed, however, that there had been no sexual tampering nor, apparently, any physical contact at all other than the knife wounds.

The knife was not found, but some six months later a twenty-four-year-old man who had been charged with the murder of another thirteen-year-old boy was questioned about the Robinson murder.

He denied it and, there being no evidence to support a charge, was never indicted. He was, however, tried and convicted on the other murder charge and sentenced to life imprisonment.

The Willich police were of the opinion that this also took care of the Robinson case.

Had they heard of the murder which took place in Essen on 4 October 1980, less than two years after the Robinson murder, they might have had reason to change their opinion.

They did not, however, and hardly anyone in Essen did either. The victim was neither rich nor famous and he was one of a great many. Essen is a large city in the heart of the industrial Ruhr district, some forty miles to the north-east of Willich. Homicide is no rarity there.

The murder took place in a junkyard and the victim, nineteen-year-old Clemens Lichtenberg, died of a crushed skull. The weapon had been an iron rod from a scrapped truck and lay near the body. There were no indications of a struggle.

Although they were unable to identify the murderer, the officers from the Essen department of criminal investigations suspected a member of one of the many street gangs so romanticized by the press. There was no known motive, and the young gangsters sometimes killed out of boredom or to demonstrate their courage.

There seemed scarcely any other explanation. Lichtenberg had not been attacked sexually and he had certainly had no money. An orphan, he had been released from the orphanage less than a month earlier, and if he had any enemies they were made with amazing speed.

Although officially unsolved, this strange, motiveless crime was to be, like the Robinson murder, regarded as cleared through another, very similar murder which took place in Essen less than a month later.

On November the first, a Saturday, eighteen-year-old Arnold Pump was beaten to death with a piece of branch in a public park in Essen, less than a half mile from where the Clemens Lichtenberg murder had taken place.

The cases were nearly identical. The victims were approximately the same age. Neither had been robbed. Neither had been molested sexually. Neither appeared to have any enemies. And both had been raised in orphanages, although not the same one.

The Essen police computer immediately called attention to these similarities and the investigation of the two cases, tentatively classed as a series, was assigned to Inspector Peter Hortig, a tall, painfully thin man with a mild expression and a nose like a knife blade.

Having gone through the autopsy reports and the reports from the technicians who had investigated at the scenes, the inspector handed the files over to his assistant, Sergeant of Detectives Ulrich Kleibel, and asked him to read them.

The sergeant, a stocky, phlegmatic man with blunt features and medium blond hair cut short at the sides, complied.

'Well?' said the inspector, when he had finished.

'The people who investigated the Lichtenberg case thought it was young street thugs,' said the sergeant. 'I don't.'

'Why?' said the inspector.

'Both killings strike me as more of an impulse,' said the sergeant. 'A street gang might slip a switchblade between his ribs or kick him to death, but I don't recall many cases where they beat somebody to death with a weapon of convenience.'

'Exactly my own conclusions,' said the inspector. 'The trouble is, if the motive wasn't just to be tough, what was it?'

'He could be crazy,' said the sergeant. 'God knows there are enough psychopaths running around the Ruhr.'

'Yes indeed,' said the inspector. 'But a psychopath nearly always has a fixation on some characteristic of the victim. Maybe it's little girls. Maybe it's women with red hair. Maybe it's one-legged postal clerks. But all the victims have some one thing in common. A homicidal psychopath doesn't kill just anybody.'

'The boys were both orphans,' said the sergeant.

'Well, I suppose it's possible,' said the inspector. 'A psychopath with a fixation on orphans? Sounds far-fetched, but then, everything in this business is.'

It was, in any case, the only theory they could come up with. Although the officers spent a considerable amount of time going over and discussing the cases, the only similarities they could find between the victims were their ages and the fact that both had been recently released from orphanages. Physically, they did not resemble each other in the least.

'Which, to me, indicates that the murderer knew them personally,' said the inspector. 'Otherwise, he wouldn't know they were orphans.'

'I disagree,' said the sergeant. 'He could have got into conversation with them and found it out.'

'No,' said the inspector. 'The autopsy reports show that both were struck down from behind and without warning. The level of adrenaline in the bloodstream was normal. They'd have been alarmed by a stranger walking around behind them like that. It was someone they knew.'

'But neither one of them had been out of the orphanage long enough to know hardly anybody,' objected the sergeant. 'They would both have had to happen to run into what was probably the only psychopath in the world with a fixation on orphans immediately they came out. It's too much of a coincidence.'

'Not if the fellow made a point of hanging around orphanages and striking up an acquaintance with the ones released,' said the inspector.

'In that case, there could be more,' said the sergeant.

The inspector nodded.

'Look into it,' he said.

The inspector's reasoning was flawless, but, unfortunately, it produced no results.

After having spent several days checking up on orphans released over the past year, the sergeant was able to say with certainty that Clemens Lichtenberg and Arnold Pump were the only two who had been murdered.

Moreover, there was no one hanging around children's homes waiting for the occupants to be released. The orphans, in fact, had a hard time getting to know anyone.

'Then it's either completely random killings or it's someone who was in the orphanage himself and knew them from there,' said the inspector.

'They weren't in the same orphange,' said the sergeant.

'Well, maybe he got transferred then,' said the inspector. 'You'll have to find out how that works. I don't know much about orphanages.'

Neither did the sergeant, but he was going to learn a good deal before he finished with the investigation.

Orphans, it seemed, were almost never transferred from one institution to the other and there was no orphan who had been in both of the homes that had housed Clemens Lichtenberg and Arnold Pump.

'The mental cases get shifted around a good deal,' reported the sergeant, 'but Lichtenberg and Pump weren't in mental institutions. They were normal.'

The sergeant had nothing else to report and there were no further leads to follow. The files were sent to the unsolved section and the inspector and his assistant turned their attention to other matters.

They had spent nearly a year on the cases and it was now 1 October 1981. Twelve days later, there would be another case which would mystify other investigators as much as the Lichtenberg and Pump cases had mystified them.

They would not, however, hear of this case for a long time as it took place far away and, indeed, in a different country altogether.

In the early evening of 13 October 1981 a house painter named Sven Jorgenson took a short cut through an alley in the town of Fåborg, Denmark.

The alley was poorly lit. Fåborg is on the western edge of the island of Fyn, which is separated from the Danish mainland by the long, narrow body of water known as the Lille Baelt. It lies far to the north and darkness had already fallen.

As a result, the house painter did not see the body of the man lying on the cobbles until he tripped over it.

Fåborg being a seaport, the painter assumed it was a drunken sailor. A closer examination, however, showed that the man was a dead sailor.

Fåborg is not a very large place and the police thought that they would not have much difficulty in solving what turned out to be a murder.

According to the findings of the autopsy, twenty-six-year-old Jan Nielsen, a merchant sailor and a native of Fåborg, had been knocked down with a powerful blow to the jaw and kicked to death. He had not been robbed or raped.

The motive was, therefore, assumed to be personal revenge. Nielsen had had a quarrel with someone, perhaps another sailor. They had fought in the alley and Nielsen had lost. His opponent had probably not intended to kick him to death.

Unfortunately for this theory, the investigations at the

scene were unable to establish any indications of a fight. Nielsen's knuckles were unmarked, meaning that he had not struck any blows himself. Even a hard blow to the body of his opponent would have produced scuffing of the knuckles by the clothing. To all appearances, the murderer had simply walked up to Nielsen, knocked him down and, perhaps, unconscious with a violent blow to the jaw and proceeded to kick him to death.

As Nielsen had bled copiously, the murderer would have had blood on his shoes.

Practically every pair of men's shoes in town were examined and the public was urged to report any sightings of a man with blood on his shoes.

No bloody shoes were found. No witnesses came forward.

The investigation then shifted to potential enemies, and an in-depth study of Nielsen's contacts, movements and activities was carried out.

By the time it was finished, the investigators knew more about Jan Nielsen than his own mother did.

They found not a single enemy. Nielsen had been a good-natured man. He had quarrelled with no one.

In the end, the police were forced to give up. There was no reason in the world for Jan Nielsen to have been murdered. Even the possibility of mistaken identity had been investigated. It too could be excluded. The community was too small for it.

Further south, things were going somewhat better for the police.

A few months after the murder of Jan Nielsen, a suspect in the murder of Arnold Pump turned up.

He was twenty-four-year-old Ralf Erb, who had been in the same orphanage as Pump. He was later transferred to another institution when it was decided that he was suffering from sufficiently severe emotional problems to require psychiatric therapy.

Erb had known Pump while he was in the orphanage and shown a keen interest in him. It was, as a matter of fact, this keen interest which got Erb transferred to a mental hospital.

Oddly enough, Erb's interest was not homosexual. Had it been, he would probably have been considered normal and left in the orphanage.

Rather, he appeared to be emotionally attached to the younger boy, whom he referred to as 'my brother'.

As Pump was not his brother, the psychologists had come to the conclusion that Erb was not right in the head.

He had, of course, been released long before Pump and was living with foster parents in Essen.

Erb had been picked up and questioned in connection with an assault case which, it turned out, he had had nothing to do with. But he had become so nervous as to arouse the suspicions of the interrogators, who began probing for what was making him nervous.

This was soon determined to be homicides involving young men and, specifically, the murder of Arnold Pump. At the mention of Pump's name, Erb broke down altogether and burst into tears.

The spectacle was striking as Erb was over six feet tall and very solidly built, with a face like an embittered bulldog.

Within this rude shell was, however, a sensitive spirit. When the interrogators checked who had handled the Pump case, and turned Erb over to Inspector Hortig, he offered only token resistance before confessing to the murder.

He was not very good on the details, but he knew where Pump had been killed and more or less how, although he offered no information that had not already appeared in the newspapers. Asked his motive for the murder, he merely stared sorrowfully at the investigators and did not reply.

'I don't think the boy's guilty,' said the inspector. 'He's a little retarded, but he's no psychopath and he doesn't know as much about the murder as we do.'

'You aren't going to go for an indictment then?' said the sergeant.

'I have to,' said the inspector. 'The damn fool's confessed.'

'Well, if he doesn't convince you, he probably won't convince the court either,' said the sergeant consolingly. 'They'll acquit him.'

'Like hell they will,' said the inspector.

He was an accurate judge of German courts. On 15 October 1982 Ralf Erb was sentenced to life imprisonment for the murder of Arnold Pump. His only comment was that he regretted it very much. By which, it was presumed, he meant the murder.

Although Erb had also confessed to the Clemens Lichtenberg murder, he was neither indicted nor tried for it. Despite his willingness to cooperate with the police, he had been unable to even find the junkyard where it had taken place and he could not identify the murder weapon. His description of Lichtenberg corresponded in no way to the young man's appearance and he did not know that he had worn glasses.

'He didn't read about the Lichtenberg case in the newspapers,' said the inspector sourly as he and the sergeant sat drinking coffee in the office following the trial.

'You think that's where he got all his information in the Pump case?' said the sergeant.

The inspector nodded.

'I was prepared to testify for the defence to that effect,' he said, 'but the boss thought not. The Lichtenberg and Pump murders are now both officially solved. Makes quite an improvement in the statistics.'

Which were, Heaven knew, bad enough. Like all the western European countries in which crime involved little risk to the criminal, West Germany was flooded with violence, rape and murder, much of it committed by people with repeated convictions for similar offences.

The inspector and the sergeant had, therefore, long since forgotten about the murders of Clemens Lichtenberg and Arnold Pump and the conviction of Ralf Erb when, on the morning of 1 February 1984, a plump, red-faced man dressed in a green loden jacket, knee-breeches, thick grey stockings and a natty green hat with a narrow brim and a feather stuck in it set off across open countryside on the outskirts of Suechteln, a small town roughly the same distance to the west of Willich as Duesseldorf is to the east.

Gustaf Schier was carrying a shotgun and the reason for his costume was that he was a hunter. Germans dress according to what they are doing. If you are going hunting, you dress the part.

Fortunately for whatever animals or birds there may have been in Gustaf Schier's game-keep that morning, he did not get far, but stumbled over something lying in the dead weeds, causing the seat of his green loden breeches to come into abrupt contact with the frozen mud.

This put Gustaf Schier into a great rage and he had plucked the offending object out of the weeds with the intention of hurling it wrathfully away when he realized that what he was holding in his hand was a human skull.

Gustaf Schier put the skull carefully back where he had found it and made straight off to report the matter to the police.

A detachment from the department of criminal investigations came out and, having searched about in the weeds a little, turned up the complete skeleton of what the medical officer later declared to be a man in his forties.

The man had come to a violent end for the skull had been smashed in with some hard, angular object such as a stone.

A few scraps of clothing and a pair of shoes were found, but no papers or anything else through which the skeleton could be identified. An expert in human bones estimated that it had been lying in the weeds for close to a year.

The police, consequently, undertook a search of the

missing person reports for the past twelve months and soon found a promising candidate.

He was forty-two-year-old Willi Fleischer, who had been a patient in the Rhineland mental clinic only four hundred yards from where the skeleton lay.

The personnel at the clinic were interrogated and stated that they had been greatly puzzled by Willi's disappearance. A gentle, low-grade moron, he was attached to the clinic, which he regarded as home, and no one could believe that he had run away.

Nor had it occurred to anyone at the time that he might have been murdered. There were few people less likely to be murdered than Willi Fleischer, who regarded everyone he encountered with a simple, child-like affection and had neither money nor enemies.

None the less, Willi Fleischer had been murdered and the skeleton was eventually identified as his.

The question now was: Who had murdered him?

As Willi, like the other patients, had been allowed to leave the clinic without supervision during the day, it could, theoretically, have been anyone. The police were, however, hoping that it had been another of the patients.

The doctors declared this to be impossible. None of the patients in the clinic was homicidal. All had been certified harmless.

As the police were aware that a startling number of murders in Germany are committed by persons certified harmless, they continued their investigation and were able to learn that Fleischer had often gone for walks with a young inmate and, indeed, some recalled that he had gone on a walk with him the day he disappeared.

The young man was, however, not a potential suspect. He had been in psychiatric institutions all his life and had been thoroughly studied by the doctors, who knew that he was incapable of murder.

'Who and where is this young man?' said the inspector in charge of the investigation.

The young man's name was Kurt Steinwegs. He was twenty-three years old, the fifth of nine children of an honest stonemason and only mildly retarded. A lovable person with a charming personality, his problem was learning difficulties which made it impossible for him to earn a living.

Steinwegs was, however, no longer in the clinic. It having been decided that his progress was sufficiently satisfactory to warrant transfer to a less confining environment, he had been sent to the Bellevue convalescent centre in the nearby Eifel mountains.

The inspector went to pay him a visit and found him fully as charming and pleasant as the personnel of the clinic had described him.

An athletic young man, a little short of six feet tall, he wore an amusing little moustache, his hair in an urchin fringe over his eyes and an engagingly toothy, largely permanent grin.

The inspector brought him back to police headquarters in Suechteln, where he plied him with biscuits, sweets and soft drinks, all of which he liked very much, and questioned him gently.

Delighted with his new friends in the police, Kurt told them everything they wanted to know.

Yes, indeed, he had killed Willi Fleischer. He had felt that the man was insulting him because he had said nothing for several minutes.

'You hit him with a stone?' said the inspector.

'Only after I had strangled him,' said Kurt cheerfully. 'I like to do it different ways. I killed the first one with a stone. I was only thirteen then.'

Whatever other flaws there might be in the mind of Kurt Steinwegs, his memory was excellent.

As the officers listened in appalled and amazed silence, he recounted in detail all six of his murders and added one that he had been planning for good measure.

The fortunate proposed victim was a gardener and, as in all other cases, a stranger to Steinwegs, who knew only that he had a wife and child. Steinwegs had been planning to murder all three of them for his first multiple homicide.

Given pencil and paper, he drew a sketch of four doughnut-shaped objects, each with a black vertical dash at the top.

These, he said, were the tyres of the gardener's truck. He had slashed all of them with a knife.

This sketch he marked with a one.

The sketch marked two was a good representation of a greenhouse with all the glass smashed. That, too, he had accomplished, said Steinwegs.

Sketch three showed three figures, one male and two female. Underneath them was written the German word for dead – '*Tot!*'

Against the number four, Steinwegs wrote DM200,000 (£70,000), which represented the amount of money he expected to realize from the murders. He was unable to explain where the money was to come from.

The gardener was contacted and Kurt's sketches proved to be accurate in every respect except for the murders, which he had not yet got around to.

So too were the sketches he drew of the murders of Ernst Dorf, Andrew Robinson, Clemens Lichtenberg, Arnold Pump, Jan Nielsen and Willi Fleischer. In every case he knew details which had never been published and were known only to the police.

He did not know the names, with the exception of Fleischer, but he knew the exact locations and dates, which made verification simple.

The murder of Jan Nielsen was thought impossible, until Steinwegs explained how he came to be in Denmark. The institution in which he had been at the time organized a sailing trip for the inmates and the ship docked for a few hours in Fåborg. The boys were allowed ashore and Steinwegs made use of his time to murder Nielsen before returning to the ship.

Ralf Erb was exonerated and released from prison, following legal proceedings by his foster parents, who complained that they had said all along that Ralf would confess to anything if pressured slightly.

As for Kurt Steinwegs, he could not, of course, be

tried. After all, his six murders had all been committed while he was an inmate of mental institutions and under treatment.

For the time being, he is not permitted to leave the institution alone, but the doctors are optimistic and report that he is making excellent progress.

He often speaks wistfully of his friends in the department of criminal investigations and some of them have been to visit him. Kurt really does have a lovable personality.

Homicidal tendencies aside, of course.

20

EQUALITY

'I see that some idiot has written up the case of the Prosse,' said Inspector Vittorio Travanca, leaning his squat, muscular body back in his swivel chair and resting his feet on the drawn-out bottom drawer of his desk.

'I do not know what a prosse is,' said his young assistant, Sergeant of Detectives Franco Verrucci. 'Is it a local idiot who has written this?'

'No,' said the inspector. 'Fortunately, it is in English so we will not be able to read it. I only saw it mentioned in a cheap magazine.'

'Perhaps, if I were to read it, I would discover what a prosse is,' said the sergeant who did not like his chief's habit of making mysteries out of commonplace things.

'A prosse is a pimp, a mezzano, someone who lives from the earnings of prostitutes,' said the inspector. 'The correct term is prosseneta, but this was no ordinary prosseneta. This was the Prosse.'

'Have pimps become so prominent that people write about them in foreign languages?' said the sergeant. 'Why not Italian?'

'We Romans are interested only in other people's pimps,' said the inspector. 'A pimp is not without honour, save in his own country.'

The sergeant contorted his dark, narrow features in a grimace of distaste. As a good communist, he found biblical quotations offensive. Also, unlike the inspector, he had not been born in Rome, but in Bari.

There followed a lengthy silence. The sergeant took out a comb, ran it carefully through his curly, medium long, blue-black hair and put it back in his pocket. The inspector gazed at the ceiling, his round, cat-like face expressionless and his lips pursed in a silent whistle.

'I've kept a transcript of the trial proceedings,' he said non-committally, getting up from the desk and going to look out of the window.

He was aware that the sergeant was dying with curiosity, but stubbornly resisting the impulse to inquire further about the Prosse.

The sergeant cleared his throat, but said nothing. He was tempted, but not ready to take the bait.

The inspector continued to regard the familiar view from the window. To his left was the greenery of the Villa Borghese, the great park in the north-east sector of Rome. To the right but out of sight was the Trevi Fountain, beloved of tourists.

'The Prosse lived down there,' said the inspector, pointing with his chin. 'You see it? Via del Tritone, number 146, third floor. A good address, but of course the Prosse had plenty of money.'

'From prostitutes?' said the sergeant, weakening in spite of himself.

'From prostitutes,' said the inspector. 'Here. I'll give you the transcript if you like. It was a murder case, of course.'

He walked back to the desk, pulled open a drawer and handed the sergeant a plain file with the words 'The Prosse' written on it.

'This is not a homicide file,' said the sergeant suspiciously, staring at it as if he were afraid that a snake would crawl out.

He was painfully familiar with the inspector's theory that a little fantasy made criminal investigations more interesting. It was possible that the Prosse was nothing but a stupid joke.

The sergeant did not approve of jokes. Like so many Marxists, he was totally lacking in humour.

'Private summation of the case for my own purposes,' said the inspector. 'Useful for training assistants.'

Still wary, but resigned, the sergeant opened the file and began to read.

The top document was titled simply, 'Personal History of the Accused'. It was in the first person and appeared to be a statement made by the Prosse to the court.

I am a native of Rome, it read, twenty-eight years of age and unmarried. My parents are respectable, middle-class, working people and I request that every effort be made to avoid their identification with this case.

My first sexual experience was at the age of eighteen and was with a young man named Alberto who was two years older than myself. The sexual contacts took place in a sleeping bag while we were on a camping trip to Lake Como.

The affair with Alberto took place in July of 1968 and continued until Christmas when I met Kathia, a German girl who was only eighteen years old, but widely experienced in sexual matters.

My affair with Kathia, short-lived as it was for she was only in Rome for a two-week holiday, altered utterly my sexual orientation and I terminated my relations with Alberto. I have never had any sexual contacts with a man since.

The claim by the prosecution that I was romantically involved with the victims is, therefore, grotesque.

From the end of 1968 to May of 1975, I engaged in many liaisons with young women, none of a permanent or significant nature. Some were, perhaps, prostitutes, but it did not occur to me to exploit them commercially.

One evening in May 1975 I had come out of a bar to get a little fresh air when my attention was attracted by a stunning young girl who was standing on the street corner soliciting the passers-by.

I engaged her in conversation and learned that her name was Francesca Lamberta. She was twenty-two years old and had been a prostitute for a little over a year and a half.

It was love at first sight for both of us, but, when I asked her to come home with me, she said that she could only stay for a short time and that I would have to pay. Otherwise, her protector would beat her.

I asked who her protector was and whether she was happy with him.

She said that he was Gianni Natalini, the barman at the Decameron Cabaret. She was not happy with him because he beat her, but she was afraid to leave him.

I said that, if she really wanted to get rid of Natalini, I would take care of it.

She did not believe me, but said that I could try if I liked. She would much prefer me as her protector.

I went to see Natalini and told him that I was taking Francesca home with me. If he caused any trouble, I would turn him in to the police. I said my uncle was a prosecuting attorney. This was not true.

I took Francesca home with me and we lived very happily. Every evening, I would drive her to the highway at the edge of the city and wait while she carried on her business. I did not ask her for the money. She gave it to me without asking.

I regarded Francesca as my wife and not my employee. I was faithful to her and had no relations with other women up until September of 1977, when I chanced to see Gina Santioni patrolling the pavement in the red-light district. She was nineteen years old with the face of a Madonna. I found her irresistible, but I resisted for two days. Then I approached her as a client, paid her regular fee and made love to her.

She was overwhelmed by my love-making and, when I asked if she would come and live with me, she said she would gladly, but that her protector would kill her.

I asked her his name and was told that he was Mauro Scalare, a procurer with several girls in his string.

I told him what I had told Gianni Natalini and took Gina home with me.

Francesca was, at first, a little jealous, but adjusted to the new arrangement once she realized that I was fully capable of taking care of the needs of both her and Gina.

We shared an extra-wide bed and made love all together. In the evening, I would drive both my girls out to

266

the highway and wait, reading or listening to music while they did their work.

Business was very good and at the end of the year I left my job. I have never considered myself a procurer. It is true that I lived off the money that Francesca and Gina gave me, but I did not ask for it. They forced it on me.

As for the murders, the first that I heard of them was when I was taken into custody by Inspector Travanca.

'Well, what do you think?' said the inspector as the sergeant slid the document under the bottom of the pile and took up the second.

'Nothing remarkable,' said the sergeant. 'A pimp like any pimp. An exploiter of the working classes. A robber capitalist. He stole them from their original pimps and forced them to work for him.'

'See what they told the court,' said the inspector.

The statements of the two prostitutes were the next documents in the file. They were short and nearly identical. Both expressed gratitude and love for their new protector. They confirmed that it was they who had insisted on turning over the money from their earnings.

'Sex is the opiate of the masses,' said the sergeant. 'I hope that they were rehabilitated and are now useful members of society.'

'They are peddling their hips in the red-light district at this very moment,' said the inspector, checking his watch. 'Unless they've contracted AIDS. You can skip the next few pages, if you like. It's only my report on the discovery of the bodies and the investigation. Probably won't interest you.'

'On the contrary,' said the sergeant, moving the prostitutes' statements to the bottom of the pile.

The date of the murders was 15 June 1978, a little over two years before the sergeant had become the inspector's assistant.

The victims, twenty-eight-year-old Gianni Natalini and twenty-six-year-old Mauro Scalare, had been found dead in the street in the centre of the red-light district and only a quarter of a mile from each other.

They had died of gunshot wounds and, according to Dr Riccardo Bellucci, the duty medical expert, at approximately the same time, between three and four in the morning.

The murders were not, however, reported until after eight o'clock, although the streets were far from empty at any time.

'Typical lack of social responsibility,' said the sergeant. 'No one wants to become involved.'

'I prefer to believe that it was reluctance to pull criminal investigations officers out of bed in the middle of the night,' said the inspector.

The sergeant pretended not to hear and continued reading.

The first documents of the investigation were the autopsy reports by Dr Bellucci. They were important as, the murders having taken place so near to each other in both time and space, it seemed probable that they were connected.

Dr Bellucci was unable to confirm this. The times of death were approximately the same and both men had been shot with a 7.65-mm calibre weapon, but, while the bullets from Scalare's body were recovered in good condition, those from the body of Gianni Natalini had struck bone and were so badly distorted that the ballistics department was unable to determine whether they had been fired from the same gun.

The only other fact established by the autopsy was that neither victim had eaten or drunk anything for at least twelve hours prior to death.

'Guess why,' said the inspector. 'It was really the solution to the case.'

The sergeant thought hard.

'They were both on diets?' he said.

The inspector looked at him sadly and shook his head. 'Keep reading,' he said.

The inspector had conducted a classical investigation,

tracing as far as possible the movements of the victims on the day preceding their deaths, their contacts, their activities and, above all, any potential enemies.

They had been immediately identified as procurers, but their whereabouts and movements during the twenty-four hours preceding the murders proved impossible to determine.

The search for enemies was more productive. Procuring in a city the size of Rome is a competitive business and Natalini and Scalare had stepped on a good many toes.

They had, however, apparently not known each other, and the only thing which they were found to have in common was that both had lost a girl to the Prosse.

The inspector had, therefore, made the arrest, searched the flat at 146 Via del Tritone and found half a box of 7.65-mm pistol ammunition, but no pistol.

'Got rid of the gun, of course,' remarked the sergeant. 'Did you get an indictment?'

The inspector nodded. 'I didn't want to, but I had to,' he said.

'But why didn't you want to?' said the sergeant. 'The fellow was obviously guilty. Natalini and Scalare were probably trying to get their slaves back so he killed them.'

'That's what the examining magistrate thought,' said the inspector. 'I never thought the Prosse was guilty. Not the type, and why would the pimps start getting their girls back at exactly the same time? They didn't lose them at the same time.'

He took a small black cigar out of the breast pocket of his jacket, stuck it in the corner of his mouth, lit it and leaned expansively back in the chair, blowing smoke at the ceiling.

'No,' he said. 'The clue was the empty stomachs. Those pimps weren't on any diet. They were as hard as rocks. Worked out in the gym every day. You have to be in shape to protect your business interests if you want to be a pimp in Rome.'

'So?' said the sergeant.

'So I put a dozen men into the area where the bodies were found,' said the inspector. 'I wanted just one report of hearing gunshot. I didn't get any.'

'Meaning?' said the sergeant, his attention fully engaged.

'Meaning they weren't shot there,' said the inspector. 'Which was what I suspected all along. The murderer shot them somewhere else, loaded the bodies into a car, drove through the district and dumped them.'

'Of course!' exclaimed the sergeant. 'But how did you work it out?'

'The empty stomachs,' said the inspector. 'They were held some where from early evening until they were killed. The murderer didn't want too many witnesses around when he dumped the bodies.'

'It all adds up,' said the sergeant, 'but why dump the bodies in the street anyway? He could have got rid of them elsewhere.'

'We never found out for certain,' said the inspector. 'It was an organization job, but the trigger that handled it couldn't be identified. I personally think that it was a sort of two-birds-with-one-stone deal. Natalini and Scalare were getting a little too successful for somebody's taste and, of course, everybody in the business knew they'd lost a girl each to the Prosse so they reckoned they'd get all three of them at one shot, the pimps dead and the Prosse stuck with the murders.'

'But it could have been the Prosse anyway,' said the sergeant. 'Didn't he get tried?'

'Charges dropped,' said the inspector. 'We were able to establish an alibi. The pimps were actually killed before midnight and she was at the beauty parlour.'

The sergeant's face abruptly took on an expression of alarm.

'She . . . ?' he said. 'Beauty parlour . . . ?'

'There's a picture on the back of the file,' said the inspector with studied carelessness. 'If you'd like a look.'

The sergeant turned the file hurriedly over.

Pasted to the back was a colour photograph of a smiling, dark-haired woman. She was very pretty and what was vulgarly termed 'built'.

The sergeant raised his eyes reproachfully to his chief's smugly smiling face.

'This is the Prosse?' he said, his voice barely audible. 'You never said she was a woman.'

'Top executive secretary before she got into the skin business,' said the inspector. 'You expect me to use sexist terms in an official document? Never heard of equality between the sexes, I suppose?'

MURDEROUS WOMEN
Where the Female is deadlier than the male.

A chilling collection of horrific crimes where women play a deadly role.

The gruesome details in these eighteen true stories – dramatically reconstructed by an outstanding crime historian from the newspaper files of three continents – prove that the female can sometimes be as deadly, if not deadlier, than the male.

STRANGE DEATHS
A chilling collection of terrifying true murders.

Fifteen true stories of the most shocking and unusual murders of this century, each one retold in frighteningly accurate detail by an outstanding historian of crime. Stories that are guaranteed to send shivers of terror down your spine.

CRYPTIC CRIMES
A chilling catalogue of mysterious murders.

Behind the closed doors and net curtains in perfectly ordinary cities, towns and villages something goes on . . . MURDER.

Reconstructed in graphic detail, here are the true stories of twenty horrific killings – baffling murder cases with strangely obscure motives. The victims were wives, grandparents, children . . . the murderers were the sort of people that you meet every day . . .

MORE BESTSELLING CRIME FROM ARROW

☐ Criminal Damage	Margaret Yorke	£3.99
☐ A Small Deceit	Margaret Yorke	£3.99
☐ Crime in Question	Margaret Yorke	£3.99
☐ Safely to the Grave	Margaret Yorke	£3.99
☐ Death on Account	Margaret Yorke	£3.50
☐ Wolfman	Ian Rankin	£3.99
☐ A Morning For Flamingos	James Lee Burke	£5.99
☐ Bad Company	Liza Cody	£3.99
☐ Head Case	Liza Cody	£3.99
☐ Going Wrong	Ruth Rendell	£4.99
☐ Kissing the Gunner's Daughter	Ruth Rendell	£4.99
☐ Wexford, An Omnibus	Ruth Rendell	£8.99

ARROW BOOKS, BOOKSERVICE BY POST, PO BOX 29, DOUGLAS, ISLE OF MAN, BRITISH ISLES

NAME _____

ADDRESS _____

_____

_____

Please enclose a cheque or postal order made out to Arrow Books Ltd. for the amount due and allow the following for postage and packing.

U.K. CUSTOMERS: Please allow 75p per book to a maximum of £7.50

B.F.P.O. & EIRE: Please allow 75p per book to a maximum of £7.50

OVERSEAS CUSTOMERS: Please allow £1.00 per book.

Whilst every effort is made to keep prices low it is sometimes necessary to increase cover prices at short notice. Arrow Books reserve the right to show new retail prices on covers which may differ from those previously advertised in the text or elsewhere.